Workbook/Laboratory Manual
to accompany

Puntos
de partida

Workbook/Laboratory Manual

to accompany

Puntos de partida

Ninth Edition

Volume 2
Capítulo 10–Capítulo 18
(Appendix 1: Capítulo 9)

Alice A. Arana
FORMERLY OF FULLERTON
COLLEGE

Oswaldo Arana
FORMERLY OF CALIFORNIA
STATE UNIVERSITY, FULLERTON

**María Francisca
Sabló-Yates**

McGraw Hill

Connect
Learn
Succeed™

The McGraw·Hill Companies

Connect
Learn
Succeed™

Published by McGraw-Hill, an imprint of The McGraw-Hill Companies, Inc., 1221 Avenue of the Americas, New York, NY 10020. Copyright © 2012, 2009, 2005, 2001, 1997, 1993, 1989, 1985, 1981. All rights reserved. No part of this publication may be reproduced or distributed in any form or by any means, or stored in a database or retrieval system, without the prior written consent of The McGraw-Hill Companies, Inc., including, but not limited to, in any network or other electronic storage or transmission, or broadcast for distance learning.

This book is printed on acid-free paper.

1 2 3 4 5 6 7 8 9 0 QDB/QDB 1 0 9 8 7 6 5 4 3 2 1

ISBN: 978-0-07-751170-8
MHID: 0-07-751170-0

Publisher and Sponsoring Editor: *Katie Stevens*
Executive Marketing Manager: *Craig Gill*
Development Editor: *Janina Tunac Basey*
Editorial Coordinators: *Sara Jaeger and Erin Blaze*
Production Editor: *Brett Coker*
Production Service: *Aaron Downey, Matrix Productions, Inc.*
Manuscript Editor: *Danielle Havens*
Cover Designer: *Preston Thomas*
Illustrators: *Harry Briggs and Dartmouth Publishing, Inc.*
Photo Researcher: *Jennifer Blankenship*
Senior Buyer: *Tandra Jorgensen*
Media Project Manager: *Sarah B. Hill*
Digital Product Manager: *Jay Gubernick*
Composition: *10/12 Palatino by Aptara®, Inc.*
Printing: *40# Abibow Equal by Quad/Graphics*

Vice President Editorial: *Michael Ryan*
Editorial Director: *William R. Glass*
Senior Director of Development: *Scott Tinetti*

The Internet addresses listed in the text were accurate at the time of publication. The inclusion of a website does not indicate an endorsement by the authors or McGraw-Hill, and McGraw-Hill does not guarantee the accuracy of the information presented at these sites.

Printed in the USA

www.mhhe.com

CONTENTS

TO THE INSTRUCTOR

Welcome to Volume 2 of the combined Workbook/Laboratory Manual to accompany *Puntos de partida, Ninth Edition!*

INTEGRATION AND ACTIVITY FLOW

- Based on feedback from instructors who teach with *Puntos*, the Workbook and Laboratory Manual, which were previously separate, have been integrated into a two-volume supplement for the Ninth Edition. With this integration, the first volume now corresponds to material covered in **Capítulos 1–9** and the second corresponds to **Capítulos 10–18.** In this edition of the Workbook/Laboratory Manual, the aural, speaking, and writing activities for each grammar and vocabulary point in the text appear together and are meant to enrich and enhance the students' learning.
- Each **Vocabulario** and **Gramática** subsection contains a progression of carefully structured and organized activities. For example, in **Capítulo 14: Las presiones de la vida moderna,** the **Las presiones de la vida académica** vocabulary subsection starts with simple matching activities. This progresses to listening and speaking activities of increasing complexity: first matching, followed by a short comprehension activity requiring simple manipulation of grammar covered in a previous chapter, concluding with a longer comprehension activity. As with all of the culminating audio activities in this Workbook/Laboratory Manual, which expose students to language in a natural and authentic context in the form of either interviews or conversations, the culminating audio activity for this subsection is based on interviews.

AUDIO ACTIVITIES

- The *Puntos* Audio Program is divided into two volumes that correspond with the two volumes of the Workbook/Laboratory Manual. It is available on audio CD as well as free-streaming audio at www.connectspanish.com.
- Audio activities in the Workbook/Laboratory Manual are easily identified by this headphones icon ꙮ.
- Students will hear a variety of native speakers in the audio activities, allowing them to become accustomed to some of the different accents, voice types, and vocabulary found in the Spanish-speaking world. The rate of speech will start out slower than native speed in the earlier chapters and will gradually increase to a moderate pace. As mentioned, many of the audio activities feature recurring characters, who will become familiar to students as they progress through the program: Miguel René (from Mexico), Karina (from Venezuela), Tané (from Cuba), and Rubén (from Spain).

ORGANIZATION/CHAPTER STRUCTURE AND FEATURES

- Each chapter of this Workbook/Laboratory Manual is based on the corresponding chapter of the textbook so that students may practice and review on their own what they are learning in class. For ease of identification, most exercises appear under the same headings as in the main text. Once a section from the textbook has been introduced, students can complete the same section in the Workbook/Laboratory Manual with the assurance that any new vocabulary or structures from later sections of that chapter will be glossed.

- **Capítulos 10–18** are organized as follows.

  - **Vocabulario: Preparación** allows students to practice the thematic vocabulary in both written and aural/oral form in a variety of contexts.
  - The expanded **Pronunciación** section contains activities that are almost entirely based on auditory cues, with, in most cases, immediate confirmation of the correct pronunciation or answer. Though **Pronunciación** sections in the main text end in **Capítulo 5,** the Workbook/Laboratory Manual has **Pronunciación** sections in every chapter.
  - **Gramática** presents a variety of written, listening, and speaking exercises on each grammar point in the corresponding section of the main text. Many of these grammar points are introduced by a **¿Recuerda Ud.?** activity, which focuses on similarities between a previously learned grammatical item and the new structure being introduced.
  - The **Un poco de todo** section starts with a cloze activity—a narrative with blanks to be filled in by the student—and provides a good opportunity for review of structures and vocabulary of the current chapter as well as previous chapters. This section also contains a culturally-based Listening Passage activity. Most Listening Passage activities begin with a pre-listening activity (**Antes de escuchar**) and conclude with a post-listening activity (**Después de escuchar**). The final activity in **Un poco de todo** is an audio activity in the form of an authentic conversation, narration, or interview that features the use of language in a natural context and provides students with additional listening and comprehension practice. This activity is frequently followed by one that gives students the opportunity to create and participate in a similar conversation based on the theme or topic of the primary audio activity.
  - The **Cultura** section consists of two activities: a map activity and a reading comprehension activity. The map activity, based on the country or countries of focus of a given chapter, provides the students with another opportunity to visualize the chapter's country of focus in relation to neighboring countries. The reading comprehension activity, based on the cultural reading in the **A leer** section of the main text (**Lectura cultural**), allows the student additional contact with the chapter theme and country of focus.
  - **Póngase a prueba** is a short quiz that focuses on some of the most mechanical aspects of the language-learning process: vocabulary, verb structures, and syntax. By taking this quiz, students can evaluate their knowledge of the more basic aspects of the language before they move on to the **Prueba corta.**
  - In the **Prueba corta** section, students will complete a test based on more contextual sentences. Audio activities follow the written ones and check students' ability to listen and respond to various situations. Immediate confirmation of the students' answers to these audio activities is provided.
  - The final section, **Puntos personales,** consists of personalized activities. In most cases, no answers are given for these activities due to their nature. The Guided Composition includes questions and/or suggested vocabulary to help students organize their thoughts before writing. **Mi diario** provides a prompt related to the theme and/or grammar in the chapter and encourages students to write freely about their own experiences. Instructors should not grade or correct **Mi diario,** but rather merely react to the content of what the student has written. It is recommended that students keep their **Mi diario** entries in a journal that is easy to carry, as this way the students can easily view their language progress. As the semester progresses and students acquire more language and vocabulary, it is expected that their entries will become more lengthy and complex. **Puntos personales** concludes with **Intercambios,** an audio activity in which students are asked to respond to thematically based questions about themselves. Although brief, this activity contains key elements of the vocabulary and grammar introduced in the chapter. All of the activities in **Puntos personales** allow students to demonstrate their ability to use in a meaningful way what they have learned in both the current and previous chapters.

OTHER NEW FEATURES OF THE NINTH EDITION

- In this edition of *Puntos*, an effort has been made to make the audio exercises less dehydrated and easier for students to process.
- In this edition, students are gradually introduced to Spanish direction lines in **Capítulos 1–4.** The direction lines appear entirely in Spanish starting with **Capítulo 5;** the only exceptions to this are the Listening Passages, where the complexity of the direction lines for this activity dictates that they remain in English.

ACKNOWLEDGMENTS

- The authors would like to express their deep appreciation to Thalia Dorwick and Ana María Pérez-Gironés for their continued leadership and guidance in this edition. We could not have done this Workbook/Laboratory Manual without their wise and perceptive comments. We also want to express our gratitude to William R. Glass, whose insightful comments on this and previous editions have helped to develop and strengthen this manual. Thanks also to Katie Stevens (Publisher) and to Scott Tinetti (Senior Director of Development) for managing every aspect of the project, from conception to development and production. Finally, we would like to thank Nina Tunac Basey, Pennie Nichols, Laura Chastain, and Danielle Havens for their tireless efforts in the content development and editing of this Workbook/Laboratory Manual.

TO THE STUDENT

Welcome to the Workbook/Laboratory Manual that accompanies *Puntos de partida,* Ninth Edition, the textbook you are using in your Spanish class. Each chapter of this supplement is based on the corresponding chapter of the textbook so that you may practice and review on your own what you are learning in class. The Workbook and Laboratory Manual activities are integrated within each section of every chapter, allowing you to practice the vocabulary and grammar points through reading, writing, listening, and speaking. In addition, most direction lines of the Workbook/Laboratory Manual are in Spanish; an exception has been made for the Listening Passage direction lines, which are in English due to their complex nature.

Throughout the audio portion of this edition, you will have the opportunity to hear a variety of accents from the Hispanic world. In the audio activities that feature different characters, you will hear Spanish as it is spoken naturally by native speakers in the form of interviews and conversations.

Here are some features of the Workbook/Laboratory Manual that you will want to keep in mind as you work with it.

- To get the most out of the Workbook/Laboratory Manual, you should complete its sections after your instructor covers the corresponding material in class. Listen to the audio as often as you need to in order to complete the activities successfully, and pay close attention to the pronunciation and the intonation of the native speakers.
- In most sections of the Workbook/Laboratory Manual, the first exercises are generally mechanical or more controlled in nature. As you do these exercises, you should focus primarily on providing the correct forms: the right form of a new verb tense, the correct question word, the exact spelling of new vocabulary, and so on. The activities that follow will require more thought and comprehension. Here's a tip: As you write your answers to all activities, read aloud what you are writing. Doing so will help you to remember the new vocabulary and structures.
- The Audio Program, which contains the listening activities from the Workbook/Laboratory Manual, is available on audio CD as well as free-streaming audio format at www.connectspanish.com. You will need the Workbook/Laboratory Manual when you listen to the Audio Program, since the activities are based on visuals and/or written cues. Audio activities in the Workbook/ Laboratory Manual are easily identified by this headphones icon .
- Each chapter of the Workbook/Laboratory Manual concludes with a section called **Puntos personales.** Answers for most of the activities in this section are not provided, given their personalized nature. In this final section you will have the opportunity to express your own opinions and answer personalized questions both orally and in writing. A recurring feature of **Puntos personales** is the Guided Composition, which includes questions and/or vocabulary to help you organize your thoughts and write a composition that is more connected. Another repeating feature is **Mi diario.** Its purpose is to encourage you to write freely in Spanish about your own opinions and experiences, using the vocabulary and structures you are currently studying, without worrying about making errors. Your instructor will read your diary or journal entries and react to them, but he or she will not grade them. Because you will be writing these **Mi diario** entries for the entire semester or quarter, it is a good idea to buy a separate notebook in which to write them. By the end of the semester or quarter, you will find that you are writing more and with greater ease in Spanish, and your journal will have a wonderful record of the progress you have made in your study of Spanish.

- An Answer Key for written activities is provided in Appendix 2, at the back of the Workbook/ Laboratory Manual. In general, answers to audio activities are on the Audio Program immediately after each item or at the end of a series of items. When not given on the Audio Program, answers to audio activities can be found in the Answer Key. Activities marked with this symbol (❖) are activities for which no answers are provided in the Answer Key, largely due to the fact that they are personalized in nature. Most activities marked with this symbol (❖) appear in the **Puntos personales** section. Here's a tip: Check your answers for each activity before proceeding to the next one. This is particularly important in activities that contain more than one **paso** (step), as in many cases, successful completion of the second **paso** is dependent on having the correct answers to the first.

We sincerely hope that your continued study of Spanish will be a satisfying experience for you!

Alice A. Arana
Oswaldo Arana
María Francisca Sabló-Yates

ABOUT THE AUTHORS

Alice A. Arana is Associate Professor of Spanish, Emeritus, at Fullerton College. She received her M.A.T. from Yale University and her Certificate of Spanish Studies from the University of Madrid. Professor Arana has also taught Spanish at the elementary and high school levels and has taught methodology at several NDEA summer institutes. She is coauthor of several McGraw-Hill supplementary materials, including the previous editions of the Workbook to accompany *Puntos de partida*, both volumes of the Workbook/Laboratory Manual to accompany *Apúntate: Español introductorio* (2010), seven editions of the Workbook/Laboratory Manual to accompany *¿Qué tal? An Introductory Course*, and the first and second editions of the Workbook/Laboratory Manual for *Puntos en breve*. She is also coauthor of the first edition of *A-LM Spanish*, of *Reading for Meaning—Spanish* and of several elementary school guides for the teaching of Spanish. In 1992, Professor Arana was named Staff Member of Distinction at Fullerton College and was subsequently chosen as the 1993 nominee from Fullerton College for Teacher of the Year. In 1994, she served as Academic Senate President.

Oswaldo Arana is Professor of Spanish, Emeritus, at California State University, Fullerton, where he taught Spanish American culture and literature. A native of Peru, he received his Ph.D. in Spanish from the University of Colorado. Professor Arana has taught at the University of Colorado, the University of Florida (Gainesville), and at several NDEA summer institutes. He is coauthor of several McGraw-Hill supplementary materials, including the previous editions of the Workbook to accompany *Puntos de partida*, both volumes of the Workbook/Laboratory Manual to accompany *Apúntate: Español introductorio* (2010), seven editions of the Workbook/Laboratory Manual to accompany *¿Qué tal? An Introductory Course*, and the first and second editions of the Workbook/Laboratory Manual for *Puntos en breve*. In addition, Dr. Arana served as a language consultant for the first edition of *A-LM Spanish*, and is coauthor of *Reading for Meaning—Spanish*, and of several articles on Spanish American narrative prose.

María Francisca Sabló-Yates holds a B.A. and an M.A. from the University of Washington (Seattle). A native of Panama, she has taught at the University of Washington and Central Michigan University (Mt. Pleasant, Michigan), and is currently an Associate Professor of Spanish at Delta College (University Center, Michigan). She is the author and coauthor of several McGraw-Hill supplementary materials, including previous editions of the *Puntos de partida* Laboratory Manual, both volumes of the Workbook/Laboratory Manual to accompany *Apúntate: Español introductorio* (2010), the first through seventh editions of the Workbook/Laboratory Manual to accompany *¿Qué tal? An Introductory Course*, and the first and second editions of the *Puntos en breve* Workbook/Laboratory Manuals.

Capítulo 10

El tiempo libre

VOCABULARIO   Preparación

Los pasatiempos, diversiones y aficiones

A. Deportes y deportistas (*athletes*). ¿Qué deportes practican estas personas?

1. Tiger Woods _____

2. Kobe Bryant _____

3. David Beckham _____

4. Lance Armstrong _____

5. Serena Williams _____

6. Alex Rodriguez _____

B. Diversiones. Identifique las actividades de las siguientes personas. Use el presente progresivo cuando sea (*whenever it is*) posible.

Marcos

Sara

Tomás

Felipe

Ernesto y Mari

Arturo

Inés y Clara

Isabel y Mario

(Continúa.)

MODELO: Inés y Clara: → Están tomando el sol.

1. Felipe: _____

2. Sara: _____

3. Marcos: _____

4. Tomás: _____

5. Mari y Ernesto: _____

6. Arturo: _____

7. Isabel y Mario: _____

 C. Gustos y preferencias

Paso 1. Ud. va a oír una serie de descripciones de lo que a varias personas les gusta hacer. Luego indique la letra de la actividad que le convendría (*would suit*) a cada persona, según lo que le gusta hacer. **¡OJO!** Hay más de una respuesta posible en algunos casos. Primero, escuche el **Vocabulario útil.**

Vocabulario útil

al aire libre   outdoors

1.	a. nadar	b. jugar al ajedrez	c. tomar el sol
2.	a. dar fiestas	b. ir al teatro	c. ir a un bar
3.	a. ir a un museo	b. hacer *camping*	c. hacer un *picnic*
4.	a. pasear en bicicleta	b. esquiar	c. correr
5.	a. jugar al fútbol	b. ir a un museo	c. ir al cine

Paso 2. Ahora va a oír las descripciones otra vez. Diga las respuestas correctas al **Paso 1,** según el modelo. Luego escuche la respuesta correcta y repítala.

MODELO: (Ud. ve) **1.** Raquel

(Ud. oye) Uno. A Raquel le gusta muchísimo ir a la playa.

(Ud. dice) A Raquel le gusta nadar y tomar el sol.

(Ud. oye y repite) A Raquel le gusta nadar y tomar el sol.

2. Diana   3. Reinaldo   4. Luci   5. Bernardo

 D. Las actividades en el tiempo libre

Paso 1. Ud. va a oír algunas descripciones sobre las actividades que hacen varias personas en su tiempo libre. Empareje el número de la descripción con el dibujo correspondiente. **¡OJO!** Hay una descripción extra.

a. _____ Marta y sus amigos   **b.** _____ Julia y sus amigos

c. _____ Rogelio   **d.** _____ Juan y sus amigos   **e.** _____ Kati y sus amigos

Paso 2. Ahora cuando oiga la letra de cada dibujo, diga lo que las personas del dibujo correspondiente están haciendo. Use los sujetos indicados y el presente progresivo, según el modelo. Luego escuche la respuesta correcta y repítala.

> MODELO: (Ud. oye) **a.**
>   (Ud. ve) **a.** Marta y sus amigos
>   (Ud. dice) Marta y sus amigos están jugando al fútbol.
>   (Ud. oye y repite) Marta y sus amigos están jugando al fútbol.

b. Julia y sus amigos   **c.** Rogelio   **d.** Juan y sus amigos   **e.** Kati y sus amigos

E. Entrevista cultural

Paso 1. Ud. va a oír una entrevista con Mauricio sobre el fútbol y otros deportes que él hace. Primero, escuche el **Vocabulario útil.** Luego escuche la entrevista.

Vocabulario útil

la liga	league
la temporada	season (sports)
los campeones	champions
el montañismo	mountain climbing
gustaría	would like
la selección	**el equipo**
el mundial	world championship (of soccer)
el maestro	teacher

Paso 2. Ahora complete el párrafo con información de la entrevista.

Mauricio es de _____,[1] _____.[2] Él _____[3] en una _____[4]

de fútbol todos los _____[5] de semana. Mauricio dice que su _____[6] es bueno,

pero que no _____[7] los campeones la temporada pasada. Además del (*In addition to*) fútbol,

Mauricio practica la _____[8] y el montañismo. En el futuro, a Mauricio le gustaría

jugar en la _____[9] de Colombia e ir a un _____[10] de fútbol. Mauricio

está estudiando para ser _____.[11]

Los quehaceres domésticos [Part 2]

A. Los quehaceres domésticos. Describa lo que están haciendo las personas en cada dibujo. Use el presente progresivo cuando sea posible.

MODELO: (Ud. ve)   →   Está sacando la basura.

1.

2.

3.

4.

1. _____

2. _____

3. _____

4. _____

B. Los aparatos domésticos. Conteste con oraciones completas.

1. ¿Para qué se usa la estufa? _____

2. ¿En qué se prepara el café? _____

3. ¿Qué hacemos con la lavadora de ropa? _____

_____

4. ¿Qué máquina usamos para lavar los platos? _____

_____

5. ¿Usamos la escoba (*broom*) para limpiar las alfombras? _____

_____

6. ¿En qué tostamos el pan? _____

_____

7. ¿Qué aparato usamos para preparar las comidas rápidamente? _____

_____

C. **Mandatos para el nuevo robot.** Imagine que Ud. y su familia tienen un nuevo robot que los va a ayudar con sus quehaceres domésticos. Dígale al robot qué debe hacer en estas situaciones. Use mandatos de **Ud.** Luego escuche la respuesta correcta y repítala.

MODELO: (Ud. oye) Uno.

(Ud. ve)

(Ud. dice) Lave los platos.
(Ud. oye y repite) Lave los platos.

2.

3.

4.

5.

D. ¿A quién le toca? Cuando oiga el número correspondiente y el nombre, diga a quién le toca hacer los quehaceres en el dibujo. Luego escuche la respuesta correcta y repítala.

MODELO: (Ud. oye)   Uno. Jorge

(Ud. ve)

(Ud. dice)   A Jorge le toca sacar la basura.
(Ud. oye y repite)   A Jorge le toca sacar la basura.

2. Graciela

3. Luis

4. Ana

5. Miguel

PRONUNCIACIÓN   *p* and *t*

Like the **[k]** sound, Spanish **p** and **t** are not aspirated as they are in English. Compare the following pairs of aspirated and nonaspirated English sounds.

pin / spin   pan / span   tan / Stan   top / stop

A. Repeticiones. Repita las siguientes palabras, imitando lo que oye.

| 1. [p] | pasar | patinar | programa | puerta | esperar |
| 2. [t] | tienda | todos | traje | estar | usted |

Ahora cuando oiga el número correspondiente, lea las siguientes palabras en voz alta. Luego escuche la pronunciación correcta y repítala.

3. una tía trabajadora   5. Tomás, toma tu té.
4. unas personas populares   6. Pablo paga el periódico.

B. Repaso: [p], [t], [k]. Ud. va a oír algunas palabras. Indique la palabra que oye.

1. **a.** pata   **b.** bata   4. **a.** dos   **b.** tos
2. **a.** van   **b.** pan   5. **a.** de   **b.** té
3. **a.** coma   **b.** goma   6. **a.** callo   **b.** gallo

C. Oraciones

Paso 1. Escriba las oraciones que oye.

1. _____

2. _____

3. _____

4. _____

Nota: Verifique sus respuestas del **Paso 1** en el Apéndice antes de empezar el **Paso 2.**

Paso 2. Ahora cuando oiga el número correspondiente, lea las siguientes oraciones en voz alta. Luego escuche la respuesta correcta y repítala.

1. Paco toca el piano para sus parientes.   3. ¿Por qué pagas tanto por la ropa?
2. Los tíos de Tito son de Puerto Rico.   4. Tito trabaja para el padre de Pepe.

GRAMÁTICA

¿Recuerda Ud.?

El pretérito

Paso 1. Complete las oraciones con el pretérito de los verbos entre paréntesis.

yo: Esta mañana _____[1] (despertarse) a las 7:00, _____[2] (ducharse), _____[3] (vestirse) y _____[4] (salir) de casa. No _____[5] (tener) tiempo para desayunar. Como (*Since*) no _____[6] (poder) encontrar estacionamiento (*parking*) en el *campus*, _____[7] (dejar: *to leave*) el coche en la calle.

Paso 2. Ahora cambie el sujeto de **yo** a **Juan.**

Juan: Esta mañana _____[1] (despertarse) a las 7:00, _____[2] (ducharse), _____[3] (vestirse) y _____[4] (salir) de casa. No _____[5] (tener) tiempo para desayunar. Como (*Since*) no _____[6] (poder) encontrar estacionamiento (*parking*) en el *campus*, _____[7] (dejar: *to leave*) el coche en la calle.

27. Talking About the Past (Part 4) • Descriptions and Habitual Actions in the Past: Imperfect of Regular and Irregular Verbs

A. Las formas del imperfecto. Complete las siguientes tablas con las formas apropiadas del imperfecto.

Los verbos regulares:

	cantar	tener	salir
yo	cantaba		
tú		tenías	
Ud.	cantaba		salía
nosotros		teníamos	
Uds.			salían

Los verbos irregulares:

	ser	ir	ver
yo	era		
tú		ibas	
Ud.			veía
nosotros	éramos		
Uds.		iban	

B. Recuerdos juveniles (*Youthful memories*). Complete la narración con la forma apropiada del imperfecto de los verbos entre paréntesis.

Cuando _____[1] (*yo:* tener) 14 años, _____[2] (*nosotros:* vivir) en el campo.[a] _____[3] (*Yo:* Ir) al colegio[b] en una ciudad cerca de casa y a veces _____[4] (*yo:* volver) tarde porque _____[5] (preferir) quedarme a jugar con mis amigos. Ellos a veces _____[6] (venir) a visitarnos, especialmente cuando _____[7] (ser) el cumpleaños de mi madre. Siempre lo _____[8] (*nosotros:* celebrar) con una gran fiesta y ese día mi padre _____[9] (hacer) todos los preparativos y _____[10] (cocinar) él mismo.[c] Nos _____[11] (visitar) parientes de todas partes y siempre _____[12] (quedarse) algunos con nosotros por dos o tres días. Durante esos días _____[13] (*nosotros:* dormir) poco porque mis primos y yo _____[14] (acostarse) en la sala de recreo y allí siempre _____[15] (haber) gente[d] hasta muy tarde. Todos nosotros lo _____[16] (pasar) muy bien. Pero esos _____[17] (ser) otros tiempos, claro.

[a]*country(side)* [b]*school* [c]*él… himself* [d]*people*

C. La mujer de ayer y la mujer de hoy. Compare la vida de la mujer de la década de los años 50 con la vida que lleva hoy día. Use los infinitivos indicados. Siga el modelo.

> MODELO: tener muchos hijos / / tener familias pequeñas →
> Antes tenía muchos hijos. Ahora tiene familias pequeñas.

1. tener menos independencia / / sentirse más libre

   _____

2. depender de su esposo / / tener más independencia económica

   _____

3. quedarse en casa / / preferir salir a trabajar

   _____

4. solo pensar en casarse (*to get married*) / / pensar en seguir su propia carrera (*own career*)

   _____

   _____

5. pasar horas cocinando / / servir comidas más fáciles de preparar

   _____

   _____

6. su esposo: sentarse a leer el periódico / / ayudarla con los quehaceres domésticos

   _____

   _____

D. Situaciones. Cambie los verbos indicados al imperfecto.

1. Nosotros *somos* muy buenos amigos de los González: _____

   nos *vemos* todos los domingos. Si ellos no *vienen* a _____ _____

   visitarnos a nuestra casa, nosotros *vamos* a la casa de ellos. _____

2. Cuando *estamos* en el Perú, nuestros sobrinos _____

   siempre nos *dan* un beso (*kiss*) cuando nos *saludan* _____ _____

   y otro beso cuando se *despiden* de nosotros. _____

3. Siempre *almuerzo* en aquel restaurante. *Sirven* la _____ _____

   mejor comida de toda la ciudad. Cuando me *ven* _____

   entrar, me *llevan* a la mejor mesa y me *traen* el menú. _____ _____

   ¡Se *come* muy bien allí! _____

E. Una despedida en el aeropuerto

Paso 1. Ud. va a oír una descripción de una despedida entre un hijo, Gustavo, que va a estudiar medicina en San Juan, Puerto Rico, y sus padres. Escuche el **Vocabulario útil** y, mientras escucha la descripción, indique las acciones y el estado en que están Gustavo y sus padres. Primero, mire la tabla.

Vocabulario útil

el correo electrónico   e-mail
despegar (avión)   to take off (*plane*)

	ESTAR EN EL AEROPUERTO	IR A SAN JUAN	ESTAR NERVIOSÍSIMO/A	ESTAR PREOCUPADO/A	SENTIRSE TRISTE
Gustavo					
la madre de Gustavo					
el padre de Gustavo					

Paso 2. Ahora va a oír algunas oraciones sobre la descripción del **Paso 1.** Indique si cada oración es cierta (**C**) o falsa (**F**).

1. C F   **2.** C F   **3.** C F   **4.** C F   **5.** C F

Nota: Verifique sus respuestas al **Paso 1** en el Apéndice antes de empezar el **Paso 3.**

Paso 3. Ahora conteste las siguientes preguntas basándose en la información que escribió en la tabla del **Paso 1.** Luego escuche la respuesta correcta y repítala.

1. …   **2.** …   **3.** …   **4.** …   **5.** …

F. Describiendo el pasado: En la escuela secundaria. Ud. va a oír algunas preguntas sobre lo que ciertas personas hacían o tenían que hacer cuando estaban en la escuela secundaria (*high school*). Conteste con las palabras que se dan. Luego escuche la respuesta correcta y repítala.

MODELO: (Ud. oye)   ¿Qué tenía que hacer Lupe?
          (Ud. ve)   tener que hacer su cama
          (Ud. dice)   Tenía que hacer su cama.
     (Ud. oye y repite)   Tenía que hacer su cama.

1. necesitar estudiar mucho
2. tener que hacer su tarea
3. necesitar limpiar su alcoba
4. esquiar en las montañas
5. jugar videojuegos
6. ir al cine

¿Recuerda Ud.?

¿Con qué palabra interrogativa se asocia la siguiente información?

PALABRA INTERROGATIVA   INFORMACIÓN

1. ¿Dónde? _____   a. a las cuatro de la tarde

2. ¿Quiénes? _____   b. de San Juan

3. ¿Cuándo? _____   c. $20.00

4. ¿De dónde? _____   d. en casa de Mari

5. ¿Cuál? _____   e. Miguel y Ana

6. ¿Cuánto? _____   f. Es el 511-2348.

7. ¿Qué? _____   g. Es un DVD.

28. Getting Information (Part 2) • Summary of Interrogative Words

A. **Situaciones.** Imagine que Ud. acaba de conocer a Rafael Pérez, un jugador de béisbol en alza (*up-and-coming*) y Ud. le hace varias preguntas. Aquí están sus respuestas. Escriba sus preguntas correspondientes a las respuestas que él da con la palabra interrogativa apropiada. Use la forma de **Ud.**

¿Qué?   ¿Dónde?   ¿Adónde?   ¿De dónde?   ¿Cómo?   ¿Cuáles?

1. —¿_____? —Me llamo Rafael Pérez.

2. —¿_____? —(Soy) De Bayamón, Puerto Rico.

3. —¿_____? —(Vivo) En el sur de California.

4. —¿_____? —Ahora voy al estadio.

5. —¿_____? —Voy a entrenarme con el equipo.

6. —¿_____? —(Mis pasatiempos favoritos) Son jugar al tenis y nadar.

¿Cuándo?   ¿Quiénes?   ¿Por qué?

7. —¿_____? —Empecé a jugar en 2000.

8. —¿_____? —(Mis jugadores favoritos) Son Albert Pujols y Alex Rodriguez.

9. —¿_____? —Porque son los mejores jugadores.

B. **Una amiga entrometida** (*nosy*). Una amiga llama a Cristina por teléfono. Complete el diálogo con las palabras interrogativas apropiadas.

AMIGA: Hola, Cristina. ¿_____[1] estás?

CRISTINA: Muy bien, gracias, ¿y tú?

AMIGA: ¡Bien, gracias! ¿_____[2] estás haciendo?

(Continúa.)

CRISTINA: Estaba estudiando con Gilberto Montero pero ya se fue.

AMIGA: ¿_____³ es Gilberto Montero?

CRISTINA: Es un amigo de la universidad.

AMIGA: ¿Ah, sí? ¿_____⁴ es?

CRISTINA: De Bogotá.

AMIGA: ¡Ah, colombiano! ¿Y_____⁵ años tiene?

CRISTINA: Veintitrés.

AMIGA: ¿_____⁶ es él?

CRISTINA: Es moreno, bajo, guapo y muy simpático.

AMIGA: ¡Aja! ¿_____⁷ regresa tu amigo a su país?

CRISTINA: En julio, pero antes vamos juntos a San Francisco.

AMIGA: ¡A San Francisco! ¿_____⁸ van a San Francisco?

CRISTINA: Porque él quiere visitar la ciudad y yo tengo parientes allí.

AMIGA: ¿Y _____⁹ van a ir? ¿En avión?

CRISTINA: No, vamos en coche.

AMIGA: ¿_____¹⁰ coche van a usar?

CRISTINA: El coche de Gilberto. ¿Qué te parece?ᵃ

AMIGA: ¡Fantástico! Adiós, Cristina. Tengo que llamar a Luisa.

ᵃ¿Qué… *What do you think?*

C. **Un correo electrónico** (*e-mail*) **de Buenos Aires.** Aquí tiene un mensaje que Sara le mandó a los Estados Unidos a Alfonso. Léalo. Luego con palabras interrogativas, escriba cinco preguntas sobre el contenido (*contents*) del mensaje o sobre lo que implica (*implies*).

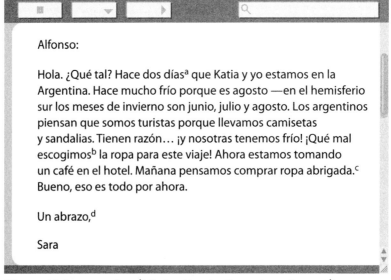

Alfonso:

Hola. ¿Qué tal? Hace dos díasᵃ que Katia y yo estamos en la Argentina. Hace mucho frío porque es agosto —en el hemisferio sur los meses de invierno son junio, julio y agosto. Los argentinos piensan que somos turistas porque llevamos camisetas y sandalias. Tienen razón… ¡y nosotras tenemos frío! ¡Qué mal escogimosᵇ la ropa para este viaje! Ahora estamos tomando un café en el hotel. Mañana pensamos comprar ropa abrigada.ᶜ Bueno, eso es todo por ahora.

Un abrazo,ᵈ

Sara

ᵃHace… *It's been two days* ᵇ¡Qué… *How badly we chose* ᶜ*warm* ᵈ*hug*

1. _____
2. _____
3. _____
4. _____
5. _____

D. ¿Qué dijiste? Su amiga Eva acaba de decirle varias cosas que Ud. no entendió bien. Indique la palabra interrogativa que Ud. usaría (*you would use*) para averiguar (*find out*) lo que le dijo Eva. Después haga una pregunta con la palabra interrogativa que indicó para obtener (*obtain*) la información que necesita. Luego escuche la respuesta correcta y repítala.

MODELO: (Ud. oye) La capital del Perú es Lima.

(Ud. ve) **a.** ¿qué? **b.** ¿cuál?

(Ud. escoge) **b.** ¿cuál?

(Ud. dice) **b.** ¿Cuál es la capital del Perú?

(Ud. oye y repite) **b.** ¿Cuál es la capital del Perú?

1. **a.** ¿qué? **b.** ¿cuál?   4. **a.** ¿qué? **b.** ¿cuál?
2. **a.** ¿qué? **b.** ¿cuál?   5. **a.** ¿qué? **b.** ¿cuál?
3. **a.** ¿qué? **b.** ¿cuál?   6. **a.** ¿qué? **b.** ¿cuál?

E. Planes para el fin de semana

Paso 1. En este diálogo, Rubén, Karina, Miguel René y Tané hacen planes para el fin de semana. Primero, escuche el **Vocabulario útil.** Luego escuche la conversación.

Karina y Rubén

Miguel René, Karina y Rubén

(Continúa.)

Tané, Karina y Rubén

Vocabulario útil

se llena con mucha gente	it gets crowded
cuadrar	to make plans (*for a period of time*)
el balón	**la pelota**
avisar	to let someone know (*something*)
¿te apuntas?	will you come?
no te preocupes	don't worry
cuídense	take care

Paso 2. Ahora conteste las preguntas, según la conversación. Luego escuche una respuesta correcta posible y repítala.

1. ... **2.** ... **3.** ... **4.** ...

Paso 3. Ahora cuando oiga el número correspondiente, haga la pregunta que corresponde a la respuesta escrita (*written*). Luego escuche la pregunta correcta y repítala. Por último (*Last*), va a oír la respuesta a su pregunta. Después de oírla, repítala.

MODELO: (Ud. ve)   **1.** Se baila salsa en el Mama Rumba.

                (Ud. oye)   Uno.

                (Ud. dice)   ¿Qué se hace en el Mama Rumba?

    (Ud. oye y repite)   ¿Qué se hace en el Mama Rumba?

    (Ud. oye y repite)   Se baila salsa en el Mama Rumba.

2. El club está en la Calle Constitución.
3. El club abre a las ocho de la noche.
4. La línea de metro que llega a la Calle Constitución es la número 5.

¿Recuerda Ud.?

Expressions of equality: **tanto/a (tantos/as)** + *noun* + **como**; *verb* + **tanto como**

1. Yo tengo cien dólares. Tú tienes cien dólares. → Yo tengo _____ dinero

   _____ tú.

2. Yo tengo tres clases. Toni tiene tres clases. → Yo tengo _____ clases _____

   Toni.

3. Yo estudio mucho. Uds. estudian mucho. → Yo estudio _____ _____ Uds.

Expressions of inequality: **más (menos)** + *adj./noun/adverb* + **que; mayor(es) / menor(es) que** + *person*

4. Yo tengo cien dólares. Tú tienes cincuenta dólares. → Yo tengo _____ dinero

   _____ tú.

5. Yo tengo tres clases. Toni tiene cuatro clases. → Yo tengo _____ clases

   _____ Toni. Toni tiene _____ clases _____ yo.

6. Yo tengo diecinueve años. Mi hermano tiene quince años. → Yo soy _____

   _____ mi hermano. Mi otro hermano tiene trece años. → Mis hermanos son

   _____ _____ yo.

29. Expressing Extremes • Superlatives

A. Opiniones sobre los deportes. Amplíe (*Expand*) la información en las siguientes oraciones, según el modelo. Luego si no está de acuerdo con la oración, escriba su opinión.

MODELO: El golf es más aburrido que la natación. (todos) →
El golf es el deporte más aburrido de todos.
No estoy de acuerdo. La natación es el deporte más aburrido de todos.

1. El béisbol es más emocionante (*exciting*) que el basquetbol. (todos)

   _____

   _____

2. Kobe Bryant es mejor jugador que LeBron James. (mundo)

   _____

   _____

3. El equipo de los Dallas Cowboys es peor que el de (*that of*) los 49ers. (todos)

   _____

   _____

(Continúa.)

4. El estadio (*stadium*) de Río de Janeiro, Brasil, es más grande que el de Pasadena. (mundo)

_____

_____

B. Las opiniones de Margarita. Ud. va a oír una narración en la cual (*in which*) Margarita da sus opiniones sobre una variedad de temas. Primero, escuche el **Vocabulario útil** y la lista de temas. Después escuche la narración. Luego escriba las opiniones de Margarita.

Vocabulario útil

acerca de	about
los disfraces	costumes
el pasatiempo	pastime
disfrutar (de)	to enjoy
¡qué lata!	what a pain!

1. la fiesta más divertida del año: _____

2. el peor mes del año: _____

3. el mejor pasatiempo de todos: _____

4. la mejor película del mundo: _____

5. el quehacer doméstico más aburrido: _____

C. Solo lo mejor... Imagine que en la quinceañera de su amiga hay todo lo mejor. Conteste las preguntas que oye con las palabras que se dan, según el modelo. Luego escuche la respuesta correcta y repítala.

> MODELO: (Ud. ve y oye) Los vestidos son elegantes, ¿no?
> (Ud. ve) fiesta
> (Ud. dice) Sí, son los vestidos más elegantes de la fiesta.
> (Ud. oye y repite) Sí, son los vestidos más elegantes de la fiesta.

1. Antonio es un chico guapo, ¿verdad? / fiesta
2. Y la comida, es muy rica, ¿no? / mundo
3. Las damas (*maids*) de honor son elegantes, ¿verdad? / todas
4. La fiesta es divertida, ¿verdad? / año

Un poco de todo

A. ¿Un día desastroso (*disastrous*) o un día de suerte (*lucky*)? Complete la siguiente narración y haga los siguientes cambios.

1. Complete la narración en el pretérito (*P:*) o el imperfecto (*I:*), según las indicaciones.
2. Cambie los verbos marcados con* por la forma del gerundio solamente: esquiar* → esquiando.

Hace cinco o seis semanas,ᵃ Fernando Sack-Soria, un joven anglohispano del sur de España,

_____¹ (*I:* pasar) unas vacaciones _____² (esquiar*) en Aspen, Colorado. Allí

_____³ (*P:* conocer) por casualidadᵇ a María Soledad Villardel, también española, pero de

Barcelona. Ella _____⁴ (*I:* visitar) a unos amigos que _____⁵ (*I:* vivir) en Aspen.

ᵃHace... *Five or six weeks ago*   ᵇpor... *by chance*

El primer encuentro[c] entre Fernando y Marisol (así llaman a María Soledad) fue casi

desastroso. Fernando _____[6] (*I: esquiar*) montaña abajo[d] a la vez[e] que

Marisol _____[7] (*I: estar*) cruzando distraída la pista de esquí.[f] Cuando

Fernando la _____[8] (*P: ver*), trató de evitar un choque.[g] _____[9] (*P: Doblar*[h])

bruscamente[i] a la izquierda y perdió el equilibrio.[j] El joven se cayó[k] y _____[10] (*P: perder*)

uno de sus esquís. Marisol paró,[l] _____[11] (*P: ponerse*) muy avergonzada y, casi sin

pensarlo, le habló… en español.

—¡Hombre, cuánto lo siento[m]! ¡No sé dónde llevaba la cabeza[n]! ¿(Tú) _____[12]

   (*P: Hacerse*) daño[ñ]?

—No, de ninguna manera! La culpa fue mía.[o] Venía muy rápido —le dijo Fernando.

—¡Por Dios! ¡Hablas español! —contestó ella muy sorprendida.

—¡Claro! Soy español, de Jerez de la Frontera.

—Y yo, de Barcelona. ¿Qué haces por aquí?

—Ya ves, _____[13] (*esperar**) a una chica guapa con quien chocar[p] en Colorado —dijo

Fernando, _____[14] (*sacudirse**[q]) la nieve y _____[15] (*sonreír**).

—¿Y tú?

—¿Yo? Estaba en las nubes,[r] como siempre, y casi te causé un accidente serio.

Para hacer corta la historia, desde ese día _____[16] (*P: hacerse*[s]) muy amigos y ahora se

mandan mensajes y se visitan cuando pueden.

[c]*meeting* [d]*montaña… down the mountain* [e]*a… at the same time* [f]*cruzando… crossing the ski slope absentmindedly*
[g]*trató… he tried to avoid a collision* [h]*To turn* [i]*sharply* [j]*balance* [k]*se… fell down* [l]*stopped* [m]*cuánto… I'm so sorry*
[n]*dónde… what I was thinking* (lit., *where I had my head*) [ñ]*hacerse… to hurt oneself* [o]*La… It was my fault* [p]*to bump into* [q]*to shake off* [r]*Estaba… My head was in the clouds* [s]*to become*

B. *Listening Passage:* ¿Cómo se pasan los fines de semana y los días de fiesta?

❖ **Antes de escuchar.** Before you listen to the passage, read the following statements about how some people spend weekends or holidays. Check those statements that are true for you and your family.

☐ Los fines de semanas son ocasiones familiares.
☐ Pasamos los fines de semana o los días de fiesta en nuestra casa de campo.
☐ Mi madre siempre prepara una comida especial los domingos.
☐ Paso el fin de semana con mis amigos y no con mi familia.
☐ Después de comer, toda la familia sale a dar un paseo por el parque.
☐ Paso el fin de semana con mis abuelos.

(Continúa.)

Listening Passage. You will hear a passage about how some Hispanics spend their weekends and holidays. First, listen to the **Vocabulario útil.** Next listen to the passage to get a general idea of the content. Then go back and listen again for specific information.

Vocabulario útil

el campo	countryside
a mediodía	at noon
se reúna	get together
se convierte	becomes
se suele elegir	it is the custom to pick
los columpios	swings
durar	to last
charlar	**hablar**
sino	rather

Después de escuchar. Read the following statements. Circle **C** if the statement is true or **F** if it is false. If, according to the passage, the statement is false, correct it.

1. C F Todos los hispanos tienen otra casa fuera de la ciudad.

_____

2. C F Normalmente los abuelos de una familia hispana no pasan tiempo con sus hijos y nietos.

_____

3. C F Los domingos, las familias hispanas almuerzan rápidamente para poder ir al cine o al teatro.

_____

4. C F Por lo general, las familias hispanas dan un paseo después del almuerzo de los domingos.

_____

C. ¿Salimos?

Paso 1. En este diálogo, Amalia y Mariela hacen planes para el fin de semana. Primero, escuche el **Vocabulario útil.** Luego escuche la conversación.

Vocabulario útil

¡pura vida!	great! (*Costa Rica*)
vos	*informal personal pronoun equivalent to* **tú** (*used in Costa Rica and most other Central American countries, as well as in Argentina and Uruguay*); *present tense* **vos** *forms are like* **vosotros** *forms without the final* **i:** **hacéis** → **hacés, queréis** → **querés, sois** → **sos.**
me encantaría	I would love to

Paso 2. Ahora Ud. va a oír algunas oraciones. Indique si las oraciones son ciertas (**C**) o falsas (**F**).

1. C F   3. C F
2. C F   4. C F

Paso 3. Ahora va a participar en una conversación similar con Teodoro. Primero, complete el diálogo con las siguientes frases. **¡OJO!** Conjugue los verbos en el tiempo presente. Segundo, haga la conversación en voz alta. Después de oír lo que Teodoro dice, lea su respuesta. Luego escuche la pronunciación correcta y repítala. Vea las repuestas correctas en el Apéndice antes de hacer la conversación en voz alta.

gracias   pero no poder   tener que estudiar

TEODORO: Oye, ¿quieres ir al cine el viernes? Ponen una película buenísima.

UD.:   Gracias, _____.[1]

TEODORO: ¿Por qué no?

UD.:   _____.[2]

TEODORO: ¡Qué lástima![a] Buena suerte[b] en el examen, pues.[c]

UD.:   _____.[3]

[a]¡Qué... *What a shame!*   [b]Buena... *Good luck*   [c]*then*

Puerto Rico

A. Mapa. Identifique Puerto Rico y su capital en el siguiente mapa.

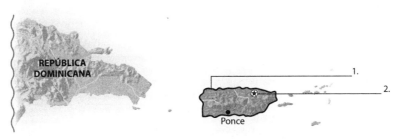
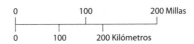

B. Comprensión. Basándose en la **Lectura cultural: Puerto Rico** de la página 314 del libro de texto, complete las siguientes oraciones.

1. A los puertorriqueños les encanta pasar su tiempo _____ en la _____.

2. Los deportes _____, como el *surfing*, son muy populares.

3. Un juego muy popular en muchos países hispanos es el _____.

4. El tiempo que se pasa hablando con la familia o amigos después de comer es la

   _____.

5. La superioridad de los argentinos en el deporte del _____ es reconocida

   (*recognized*) mundialmente.

6. La cultura puertorriqueña evoca las tradiciones de los _____, habitantes originarios,

   los africanos y los _____.

7. El Viejo San Juan refleja especialmente la cultura _____, con el antiguo Fuerte

   llamado San Felipe del Morro, la Catedral, las calles adoquinadas y los edificios de estilo

   _____.

8. La palabra _____, para referirse a los puertorriqueños, viene de la herencia taína.

9. La pequeña rana que es propia (*native*) de la Isla se llama el _____.

PÓNGASE A PRUEBA

A. Imperfecto de los verbos regulares e irregulares

1. Complete la siguiente tabla.

	cantar	ir	leer	ser	ver
yo	*cantaba*				
nosotros					

2. Empareje los siguientes usos del imperfecto con los ejemplos.

   1. _____ to express *time* in the past

   2. _____ to describe a repeated or habitual action in the past

   3. _____ to describe an action that was in progress when something else happened

   4. _____ to express age in the past

   5. _____ to describe ongoing physical, mental, or emotional states in the past

   6. _____ to describe two simultaneous past actions in progress

   a. ¿Tú estudiabas mientras Juan miraba la televisión?.

   b. Tenía 8 años.

   c. Cenaba con mis padres cuando llamaste.

   d. Eran las doce.

   e. Siempre comíamos a las seis.

   f. No me gustaba practicar.

B. **¿*Qué o cuál(es)?*** Complete la pregunta con la palabra interrogativa apropiada.

1. ¿_____ significa (*means*) ciclismo?

2. ¿_____ es tu teléfono?

3. ¿_____ son tus libros?

4. ¿_____ restaurante me recomiendas?

5. ¿_____ es el mejor restaurante de la ciudad?

C. **Superlatives.** Complete las oraciones.

1. (*happiest*) Soy _____ persona _____ feliz _____ mundo.

2. (*best*) Son los _____ jugadores _____ equipo.

3. (*worst*) Es el _____ estudiante _____ _____ clase.

PRUEBA CORTA

A. **El imperfecto.** Complete el párrafo con el imperfecto de los verbos entre paréntesis.

Cuando Mafalda _____[1] (ser) una niña pequeña, ella no _____[2] (asistir) a la escuela. Siempre _____[3] (estar) en casa con su madre, y a veces la _____[4] (ayudar) con los quehaceres domésticos. Muchas veces, durante el día, otras niñas que _____[5] (vivir) cerca _____[6] (ir) a visitarla y todas _____[7] (jugar) en el patio de su casa. Su mamá les _____[8] (servir) galletas y leche y cuando todas sus amigas _____[9] (cansarse[a]) de jugar, ellas _____[10] (volver) a casa.

[a]*to become tired*

B. **Las palabras interrogativas.** Complete las preguntas con la palabra o frase interrogativa apropiada.

1. ¿_____ van Uds. ahora? ¿A casa o al centro?

2. ¿_____ es la chica de pelo rubio?

3. ¿_____ se llama la profesora de francés?

4. ¿_____ están los otros estudiantes? No los veo.

5. ¿_____ es tu clase favorita este semestre?

6. ¿_____ pagaste por tu nuevo coche?

C. Los superlativos. Exprese en español las siguientes frases.

1. (*best*) Es _____ jugador _____ equipo

2. (*best*) Son _____ estudiantes _____ clase.

3. (*worst*) Fue _____ día _____ mi vida.

4. (*best*) Es _____ película _____ año.

5. (*most exciting*) Es _____ deporte _____ emocionante _____ todos.

D. Recuerdos. Ud. va a oír una narración en la que la narradora habla de su vida cuando era niña. Luego va a oír algunas preguntas sobre la narración. Indique la mejor respuesta a cada pregunta.

1. **a.** Trabajaba en Panamá.   **b.** Vivía en Panamá.
2. **a.** Hacía muchísimo calor.   **b.** No hacía mucho calor.
3. **a.** Jugaba béisbol.   **b.** Patinaba con sus amigos.
4. **a.** Iba al cine.   **b.** Iba al centro.
5. **a.** Patinaba con sus padres.   **b.** Patinaba con sus amigos.
6. **a.** Daba paseos en el parque.   **b.** Daba paseos en la playa.
7. **a.** Su quehacer favorito era lavar los platos.   **b.** No le gustaba lavar los platos.

E. Una niñez feliz. Cuando oiga el número correspondiente, forme oraciones con las palabras que se dan. Use el imperfecto de los verbos. Si el sujeto está entre paréntesis, no lo use. Luego escuche la respuesta correcta y repítala.

MODELO: (Ud. ve)   **1.**   (yo) / ser un niño muy feliz
                (Ud. oye)   Uno.
                (Ud. dice)   Era un niño muy feliz.
      (Ud. oye y repite)   Era un niño muy feliz.

2. cuando (yo) ser niño / vivir en Colombia
3. mi familia / tener una casa bonita en Medellín
4. mi hermana y yo / asistir a las escuelas públicas
5. me gustar / jugar con mis amigos
6. todos los sábados / mi mamá y yo / ir de compras
7. los domingos / (nosotros) reunirnos con nuestros abuelos

PUNTOS PERSONALES

❖ **A. Hablando de deportes y quehaceres domésticos.** Conteste las preguntas con oraciones completas.

1. Cuando era estudiante de la escuela secundaria (*high school*), ¿qué hacía Ud. en su tiempo libre?

_____

_____

2. ¿Practicaba algún deporte? ¿Entrenaba con un equipo de la escuela? ¿Con qué frecuencia ganaba su equipo?

_____

_____

3. ¿Qué hace en su tiempo libre ahora?

_____

_____

4. ¿Practica Ud. algún deporte? ¿Cuál?

_____

_____

5. ¿Qué quehaceres domésticos le tocaba hacer a Ud. cuando era estudiante de la escuela secundaria?

_____

_____

6. ¿Cuál de los quehaceres le gustaba menos? ¿Se queja porque todavía le toca hacerlo a Ud. o ahora le toca hacerlo a otra persona?

_____

_____

7. ¿Qué quehaceres domésticos le toca hacer ahora?

_____

_____

❖ B. Su pasado

Paso 1. Conteste las preguntas sobre su vida cuando tenía 15 años.

1. ¿Dónde y con quién vivía Ud.? _____

_____

2. ¿A qué escuela asistía? _____

_____

3. ¿Cómo se llamaba su maestro (teacher) preferido / maestra preferida en la escuela secundaria? ¿Cómo era él/ella? _____

_____

4. ¿Qué materia le gustaba más? _____

_____

(Continúa.)

5. ¿Qué tipo de estudiante era? ¿Siempre recibía buenas notas (*grades*)? _____

_____

6. ¿Qué deportes practicaba? _____

_____

7. Generalmente, ¿qué hacía después de volver a casa? _____

_____

8. Y los fines de semana, ¿qué hacía? _____

_____

Paso 2. Ahora va a oír las mismas preguntas del **Paso 1.** Contéstelas con las respuestas que escribió en el **Paso 1.**

1. ... **2.** ... **3.** ... **4.** ... **5.** ... **7.** ... **8.** ...

❖ **C. Opiniones.** Use el superlativo para dar su opinión sobre los siguientes temas.

MODELO: una persona inteligente: → ¡Yo soy la persona más inteligente de la clase!

1. una ciudad interesante: _____

_____

2. una experiencia emocionante (*exciting*): _____

_____

3. un deporte violento: _____

_____

4. una persona simpática: _____

_____

D. El tiempo libre

Paso 1. En esta entrevista, Rubén, Karina, Miguel René y Tané hablan de lo que les gusta hacer en su tiempo libre. Escuche el **Vocabulario útil** y la entrevista. Luego indique a quién le gusta hacer las siguientes actividades.

Vocabulario útil

platicar   hablar

	Rubén	Karina	Miguel René	Tané
bailar				
descansar				
dormir				
hablar con sus amigos				
ir a tomar un café				
ir a un bar				
ir al cine				
ir de compras				
leer				
salir con sus amigos				
ver sus fotos				

❖ **Paso 2.** Ahora conteste por escrito la siguiente pregunta.

¿Cuáles de las actividades que les gusta hacer a Rubén, Karina, Miguel René y Tané le gusta hacer a Ud. también?

_____

_____

_____

_____

❖**E.** **Guided Composition.** En una hoja aparte, use los siguientes verbos y frases en el orden dado (*given*) para escribir una composición en el imperfecto. En esta composición va a describir un día típico de cuando Ud. era estudiante de la escuela secundaria. Use frases como **casi siempre, nunca, muchas veces** y **generalmente.**

1. despertarse
2. bañarse / ducharse
3. cepillarse los dientes
4. vestirse
5. desayunar
6. despedirse
7. ir a la escuela
8. asistir a clases
9. almorzar
10. conversar y reírse con los amigos
11. volver a casa
12. estudiar
13. sentarse a cenar a las seis
14. si no tener que estudiar
15. mirar la televisión
16. leer
17. decirle «buenas noches» a _____
18. quitarse la ropa
19. acostarse

❖F. **Mi diario.** ¿Qué quehaceres domésticos le tocaba hacer a Ud. cuando estaba en la escuela secundaria? ¿Con qué frecuencia debía hacerlos? Escriba algo en su diario sobre estos quehaceres.

MODELO: Yo debía hacer mi cama todos los días, ¡y lo hacía! También tenía que…

❖ G. **Intercambios.** Escuche las siguientes preguntas y contéstelas por escrito.

1. _____

_____

2. _____

_____

_____

3. _____

_____

4. _____

_____

5. _____

_____

Capítulo 11

La salud

VOCABULARIO Preparación

La salud y el bienestar

A. Las partes del cuerpo humano. Complete las oraciones con las partes del cuerpo humano. ¡OJO! ¡Cuidado con el artículo definido!

boca	dientes	nariz	pulmones
cerebro	estómago	oídos	
corazón	garganta	ojos	

1. Hablamos con _____ y pensamos con _____.

2. Vemos con _____ y oímos con _____.

3. Respiramos con _____ y _____.

4. La sangre (*blood*) pasa por _____.

5. Tragamos (*We swallow*) la comida por _____.

6. La comida se digiere (*is digested*) en _____.

7. Masticamos (*We chew*) con _____.

B. Asociaciones. Ud. va a oír algunas actividades. Indique la parte del cuerpo humano que Ud. asocia con cada actividad. ¡OJO! Hay más de una respuesta posible en algunos casos.

1. los pies	las piernas	los dientes	los brazos
2. los pulmones	los dedos del pie	la nariz	los ojos
3. los pulmones	la boca	las manos	las piernas
4. los dientes	la garganta	el corazón	la boca
5. los ojos	los pulmones	las piernas	el estómago
6. la nariz	los oídos	las orejas	los dedos

C. Algunas partes del cuerpo humano. Identifique las partes del cuerpo humano cuando oiga el número correspondiente. Use **Es...** o **Son...** y el artículo definido apropiado (**el, la, los** o **las**). Luego escuche la respuesta correcta y repítala.

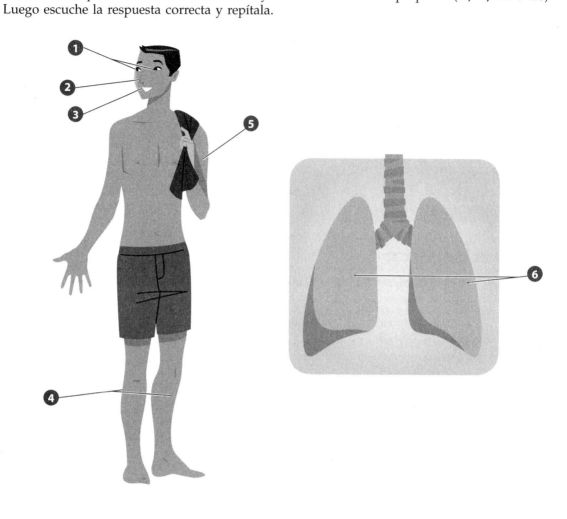

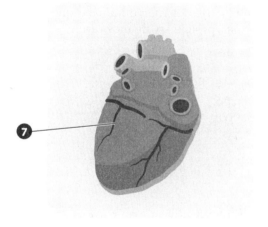

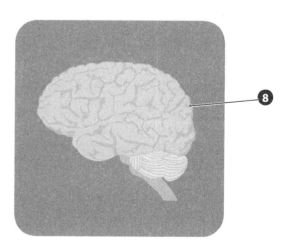

D. **¿Saludable** (*Healthy*) **o no?** Conteste las preguntas, según los dibujos.

1.

    a. ¿Qué hace Angélica?

    _____

    b. ¿Qué tipo de vida lleva?

    _____

    c. ¿Hace Ud. tanto ejercicio como ella?

    _____

2.

    a. ¿Se cuida mucho este hombre?

    _____

    b. ¿Qué debe dejar de hacer?

    _____

    c. ¿Debe hacer más ejercicio?

    _____

E. **¿Practica Ud. algún deporte? ¿Por qué?**

Paso 1. Varios estudiantes hispanos van a hablar acerca de (*about*) los deportes que practican y de por qué los practican. Primero, escuche el **Vocabulario útil.** Luego escuche la narración y escriba el deporte o los deportes que cada estudiante practica. Después escuche otra vez y escriba la razón por la cual (*for which*) cada estudiante practica el deporte.

Vocabulario útil

emocionante	exciting
entretenido/a	entertaining, fun
que uno se engorde	that one get fat
mantenerse en forma	to stay in shape

PERSONA	DEPORTE(S)	RAZÓN POR LA CUAL SE PRACTICA
Clara		
Antonio		
Gabriela		
Patricia		
Teresa		
José		
Xiomara		
Erick		

Nota: Verifique sus respuestas al **Paso 1** en el Apéndice antes de empezar los **Pasos 2** y **3**.

Paso 2. Ahora conteste las siguientes preguntas, según la tabla.

1. ¿Cuál es el deporte más popular entre los estudiantes que contestaron las preguntas?

_____

2. ¿Cuántas de las personas mencionan entre sus razones la salud o los beneficios para el cuerpo?

_____

Paso 3. Ahora va a oír algunas preguntas. Contéstelas con información de la tabla del **Paso 1.** Luego escuche la respuesta correcta y repítala.

1. ... 2. ... 3. ... 4. ... 5. ...

F. ¿Una vida sana? En esta entrevista, Tané, Karina, Miguel René y Rubén hablan de lo que hacen para cuidar su salud. Primero, escuche el **Vocabulario útil.** Luego escuche la entrevista e indique con la primera letra del nombre de la persona (**T** [Tané], **K** [Karina], **MR** [Miguel René] y **R** [Rubén]) quién hace cada acción. ¡**OJO!** A veces hay más de una persona para una acción.

Vocabulario útil

la alimentación	diet
seco/a	dry
la grasa	fat

Tané

Karina

Miguel René

Rubén

1. No fuma. _____
2. Toma mucha agua. _____
3. Come una alimentación balanceada. _____
4. Nunca o casi nunca hace ejercicio. _____
5. Hace mucho ejercicio. _____
6. Lleva una vida sana. _____

En el consultorio del médico

A. **Los enfermos.** Conteste las preguntas, según los dibujos. Use la forma apropiada de las palabras de la lista.

consultorio   ponerle una inyección   tomarle la temperatura

hacerle preguntas   tener dolor de cabeza
   sobre su salud
                          tener dolor de estómago
lavarse las manos

1.

2.

1. a. ¿Dónde está el chico? _____

    b. ¿Qué le hace la enfermera? _____

    c. ¿Qué le va a hacer el médico? _____

2. a. ¿Qué tiene la mujer? _____

    b. ¿Qué hace la médica? _____

    c. ¿Qué hace el enfermero? _____

B. **Cuestiones de salud.** Complete las oraciones con la forma apropiada de las palabras de la lista.

abrir la boca   fiebre   pastillas

antibióticos   hacer ejercicio   respirar

comer comidas sanas   jarabe   sacar la lengua

cuidarse   llevar lentes   tos

dormir lo suficiente

1. Cuando el médico nos examina la garganta, tenemos que _____ y

    _____.

2. Cuatro de las cosas que debemos hacer para llevar una vida sana son _____,

    _____, _____ y _____.

3. Cuando tenemos un resfriado, no podemos _____ bien, tenemos

    _____ y tenemos _____.

4. Generalmente, el doctor / la doctora receta (*prescribes*) un _____ para la tos.

5. Si no vemos bien, es necesario _____.

6. Si tenemos una infección, el médico / la médica nos da _____.

C. **Para completar.** Ud. va a oír una serie de oraciones incompletas. Escoja la letra de la palabra o frase que mejor completa cada oración.

1. a. ponerle una inyección   b. respirar bien
2. a. guardamos cama   b. nos sacan una muela
3. a. una tos   b. un jarabe
4. a. frío   b. un resfriado
5. a. una receta   b. una gripe
6. a. fiebre   b. dolor de garganta

D. Hablando de problemas de salud

Paso 1. En cada dibujo, una persona tiene algún problema de salud. Escriba el problema que tiene cada persona. El dibujo número 1 está parcialmente hecho (*done*). Los círculos son para el **Paso 2.**

Darío

Rebeca

1. ◯ Darío tiene dolor de _____.

   (A Darío le duele el _____.)

2. ◯ _____

   _____

Toño

Gabi

3. ◯ _____

   _____

4. ◯ _____

   _____

Nota: Verifique las respuestas al **Paso 1** en el Apéndice antes de empezar el **Paso 2.**

Paso 2. Ahora va a oír las recomendaciones de la médica. Escriba la letra de la recomendación en el círculo del dibujo correspondiente.

E. En la farmacia

En este diálogo, el farmacéutico habla con Juan Carlos, que todavía está enfermo. Primero, escuche el **Vocabulario útil.** Luego escuche la conversación y conteste las siguientes preguntas por escrito.

Vocabulario útil

es importante que tomes	it's important that you take
no dejes de	don't stop
en cuanto	as soon as
manejar	to drive
que te sientas mejor	I hope you feel better

1. ¿Cuáles son los síntomas de Juan Carlos?

   _____

2. ¿Cuándo fue al médico?

   _____

3. ¿Qué le recetó el médico?

   _____

4. ¿Qué no puede hacer Juan Carlos si toma el jarabe?

   _____

5. ¿Qué va a hacer Juan Carlos al llegar (*when he arrives*) a casa?

   _____

🎧 PRONUNCIACIÓN s, z, ce, and ci

El sonido [s]

- The [s] sound in Spanish can be spelled several different ways and has several variants, depending on the country or region of origin of the speaker. Listen to the difference between the pronunciation of the [s] sound in two distinct Spanish-speaking areas of the world.

Spain:	Vamos a llamar a Susana este lunes.
Latin America:	Vamos a llamar a Susana este lunes.
Spain:	Cecilia siempre cena con Alicia.*
Latin America:	Cecilia siempre cena con Alicia.
Spain:	Zaragoza Zurbarán zapatería*
Latin America:	Zaragoza Zurbarán zapatería

- Notice also that in some parts of the Hispanic world, in rapid speech, the [s] sound becomes aspirated at the end of a syllable or word. Listen as the speaker pronounces these sentences.

    ¿Hasta cuándo vas a tomar las pastillas?   Les recetamos los antibióticos.

A. Repeticiones. Repita las siguientes palabras, imitando lo que oye.

1. salud	pastel	consultorios	años
2. cerebro	hacer	quince	trece
3. ciencias	medicina	inyección	situación
4. corazón	azul	brazos	perezoso

Ahora cuando oiga el número correspondiente, lea las siguientes palabras, frases y oraciones. Luego escuche la pronunciación correcta y repítala.

- **5.** los ojos
- **6.** las orejas
- **7.** unas médicas españolas
- **8.** unas soluciones científicas
- **9.** No conozco a Luz Mendoza de Pérez.
- **10.** Los zapatos de Cecilia son azules.

B. Repaso.[†] Ud. va a oír una serie de palabras que se escriben con **c** o con **q**. Indique la letra que se usa para escribir cada palabra. ¡OJO! Las palabras que va a oír son desconocidas (*unknown*). Preste (*Pay*) atención a los sonidos que oye.

1. c q   **2.** c q   **3.** c q   **4.** c q   **5.** c q   **6.** c q

---

*In much of Spain, **z** and **c** [+ **e** or **i**] are pronounced as θ, which is similar to the English *th* in *think*.
[†]As you have seen, the pronunciation of the Spanish **c** depends on the spelling, where the **c** of **carro, como,** and **cumplir** is [k], and that of **cien** and **cero** is [s] (or θ in much of Spain). To review the spelling and pronunciation of the [k] sound in Spanish, see **Pronunciación:** *c and qu,* on p. 227 of **Appendix 1: Capítulo 9** of this Workbook/Laboratory Manual.

GRAMÁTICA

¿Recuerda Ud.?

A. Escriba la forma indicada del verbo en el imperfecto (**I**) y en el pretérito (**P**).

	I	P
1. cuidarse (nosotros)	_____	_____
2. comer (nosotros)	_____	_____
3. hacer (yo)	_____	_____
4. ser (tú)	_____	_____
5. decir (ellos)	_____	_____
6. saber (yo)	_____	_____
7. jugar (yo)	_____	_____
8. ir (él)	_____	_____
9. poner (Ud.)	_____	_____
10. venir (tú)	_____	_____

B. ¿Imperfecto (**I**) o pretérito (**P**)?

1. _____ To talk about age (with **tener**) or to tell time in the past (**Gramática 27**)

2. _____ To tell about a repeated habitual action in the past (**Gramática 27**)

3. _____ To narrate an action in progress in the past (**Gramática 27**)

4. _____ To describe an action that was completed or begun in the past (**Gramática 23, 24, 25**)

30. Narrating in the Past (Part 5) • Using the Preterite and the Imperfect

A. Otra pequeña historia. Complete el siguiente párrafo con verbos de la lista.

dije	entró	llegué
dijo	era	sentía
dio	eran	tenía
dolían	examinó	

_____[1] las dos en punto cuando (yo) _____[2] al consultorio de la doctora.

Después de veinte minutos la doctora _____[3] y me preguntó qué _____[4]

Le _____[5] que me _____[6] la cabeza y la garganta. Ella me _____[7]

la garganta y la lengua y me _____[8] que no _____[9] nada serio. Me

_____[10] unas pastillas para la garganta y me dijo que volviera[a] en tres días si no me

_____[11] mejor.

[a]_I should return_

B. De viaje. Ud. va a oír algunas oraciones sobre un viaje que hizo Maribel. Primero lea las oraciones escritas. Cuando oiga cada una de las oraciones narradas, escoja el verbo correcto para completar la oración escrita.

1. Por eso _compré / compraba_ un boleto de ida y vuelta.
2. Odio hacer escalas y no _quise / quería_ pasar mucho tiempo en el aeropuerto.
3. No _quise / quería_ sentarme al lado de la ventanilla.
4. _Me desperté / Me despertaba_ muy tarde.
5. Por eso lo _facturé / facturaba_.
6. _Estaba / Estuve_ muy cansada.

C. La última enfermedad. En esta entrevista, Rubén, Tané, Miguel René y Karina hablan de su última enfermedad. Primero, escuche el **Vocabulario útil**. Después escuche la entrevista e indique a quién le pasaron las varias cosas con la primera letra del nombre de la persona: **R** (Rubén**)**, **T** (Tané), **MR** (Miguel René) y **K** (Karina).

Vocabulario útil

el tratamiento	treatment
hace _____ meses	_____ months ago
la varicela	chicken pox
que no me rascara	not to scratch myself
para evitar las cicatrices	to avoid scars
las manos atadas	my hands tied up
la vacuna	vaccine
la intoxicación	allergic reaction

Rubén

Tané

Miguel René

Karina

1. _____ Se enfermó hace cuatro meses.

2. _____ Se enfermó cuando tenía 19 años.

3. _____ Se enfermó hace ocho meses.

4. _____ Se enfermó hace dos meses.

5. _____ Tuvo varicela.

6. _____ Tuvo gripe.

7. _____ Tuvo una reacción alérgica a un repelente de mosquitos.

8. _____ Tuvo asma.

9. _____ El doctor le recomendó tomar antibióticos.

10. _____ Le recomendaron vacunas antialérgicas.

11. _____ El doctor le dijo que no se rascara para evitar las cicatrices.

12. _____ El doctor le recomendó un antialérgico.

D. **Oraciones emparejadas** (*paired*). Empareje las expresiones en español con las explicaciones en inglés.

1. _____ No **pudo** abrir la puerta.   **a.** tried and failed
   _____ No **podía** abrir la puerta.   **b.** was unable to

2. _____ No **quiso** ir.   **a.** didn't want to go (but may have gone)
   _____ No **quería** ir.   **b.** refused to go (and didn't)

3. _____ **Supe** del accidente.   **a.** I knew about the accident.
   _____ **Sabía** del accidente.   **b.** I learned (found out about) . . .

4. _____ **Estuve** allí a las dos.   **a.** I was (already) there at two.
   _____ **Estaba** allí a las dos.   **b.** I was (got) there . . .

5. _____ **Conocí** a tu hermana.   **a.** I met (became acquainted with) . . .
   _____ No **conocía** a tu hermana.   **b.** I didn't know . . .

6. _____ **Tuvimos** que salir.   **a.** We were supposed to go out (but no indication of
   _____ **Teníamos** que salir.   whether we did).
                                           b. We had to go out and did.

7. _____ **Fue** a comprar aspirinas.   **a.** He went to buy . . .
   _____ **Iba** a comprar aspirinas.   **b.** He was going to buy . . .

E. **Un episodio de la niñez**

Paso 1. Indicate which tense should be used under the following circumstances: the preterite or the imperfect. Determining which tense should be used under these circumstances will help you decide which tense to use in **Paso 2,** in which you will complete a narration with the preterite or the imperfect.

1. Scan the first paragraph of the narration. As you will see, it is a description (it sets the scene) of the narrator's life when he or she was 12 years old. Which tense will you use? *preterite / imperfect*

2. Scan the second paragraph. Most of it tells what happened: various people *traveled, stayed* with their grandmother, and so on. Which tense will you use? *preterite / imperfect*

3. In the second paragraph, the verb **ir** is used to describe a situation, not to report an action. The English equivalent is: *Everything was going well.* Which tense will you use? *preterite / imperfect*

4. In this paragraph, does **saber** mean *knew* or *found out*? Because the meaning is probably *found out*, which tense will you use? *preterite / imperfect*

5. Does **querer** mean *wanted to* or *tried*? Since the meaning is probably *wanted to*, which tense will you use? *preterite / imperfect*

6. Since **asegurar** tells what the grandmother *did*, which tense will you use? *preterite / imperfect*

7. Since **estar bien** describes how the narrator's sister was feeling, which tense will you use? *preterite / imperfect*

Paso 2. Ahora complete las oraciones con la forma apropiada del pretérito o imperfecto de los verbos entre paréntesis.

Cuando yo _____¹ (tener) 12 años, _____² (vivir) con mis dos herma-

nas y mis padres en Fresno, donde yo _____³ (asistir) a una escuela privada. Mi

papá _____⁴ (trabajar) en el Banco de América y mi mamá _____⁵

(quedarse) en casa.

Una vez, mis padres _____⁶ (viajar) a Europa. Mis hermanas y yo

_____⁷ (quedarse) con nuestra abuela. Todo _____⁸ (ir) bien hasta que

un sábado por la tarde mi hermana menor _____⁹ (romperse[a]) la nariz. Cuando mis

padres _____¹⁰ (saber) del accidente, _____¹¹ (querer) volver, pero mi

abuela les _____¹² (asegurar[b]) que no era necesario porque mi hermana

_____¹³ (estar) bien.

[a]*to break* [b]*to assure*

F. **¿El pretérito o el imperfecto?** Indique el verbo correcto para completar cada una de las oraciones.

1. Nosotros *supimos / sabíamos* que Francisco *tuvo / tenía* un accidente cuando nos lo contó Mario.
2. Carmela nos llamó para decirnos que no *se sintió / se sentía* bien y que *fue / iba* a quedarse en casa.
3. Raúl no *pudo / podía* estudiar anoche porque se le apagaron las luces. Por eso, *fue / iba* a estudiar en la biblioteca donde afortunadamente (*fortunately*) había luz.
4. Yo no *pude / podía* salir anoche porque *tuve / tenía* fiebre.
5. Yo *estuve / estaba* en el consultorio del médico a las nueve en punto, pero él todavía no *estuvo / estaba* allí.
6. Le prometí al doctor que *fui / iba* a dejar de fumar… ¡y pronto!

G. **¿Un sábado típico?** Ud. va a oír una serie de oraciones que describen la rutina normal de Carlos los sábados. Forme oraciones nuevas para decir lo que Carlos hizo el sábado pasado. Empiece (*Begin*) cada oración con **El sábado pasado...** Luego escuche la respuesta correcta y repítala.

MODELO: (Ud. ve y oye) Todos los sábados, Carlos se despertaba a las siete.
     (Ud. oye) Ocho. →
     (Ud. dice) El sábado pasado, se despertó a las ocho.
     (Ud. oye y repite) El sábado pasado, se despertó a las ocho.

1. Todos los sábados, iba al centro comercial.
2. Todos los sábados, tomaba té por la mañana.
3. Todos los sábados, visitaba a su madre.
4. Todos los sábados, se acostaba temprano.

H. ¿Qué estaban haciendo? Exprese lo que se ve en los dibujos con los verbos indicados. Use el pasado progresivo del primer verbo y el pretérito del segundo.

MODELO: llorar / encontrarlos → Los niños estaban llorando cuando su madre los encontró.

1.

pegarse (*hitting each other*) / verlos

_____

_____

_____

2.

dormir / sonar (*to ring*)

_____

_____

_____

3.

despedirme / entrar

_____

_____

_____

I. **¿Qué tenía el Sr. Correa?** Complete la narración con la forma apropiada del pretérito o imperfecto de los verbos entre paréntesis.

El lunes pasado, cuando Jorge Correa _____ [1] (despertarse),

_____ [2] (decir) que no _____ [3] (sentirse) bien. No

_____ [4] (poder) dormir durante toda la noche. También, le

_____ [5] (doler) el pecho.[a] Inmediatamente _____ [6] (*él:* hacer)

una cita con el médico. _____ [7] (*Él: Estar*) muy nervioso porque

_____ [8] (temer[b]) algo serio, como un ataque al corazón. El doctor lo

_____ [9] (examinar) y le _____ [10] (decir) que no

_____ [11] (ser) nada grave, que solamente _____ [12] (estar)

muy cansado, que _____ [13] (deber) dormir más y comer mejor. El doctor le

_____ [14] (dar) unas vitaminas y unas pastillas para dormir. Y cuando el

Sr. Correa _____ [15] (llegar) a casa, ya _____ [16]

(sentirse) mucho mejor.

[a]*chest* [b]*to fear*

J. **Una decisión difícil**

Paso 1. Ud. va a oír algunas oraciones sobre la decisión de Laura de dejar (*leave*) su pueblo (*hometown*). Después de cada oración, va a oír una expresión temporal. Haga una oración nueva con la expresión temporal al principio (*beginning*) de la oración. Luego cambie el verbo en cursiva (*italics*) al pretérito o imperfecto, según el contexto. Por último (*Last*), escuche la respuesta correcta y repítala.

MODELO: (Ud. ve) *Vivimos* en un pequeño pueblo en las montañas.

(Ud. oye) De niña

(Ud. dice) De niña, vivíamos en un pequeño pueblo en las montañas.

(Ud. oye y repite) De niña, vivíamos en un pequeño pueblo en las montañas.

1. Mi madre *trabaja* en una tienda.
2. Mi padre *trabaja* en un banco.
3. *Vamos* a la ciudad y *compramos* cosas que no *podemos* encontrar en nuestro pueblo.
4. *Empiezo* a asistir a la universidad de la ciudad.
5. *Decido* dejar mi pueblo para siempre.
6. Mis padres *están* tristes porque yo ya no *vivo* con ellos.

Paso 2. Va a oír algunas preguntas. Contéstelas con la información del **Paso 1.** Luego escuche una respuesta posible y repítala.

1. … 2. … 3. … 4. …

¿Recuerda Ud.?

Los usos de *que, qué, lo que* **y** *quién.* Complete las oraciones con la palabra apropiada de la lista. Algunas palabras se usan más de una vez.

que   qué   lo que   quién

1. —¿ _____ es esto? —Es un libro _____ me regaló Anita.

2. —¿Con _____ hablabas? —Con la chica _____ me regaló este libro.

3. —¿Necesitas algo más? —No, _____ necesito es tiempo para descansar.

4. —_____ no entiendo es cómo te enfermaste.

31. Recognizing *que, quien(es), lo que* • Relative Pronouns

A. La salud es lo que importa. Ud. va a oír un anuncio (*ad*). Después complete las oraciones con **que, quien(es)** o **lo que.**

¿Sabe Ud. _____[1] debe hacer para ser saludable emocionalmente? ¿Vive Ud. la vida

_____[2] debe vivir? Para estar seguro de _____[3] necesita para la salud física, con-

sulte con un doctor en _____[4] confía. Pero, para lograr un estado de bienestar mental,

hágase estas preguntas:

• ¿Hay personas con _____[5] puedo hablar si tengo problemas?

• ¿Qué métodos uso para combatir el estrés _____[6] me causan los problemas diarios?

B. Lo que me pasó en el hospital. Complete las oraciones lógicamente con **que, quien(es)** o **lo que.**

1. Esa es la medicina _____ me recetó (*prescribed*) el doctor.

2. ¿Te acuerdas de las pastillas tan caras de _____ te hablé el otro día? Pues ese es el

   doctor _____ me las recetó.

3. El doctor con _____ conversabas antes es especialista en los pulmones.

4. Esos son los pacientes de _____ te hablaba.

5. Las enfermeras a _____ les mandé flores me cuidaron en el hospital.

6. El joven _____ visitó a doña Mercedes en el hospital es el sobrino a

   _____ llamaron por teléfono cuando ella se enfermó.

7. A veces los pacientes no comprendían _____ decían los médicos.

C. Más sobre el hospital. Combine las oraciones y evite la repetición innecesaria. Use el pronombre relativo correcto: **que** o **quien.**

MODELO: Esa es la doctora. Mi amigo me habló de la doctora. →

Esa es la doctora de quien me habló mi amigo.

1. Esa es la doctora. La doctora me cuidó cuando me resfrié gravemente.

   _____

2. Aquella es la paciente. Yo te hablaba de ella ayer.

   _____

3. Esa es Susana Preciado. Compartí (*I shared*) mi cuarto con Susana Preciado.

   _____

4. Estas son las flores. Me mandaron estas flores al hospital.

   _____

5. ¡Esta es la cuenta! ¡Recibí la cuenta hoy!

   _____

¿Recuerda Ud.?

Los pronombres reflexivos. Complete las oraciones con el pronombre reflexivo apropiado.

1. yo _____ levanto

2. tú _____ despides

3. Ud./él/ella _____ viste

4. nosotros/as _____ divertimos

5. Uds./ellos/ellas _____ acuestan

---

32. Expressing *each other* • Reciprocal Actions with Reflexive Pronouns

A. Entre profesor y estudiantes. ¿Entre quiénes ocurre lo siguiente: entre el profesor y los estudiantes o entre los estudiantes solamente?

	ENTRE EL PROFESOR Y LOS ESTUDIANTES	ENTRE LOS ESTUDIANTES
1. Se respetan mucho.	☐	☐
2. Se escuchan con atención.	☐	☐
3. Se ayudan con la tarea.	☐	☐
4. Se ven en la cafetería.	☐	☐
5. Se hablan por teléfono.	☐	☐
6. Se mandan mensajes.	☐	☐
7. Se comunican por e-mail.	☐	☐

B. ¿Qué hacen estas personas?

Paso 1. Cuando oiga el número correspondiente, diga lo que hacen las personas en cada dibujo. Va a describir acciones recíprocas. Luego escuche una respuesta posible y repítala.

1. besarse

2. hablarse por teléfono

3. darse la mano

4. quererse

Paso 2. Ahora, escriba oraciones sobre otra acción recíproca entre las personas de los dibujos del **Paso 1.** Use el pronombre reflexivo apropiado. Los números se refieren a los dibujos del **Paso 1.**

MODELO: **1.** abrazar → Verónica y Armando se abrazan.

2. también mandar mensajes _____

3. saludar _____

4. mirar _____

Nombre _____ Fecha _____ Clase _____

Un poco de todo

A. Un caso de apendicitis. Complete el diálogo entre Alicia y Lorenzo con verbos en el pretérito o imperfecto o con otras palabras necesarias.

LORENZO: ¿Y qué _____[1] (ser) lo más divertido de tu año en Venezuela?

ALICIA: No lo vas a creer, pero fue un ataque de apendicitis que _____[2] (*yo:* tener) en la primavera, la primera semana que _____[3] (estar) allí.

LORENZO: ¿Qué te pasó?

ALICIA: Pues, el lunes cuando _____[4] (levantarme), me _____[5] (sentir) un poco mal, pero no _____[6] (querer) perder el tiempo en el consultorio de un médico. Por la tarde, mi temperatura _____[7] (ponerse) muy alta y me _____[8] (doler) el estómago. Esa noche _____[9] (dormir) muy mal y a la mañana siguiente _____[10] (empezar) a vomitar.

LORENZO: ¿Por qué no _____[11] (llamar) a tus amigos, _____[12] Sres. Durango?

ALICIA: No los _____[13] (conocer) todavía. Pero sí _____[14] (llamar) _____[15] la dependienta del hotel. Cuando me vio, ella _____[16] (llamar) una ambulancia y me _____[17] (*ellos:* llevar) al hospital.

LORENZO: Pues, no veo _____[18] cómico de todo eso.

ALICIA: Espera. Por fin me operaron, y cuando me _____[19] (despertar) de la operación, repetía constantemente en español: «No puedo hablar español… » Por lo visto,[a] _____[20] único que me preocupaba era _____[21] español, pues no lo _____[22] (hablar) bien en aquel entonces.[b] Las enfermeras y _____[23] doctor Castillo se rieron mucho.

[a]Por… *Apparently*   [b]en… *in those days*

B. *Listening Passage:* **El sistema médico en los países hispanos**

❖ **Antes de escuchar.** Do the following prelistening activity. Read the statements about medical systems. Check those that you think apply only to the country in which you live.

1. ☐ El sistema médico está controlado por el gobierno (*government*).
2. ☐ Hay una gran cantidad de compañías de seguro (*insurance companies*).
3. ☐ Hay pocas compañías de seguro.
4. ☐ Cada persona paga los gastos médicos de acuerdo con (*according to*) su salario y no de acuerdo con el tipo de seguro que tiene.
5. ☐ Cualquier (*Any*) persona tiene derecho (*right*) al mejor tratamiento médico posible.
6. ☐ Hay muchas personas que no tienen acceso a tratamiento médico, ya sea (*be it*) por falta de (*lack of*) dinero o porque no tienen seguro médico.

(Continúa.)

7. ☐ A veces, es necesario esperar mucho tiempo para ver al médico.

8. ☐ A veces hay mucha demanda, pero hay pocos servicios y personal disponibles (*available personnel*).

Listening Passage. Now you will hear a passage about the medical systems in most of the Hispanic world. First listen to the **Vocabulario útil** and read the true/false statements in **Después de escuchar** to know what information to listen for. Then listen to the passage.

Vocabulario útil

los ciudadanos	citizens
implicar	to imply
proveer	to provide
la cobertura	coverage
las ventajas	advantages
cobrar	to charge
sin embargo	however
las desventajas	disadvantages
tender a disminuir	to tend to diminish or reduce
trate	treat
en resumen	in summary
el quebradero de cabeza	problem, something that requires great thought

Después de escuchar. Indicate whether the following statements are true (**C**) or false (**F**), according to the passage. Correct the false statements.

1. C F El sistema médico más común en los países hispanos es el privado.

   _____

2. C F El gobierno no controla el sistema médico en muchos países hispanos.

   _____

3. C F En un sistema de medicina socializada, todos tienen derecho a recibir tratamiento médico.

   _____

4. C F Una de las desventajas de la medicina socializada, especialmente en países menos ricos, es que a veces no hay suficientes servicios o suficientes doctores.

   _____

C. **En el consultorio**

Paso 1. En este diálogo, una niña, Marta, está enferma. Su madre la lleva al consultorio de la Dra. Méndez. Escuche el diálogo. Luego va a oír algunas oraciones. Indique si son ciertas (**C**) o falsas (**F**). Si la información no se da, marque **ND** (No lo dice).

1. C F ND   4. C F ND

2. C F ND   5. C F ND

3. C F ND   6. C F ND

Paso 2. Ahora va a participar en una conversación similar en la cual *(in which)* Ud. hace el papel *(you play the role)* del paciente. Antes de escuchar, complete el diálogo con las siguientes frases. Debe conjugar los verbos. **¡OJO!** Las frases que se dan no están en el orden correcto. Verifique las repuestas correctas en el **Apéndice** antes de hacer la conversación en voz alta. Luego haga la conversación en voz alta. Después de oír lo que la doctora dice, lea su respuesta. Por último, escuche la pronunciación correcta y repítala.

el lunes pasado
no tener fiebre
estar muy cansado/a
dolor de cabeza

DOCTORA: Siéntese, por favor. ¿Qué le ocurre?

UD.: Bueno, tengo _____¹

y _____.²

DOCTORA: ¿Cuando empezó a tener estos síntomas?

UD.: _____.³

DOCTORA: Bueno, le voy a tomar la temperatura. Si tiene fiebre, le voy a recomendar que guarde

cama por uno o dos días y que tome un antibiótico.

UD.: Y, ¿si _____⁴?

DOCTORA: Entonces le voy a recomendar que tenga paciencia. Es posible que solo sea un resfriado.

CULTURA

Venezuela

A. Mapa. En el siguiente mapa, identifique Venezuela y la capital de ese país.

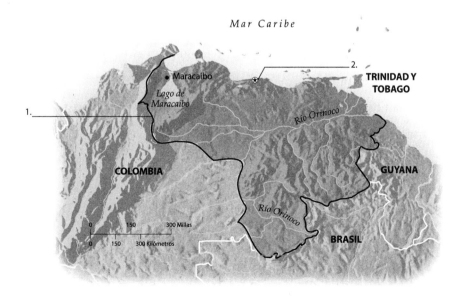

B. Comprensión. Complete las oraciones con información de la **Lectura cultural: Venezuela** de la página 344 del libro de texto.

1. El sistema de salud de Venezuela es _____ y gratuito.

2. El sistema de servicios médicos públicos, también conocido como la seguridad

   _____, se pagan con impuestos (*taxes*).

3. Este sistema sirve especialmente a la gente (*people*) de la clase trabajadora que no puede

   _____ un seguro médico privado.

4. También existe la posibilidad de tener atención médica _____ a través de empleadores (*employers*).

5. En general, el cuidado médico privado de Venezuela es mucho más _____ que en los Estados Unidos.

6. Tres de los países de Latinoamérica que ofrecen ayuda médica a todos sus ciudadanos son

   _____, _____ y _____.

7. El sistema nacional de seguridad social de España contribuye a que los españoles tengan

   (*have*) una de las esperanzas de vida (*life expectancies*) más _____ del mundo.

8. Venezuela tiene la reputación de ser «el país de las mujeres bellas» porque las venezolanas

   han obtenido (*have won*) varias veces el título de _____ y _____.

9. La arepa, un plato típico de Venezuela parecido a la _____, tiene como ingrediente principal harina de maíz blanco.

PÓNGASE A PRUEBA

A. Usando el pretérito y el imperfecto. ¿Se debe usar el pretérito (**P**) o el imperfecto (**I**)?

1. _____ para hablar de una acción habitual o repetida (*repeated*) en el pasado

2. _____ para hablar de una acción que empieza o termina en el pasado

3. _____ para dar una descripción

4. _____ para dar la hora en el pasado o hablar de la edad con **tener** en el pasado

5. _____ para hablar de una acción en progreso en el pasado

B. Los pronombres relativos

1. **¿Que, quien(es)** o **lo que?**

   a. _____ Se usa después de una preposición (**a, de, con, por, para**) para hablar de personas.

   b. _____ Se refiere a personas o cosas.

   c. _____ Se refiere a una idea o situación.

2. Justifique el uso de cada pronombre relativo. Use las letras que se dieron para las explicaciones del ejercicio anterior.

1. _____ No entiendo <u>lo que</u> quieres decir (*you mean*).

2. _____ ¿Dónde están las aspirinas <u>que</u> compraste?

3. _____ Esas son las personas <u>con quienes</u> viajamos.

4. _____ ¿<u>De quiénes</u> están hablando?

5. _____ ¿Es ella la mujer <u>que</u> te prestó el dinero?

C. **Acciones recíprocas con pronombres reflexivos.** Combine las dos oraciones con un pronombre reflexivo para indicar que es una acción recíproca.

1. Mi novio/a me quiere. Yo quiero a mi novio/a.

   _____

2. Mi mejor amigo me conoce bien. Yo conozco bien a mi mejor amigo.

   _____

3. Marta llama a sus padres todos los domingos. Sus padres llaman a Marta todos los domingos.

   _____

PRUEBA CORTA

A. **El trabajo.** Complete las oraciones con la forma correcta del pretérito o del imperfecto del verbo entre paréntesis, según el contexto.

Cuando yo _____[1] (ser) niño, no _____[2] (tener) que trabajar porque mis

padres _____[3] (pagar) todos mis gastos.[a] Una vez, el dueño de un restaurante me

_____[4] (preguntar) si yo _____[5] (querer) ayudarlo los fines de semana,

pero yo no _____[6] (poder) hacerlo porque mis padres no _____[7]

(darme) permiso.[b] Ellos _____[8] (creer) que yo _____[9] (ser) muy joven

para trabajar. Más tarde, cuando _____[10] (*yo:* tener) 15 años, _____[11]

(conseguir) un empleo y finalmente _____[12] (empezar) a ganar mi propio[c] dinero.

[a]*expenses* [b]*permission* [c]*own*

B. ¿*Que, quien(es)*, o *lo que*? Complete las oraciones lógicamente con **que, quien(es)**, o **lo que.**

1. ¿Son estos los antibióticos _____ tienes que tomar?

2. Ayer conocí a la enfermera de _____ me hablaste.

3. Los pacientes hicieron _____ les dijo el doctor.

4. Ese es el especialista a _____ consultó mi padre.

5. ¿Ya vino la muchacha _____ conocimos ayer?

C. Acciones recíprocas. Complete cada oración con la forma apropiada del presente del verbo entre paréntesis para indicar que la acción es recíproca.

1. A veces, cuando los amigos _____ (despedir), _____ (dar) la mano.

2. Muchos padres e hijos _____ (hablar) por teléfono cuando viven lejos.

3. Las relaciones siempre son mejores entre los jefes y los empleados cuando _____ (respetar).

4. Tradicionalmente, los novios no _____ (ver) antes de la ceremonia de la boda (*wedding*).

5. Los buenos amigos _____ (ayudar) frecuentemente.

D. Una enfermedad muy grave. Cuando oiga el número correspondiente, forme oraciones con las palabras que se dan y en el orden en el cual (*in which*) se dan. Use el pretérito o el imperfecto de los verbos, según el contexto. Si el sujeto está entre paréntesis, no lo use. Luego escuche la respuesta correcta y repítala.

MODELO:　　　　　　　(Ud. ve)　**1.** el mes pasado / (yo) enfermarse gravemente
　　　　　　　　　　　(Ud. oye)　Uno.
　　　　　　　　　　　(Ud. dice)　El mes pasado me enfermé gravemente.
　　　　(Ud. oye y repite)　El mes pasado me enfermé gravemente.

2. (yo) estar en el trabajo / cuando de repente / (yo) sentirse muy mal
3. (yo) estar mareado / y (yo) tener fiebre muy alta
4. mi jefe (*boss*) / llamar al hospital inmediatamente
5. la ambulancia / llevarme al hospital / en seguida
6. (yo) tener que pasar / cuatro días en el hospital

❖ PUNTOS PERSONALES

A. Su salud. Vamos a hablar de su salud. Conteste con oraciones completas.

1. ¿Lleva Ud. anteojos o lentes de contacto? ¿Ve Ud. bien sin ellos?

_____

_____

2. ¿Duerme Ud. lo suficiente? ¿Cuántas horas duerme por lo general?

_____

_____

3. ¿Qué deportes practica Ud.? ¿Levanta pesas o hace ejercicios aeróbicos?

_____

_____

4. ¿Come Ud. comidas sanas? ¿Qué cosas come Ud. generalmente?

_____

_____

5. ¿Qué le pasa a Ud. cuando no se cuida?

_____

_____

B. **Opiniones.** Conteste las preguntas, según su opinión.

1. ¿Qué es lo bueno (o lo malo) de vivir cerca de una playa? _____

_____

2. ¿Qué es lo mejor de dejar de fumar? _____

_____

3. ¿Qué es lo peor de resfriarse? _____

_____

4. ¿Qué es lo malo de ir al dentista? _____

_____

C. **La reciprocidad.** Describa las acciones y sentimientos recíprocos entre Ud. y su mejor amigo/a. Use por lo menos cinco de los verbos de la siguiente lista.

admirar	hablar	querer
ayudar	llamar	respetar
escribir	prestar (ropa, dinero)	saludar

MODELO: Nos vemos por lo menos (*at least*) tres veces por semana.

_____

_____

_____

_____

D. Preguntas personales

Paso 1. Ud. va a oír una breve narración sobre cada uno de los siguientes temas:

1. lo que se debe hacer para ser saludable emocionalmente
2. lo que se debe hacer cuando se tiene problemas
3. lo que se debe hacer para combatir el estrés que causan los problemas diarios

Paso 2. Ahora va a oír algunas preguntas sobre los temas del **Paso 1.** Contéstelas por escrito, según su propia (*own*) opinión o experiencia.

1. _____
   _____

2. _____
   _____

3. _____
   _____

E. Guided Composition. En una hoja aparte, escriba una composición de tres párrafos sobre cómo cuida Ud. su salud.

Primer párrafo: Sus hábitos personales

- ¿Hace ejercicio? ¿Qué tipo de ejercicio hace? ¿Cuántas veces por semana?
- ¿Practica deportes? ¿Cuáles?
- ¿Come comidas sanas? Dé ejemplos.
- ¿Con qué frecuencia visita Ud. al médico y al dentista?
- ¿Fuma?
- ¿Con qué frecuencia visita Ud. al médico y al dentista?

Segundo párrafo: ¿Qué hace cuando tiene problemas de salud como los siguientes?

- dolor de cabeza, de garganta
- una tos persistente
- una fiebre
- le molestan los ojos

Tercer párrafo: Plan de salud

- ¿Qué plan tiene para mejorar (*improve*) su salud? ¿O se siente satisfecho/a (*satisfied*) con su salud?

F. Mi diario

Escriba sobre la última vez que Ud. se resfrió. Mencione lo siguiente:

- cuándo ocurrió
- los síntomas que tenía
- lo que hizo para mejorarse
- cuánto tiempo le duró (*lasted*) el resfriado

Si Ud. no se ha resfriado nunca (*If you've never had a cold*), explique este fenómeno en su diario y diga además lo que Ud. hace para mantenerse tan sano/a.

G. Intercambios. Escuche las siguientes preguntas y contéstelas por escrito.

1. _____
   _____

2. _____
   _____

3. _____
   _____

Capítulo 12

Conectad@s

VOCABULARIO   Preparación

La ciudad y el barrio

A. Nuestro apartamento. Complete el párrafo con la forma apropiada de las palabras de la lista.

afueras	calefacción	piso
alquilar	centro	planta baja
alquiler	dirección	portero
anciano	dueño	vecino
ascensor	electricidad	vista
barrio	inquilino	

Mi compañero y yo acabamos de _____[1] un apartamento en Nueva York. Nuestra

nueva _____[2] es 154 E. 16th St. Nos gusta este _____[3] porque es

relativamente tranquilo y limpio. El _____[4] del apartamento no es muy caro porque

está en el tercer[a] _____[5] y el edificio de apartamentos no tiene _____.[6]

Tampoco tiene muy buena _____,[7] pero eso no nos importa. Lo importante es que,

como[b] el edificio está en el _____[8] de la ciudad, podemos ir caminando a todas

partes. Nos gusta más vivir en el centro que en las _____[9] porque todo es más

conveniente. Al lado de nuestro edificio hay una residencia para _____[10] y, cuando

hace buen tiempo, se ve a mucha gente mayor[c] sentada[d] en los bancos[e] tomando el sol.

En nuestro edificio nosotros, los _____,[11] pagamos el gas, la

_____[12] y la _____,[13] y los _____[14] pagan el agua.

Una de las ventajas[f] de vivir en este edificio es que hay un _____[15] que vive en

la _____[16] y lo cuida[g] todo. Todavía no conocemos bien a nuestros

_____,[17] pero el portero dice que todos son muy amables.

[a]*third* [b]*since* [c]gente... *elderly people* [d]*seated* [e]*benches* [f]*advantages* [g]lo... *takes care of*

B. Definiciones

Paso 1. Ud. va a oír algunas definiciones. Escoja la palabra que se define.

1. **a.** la inquilina   **b.** la residencia
2. **a.** las afueras   **b.** el alquiler
3. **a.** el barrio   **b.** la vecina
4. **a.** el portero   **b.** el ascensor
5. **a.** mudarse   **b.** alquilar
6. **a.** la residencia de ancianos   **b.** la vista
7. **a.** el segundo piso   **b.** el primer piso

Paso 2. Ahora va a oír las definiciones otra vez. Cuando las oiga, diga la respuesta. Luego escuche la respuesta correcta y repítala. Empiece cada oración con **Es…**

MODELO: (Ud. oye)   Uno. La persona que alquila un apartamento o una casa.
                 (Ud. dice)   Es la inquilina.
        (Ud. oye y repite)   Es la inquilina.

2. …   3. …   4. …   5. …   6. …   7. …

C. Vocabulario útil para hablar de viviendas

Paso 1. En esta entrevista Alexander habla de su trabajo en Costa Rica. No se da una lista de **Vocabulario útil.** Ud. va a emparejar las palabras con sus definiciones correspondientes. Primero, escuche la entrevista. Luego empareje las palabras y frases con sus definiciones.

_____ **1.** pasos (*steps*) burocráticos

_____ **2.** casas que están separadas de otras casas (*free-standing*)

_____ **3.** que tiene muebles

_____ **4.** animales que ponen (*lay*) huevos y que también se comen

_____ **5.** tierras (*land*), viviendas (*housing*) y edificios que se pueden comprar, vender y alquilar

_____ **6.** ir lejos de un lugar

_____ **7.** personas

_____ **8.** con más espacio

a. los bienes raíces
b. los trámites
c. alejarse
d. las casas particulares
e. las aves (*birds*) de corral
f. la gente
g. amueblado/a
h. amplio/a

Paso 2. Escuche la entrevista otra vez. Luego complete los siguientes párrafos con información de la entrevista. También se usan algunas palabras del **Paso 1.**

Alexander Borbón trabaja para una compañía de _____[1] en _____[2] (ciudad). Básicamente, lo que él hace es _____[3] casas y ayudar con los _____[4] para comprarlas o alquilarlas.

La _____[5] típica en Costa Rica varía mucho. En el _____[6] hay muchos _____[7] y condominios. Los condominios pueden estar _____[8] o sin muebles. Pero en las afueras, hay casas que tienen un _____[9] más amplio con _____[10] de corral.

Tengo… Necesito… Quiero… (Part 3)

A. Cosas electrónicas. Complete las oraciones con la palabra apropiada.

bajar   fotocopia   guardar   pantalla
correo electrónico   grabar   imprimir   remoto

1. Por favor, mándeme la información a mi _____ personal.

2. Acabamos de instalar una televisión de _____ plana. El control

   _____ es un modelo universal y funciona muy bien.

3. La primera cosa que necesitas recordar es _____ tu documento antes de apagar

   la computadora.

4. Es buena idea hacer una _____ de la primera página de tu pasaporte antes de

   viajar.

5. Me gustaría _____ el concierto de Juanes, pero si me ven, me van a echar

   (*throw out*) del teatro.

6. Necesito _____ este documento del Internet; más tarde puedo

   _____lo para leerlo con tranquilidad.

B. Maravillas y problemas de la tecnología. Complete las oraciones con la forma apropiada de las palabras de la lista.

almacenar   cámara   DVD   GPS   parada
app   contraseña   entrar en Facebook   impresora   teléfono fijo
buzón de voz   descargar   fallar

1. Una vez me _____ la computadora y, como (*since*) no recordé

   _____ mi trabajo, lo perdí todo.

2. Prefiero ver películas en el Internet en vez de (*instead of*) comprar un _____.

3. Con mi _____ digital y esta buena _____ puedo imprimir mis

   propias (*own*) fotos.

4. El otro día no pude _____ porque olvidé mi _____.

5. Primero, llámeme al _____. Si no contesto, llámeme al teléfono celular. Si todavía

   no contesto, déjeme un mensaje en el _____.

6. La semana pasada _____ el _____ de Twitter en mi teléfono

   celular.

7. Si no tuviera (*I didn't have*) _____ en mi teléfono celular, nunca encontraría

   (*would I find*) las _____ del autobús.

C. Cosas del trabajo. Imagine que Ud. habla con un amigo sobre algunos problemas de su trabajo. Complete las oraciones con la forma apropiada de las palabras de la lista.

aumento	conseguir	funcionar	manejar
cambiar de trabajo	fallar	jefe/a	sueldo

1. Si la _____ no me da un _____ de sueldo, voy a

   _____. Pero antes de dejar (*quitting*) mi trabajo, debo _____ otro.

2. Del _____ que gano (*I earn*) cada mes, el gobierno (*government*) me quita

   (*takes away*) el 20%.

3. ¡Qué lata! (*What a pain!*) Ayer la computadora de la oficina _____, y fue imposible

   terminar el trabajo.

4. Esta mañana tuve que _____ mi moto para ir a la oficina porque mi coche no

   _____.

D. Identificaciones. Cuando oiga el número correspondiente, identifique las siguientes cosas. Empiece cada oración con **Es un...** o **Es una...** Luego escuche la respuesta correcta y repítala.

MODELO: (Ud. oye) Uno.
               (Ud. dice) Es una impresora.
         (Ud. oye y repite) Es una impresora.

2. ...   **3.** ...   **4.** ...   **5.** ...   **6.** ...

PRONUNCIACIÓN ñ and ch

- The pronunciation of the letter **ñ** is similar to the sound [ny] in the English words *canyon* and *union*. However, in Spanish it is pronounced as one single sound. Listen to the pronunciation of the following words.

  Toño   montaña   araña   uña   Logroño

- In Spanish, when the letters **c** and **h** are combined, they are pronounced like the English *ch* in *church*. Listen to the pronunciation of the following words.

  derecho   coche   anoche   luchar   charco

A. **Repeticiones.** Repita las siguientes palabras, imitando lo que oye.

   1. cana / caña   sonar / soñar   mono / moño   tino / tiño   cena / seña
   2. año   señora   cañón   español   pequeña   compañero

Ahora, cuando oiga el número correspondiente, lea las siguientes oraciones. Luego escuche la pronunciación correcta y repítala.

   3. El Sr. Muñoz es de España.
   4. Los niños pequeños no enseñan español.
   5. La Srta. Ordóñez tiene 20 años.
   6. El cumpleaños de la Sra. Yáñez es mañana.

B. **Más repeticiones.** Repita las siguientes palabras, imitando lo que oye.

   1. mucho   muchacho   Conchita   Chile   mochila   hache

Ahora, cuando oiga el número correspondiente, lea las siguientes oraciones. Luego escuche la pronunciación correcta y repítala.

   2. Siga derecho por la calle Atocha.
   3. Los muchachos compraron mucha leche.
   4. Ese coche es del estudiante chileno.
   5. Necesito una cuchara para el chocolate.

C. **A escoger.** Va a oír algunas palabras. Escoja la palabra que oye.

   1. **a.** pena   **b.** peña
   2. **a.** una   **b.** uña
   3. **a.** Lena   **b.** leña
   4. **a.** suena   **b.** sueña
   5. **a.** mono   **b.** moño

D. **Oraciones.** Ud. va a oír algunas oraciones que tienen palabras con los sonidos **ñ** y **ch.** Preste atención y escriba lo que oye.

   1. _____
   2. _____
   3. _____
   4. _____
   5. _____

GRAMÁTICA

¿Recuerda Ud.?

A. Los mandatos: *Ud.* y *Uds.* Escriba la forma indicada del mandato formal. Preste atención a la posición de los pronombres de complemento directo, indirecto y reflexivo.

1. dejarlo   <u>Déjelo</u> Ud.   No <u>lo deje</u> Ud.

2. escribirlo   _____ Uds.   No _____ Uds.

3. jugarlo   _____ Ud.   No _____ Ud.

4. decírmelo   _____ Ud.   No _____ Ud.

5. dárselo   _____ Uds.   No _____ Uds.

B. ¿Cómo se dice en español? Traduzca (*Translate*) los siguientes mandatos de inglés a español, según la forma indicada del verbo.

1. irse, Uds.: *Don't leave yet* (todavía).   _____

2. conseguir, Ud.: *Get another job.*   _____

3. cansarse, Uds.: *Don't get tired.*   _____

4. olvidarse, Ud.: *Don't forget.*   _____

33. Influencing Others (Part 2) • *Tú* (Informal) Commands

A. ¡Escúchame, Anita! Déle mandatos afirmativos o negativos a su compañera Anita. ¡OJO! ¡Cuidado con los acentos y la posición de los pronombres!

1. (Subir) _____ la calefacción.

2. (cambiar) No _____ tanto el canal.

3. (usar) No _____ ese teléfono ahora; _____ tu teléfono celular.

4. (Apagar) _____ las luces (*lights*) antes de acostarte.

5. (quejarse) No _____ tanto del trabajo. ¡Por lo menos, tienes trabajo!

6. (mandarle) No _____ un correo electrónico; _____ un fax.

7. (Prestarme) _____ tus llaves, por favor.

8. (Decirme) _____ la verdad; no _____ tonterías. (*nonsense*)

B. Más mandatos. Déles mandatos apropiados, afirmativos o negativos, a sus amigos y a varios miembros de su familia.

    MODELO: Rosa nunca me escucha. → Rosa, escúchame.

1. Susana juega en la sala.   Susana, no _____.

2. José no deja de mandar mensajes.   José, _____.

3. Juan siempre llega tarde.   Juan, no _____.

4. Carmela se viste muy mal.   Carmela, _____.

5. Tito no se lava las manos antes de comer.   Tito, _____.

6. Jorge es pesado (*a pain*).   Jorge, no _____.

7. Miguel pone los pies en el sofá.   Miguel, no _____.

8. David toca la pantalla.   David, no _____.

9. Alex no tiene cuidado (*is not careful*) al (*upon*) cruzar la calle.   Alex, _____.

C. A la hora de cenar. Leonor le hace unas preguntas a su mamá, quien le contesta con un mandato informal. Complete los dos mandatos posibles. Use pronombres del complemento directo e indirecto para evitar la repetición innecesaria.

    MODELO: ¿Preparo la ensalada? → Sí, prepárala./No, no la prepares.

1. ¿Pongo la mesa?

    Sí, _____ No, _____

2. ¿Le sirvo leche a Claudia?

    Sí, _____ No, _____

3. ¿Te traigo la otra silla?

    Sí, _____ No, _____

4. ¿Te lavo los platos?

    Sí, _____ No, _____

D. Encuesta: Los mandatos de sus padres. Ud. va a oír algunos mandatos. Indique si cada mandato es uno de los que sus padres le daban a Ud. cuando era niño/a. Escoja respuestas que son correctas, según su propia (*own*) experiencia.

MANDATOS AFIRMATIVOS

1. ☐ Sí ☐ No   3. ☐ Sí ☐ No
2. ☐ Sí ☐ No   4. ☐ Sí ☐ No

MANDATOS NEGATIVOS

5. ☐ Sí ☐ No   7. ☐ Sí ☐ No
6. ☐ Sí ☐ No   8. ☐ Sí ☐ No

E. La vida doméstica de la Cenicienta (*Cinderella*). Haga el papel (*Play the role*) de la madrastra (*stepmother*) y dígale a la Cenicienta lo que debe hacer antes de ir al baile. Use los verbos que oye para darle mandatos informales afirmativos. Luego escuche la respuesta correcta y repítala.

MODELO: (Ud. oye) Uno. lavar los platos
(Ud. dice) Lava los platos.
(Ud. oye y repite) Lava los platos.

2. ... **3.** ... **4.** ... **5.** ...

F. ¡No lo hagas! Imagine que Ud. es el padre o la madre de la chica que se ve en los dibujos. Cuando oiga el número correspondiente, dígale que no haga (*not to do*) las acciones que se ven en cada dibujo. Use mandatos informales negativos. Luego escuche la respuesta correcta y repítala.

MODELO: (Ud. oye) Uno.
(Ud. ve)

1. pegarle a Isabel
(Ud. dice) No le pegues a Isabel.
(Ud. oye y repite) No le pegues a Isabel.

2. saltar (*to jump*) / cama   **3.** poner / mesa

4. pasear en bicicleta / sin casco   **5.** escribir / pared

34. Expressing Subjective Actions or States • Present Subjunctive (Part 1): An Introduction

A. Formas. Complete la siguiente tabla con las formas apropiadas de los verbos en el presente de subjuntivo.

YO	YO/UD. (SUBJUNCTIVE)	NOSOTROS (SUBJUNCTIVE)
llego	que *llegue*	que _____
empiezo	que _____	que *empecemos*
conozco	que *conozca*	que _____
juego	que _____	que *juguemos*
consigo	que *consiga*	que _____
divierto	que *divierta*	que _____
duermo	que _____	que *durmamos*

B. ¡Termínelo Ud.! Indique cuáles de las opciones son correctas en cada caso. **¡OJO!** Hay dos opciones posibles en cada caso.

1. Prefiero…
   a. quedarme en casa.
   b. que te quedas en casa.
   c. que te quedes en casa.

2. No me gusta…
   a. que sales sin mí.
   b. que salgas sin mí.
   c. salir solo.

3. Es importante…
   a. mandar este fax hoy.
   b. que mandemos este fax hoy.
   c. que mandamos este fax hoy.

4. Me alegro de…
   a. que estés aquí.
   b. estar aquí.
   c. que estás aquí.

5. Queremos…
   a. encontrarnos allí.
   b. que nos encuentras allí.
   c. que nos encuentres allí.

6. Dudo…
   a. que él sabe resolver el problema.
   b. que él sepa resolver el problema.
   c. poder resolver el problema.

C. Ideas incompletas. Haga oraciones y cambie el infinitivo por la forma apropiada del subjuntivo.

1. Espero que Ud. … _____ (poder) acabar hoy.

   no se _____ (olvidar) de almacenar la información.

   _____ (saber) usar esta computadora.

2. Dudo que ellos… _____ (empezar) hoy.

   nos _____ (mandar) el fax hoy.

   nos _____ (decir) todos sus problemas.

3. Insisten en que tú… _____ (llegar) a tiempo.

   _____ (ser) más responsable.

   _____ (buscar) otro modelo más económico.

(Continúa.)

4. No quieren que nosotros… _____ (ir) solos.

_____ (alquilar) un apartamento en este barrio.

_____ (perder) mucho tiempo.

 D. ¿Qué quiere Arturo?

Paso 1. Arturo va a hablar de lo que él quiere que hagan sus hermanos. Primero, escuche el **Vocabulario útil.** Luego escuche a Arturo e indique en la siguiente tabla lo que Arturo quiere que haga o no haga cada hermano.

Vocabulario útil

compartir	to share
la dichosa	the lucky one
la queja	complaint
bajar	to lower

PERSONA	NO JUGAR CON SU WII HASTA LAS DOCE DE LA NOCHE	NO USAR SU COCHE	PRESTARLE SU iPAD	BAJARLE EL VOLUMEN A SU MÚSICA
su hermana				
su hermano menor				
sus hermanitos				

Nota: Verifique sus respuestas al **Paso 1** en el Apéndice antes de empezar el **Paso 2.**

Paso 2. Ahora conteste las preguntas que oye con información de la tabla que completó en el **Paso 1.** Luego escuche la respuesta correcta y repítala.

1. …   **2.** …   **3.** …   **4.** …

 E. ¿Qué quieren? Ud. va a oír algunas preguntas. Primero, escuche el **Vocabulario útil.** Luego escuche las preguntas y contéstelas con la forma del presente de subjuntivo del verbo en las oraciones que se dan.

Vocabulario útil

el/la empleado/a   employee

MODELO:	(Ud. ve)	**1.** Sara no llega a tiempo.
	(Ud. oye)	Uno. ¿Qué quiere la jefa?
	(Ud. dice)	Quiere que Sara llegue a tiempo.
	(Ud. oye y repite)	Quiere que Sara llegue a tiempo.

2. Lucía no guarda los documentos.
3. Uds. no hacen su trabajo.
4. Nosotros no cambiamos la tinta (*ink*) de la impresora.
5. Los secretarios no imprimen los documentos.
6. El jefe no les da un aumento de sueldo.

35. Expressing Desires and Requests • Use of the Subjunctive (Part 2): Influence

A. Jefes y empleados (*employees*)

Paso 1. Complete cada oración con la forma apropiada del presente de subjuntivo.

1. La jefa: Insisto en que mis empleados…

   (decir la verdad) _____

   (llegar a tiempo) _____

   (aceptar responsabilidad) _____

   (saber usar la computadora) _____

   (no entrar en Facebook en el trabajo) _____

2. El empleado: Es importante que mi trabajo…

   (resultar interesante) _____

   (gustarme) _____

   (no estar lejos de casa) _____

   (darme oportunidades para avanzar [*advance*]) _____

Paso 2. Ahora complete estos comentarios con la forma apropiada del verbo entre paréntesis: el infinitivo, el presente de indicativo o el presente de subjuntivo.

1. (trabajar): Mi jefe es exigente (*demanding*) y antipático; quiere que (nosotros)

   _____ este sábado, pero ya tengo otros planes y no quiero _____.

2. (almorzar): Nuestro director prefiere que (nosotros) _____ en la oficina, pero yo

   prefiero _____ en el parque.

3. (traer): No puedes _____ tu gato a la oficina. La jefa prohíbe que (nosotros)

   _____ mascotas al trabajo.

4. (pedir): En la oficina no permiten que (nosotros) _____ vacaciones en verano.

   Por eso, voy a _____ mis dos semanas en enero.

5. (obtener): Si yo no _____ un trabajo de tiempo completo (*full-time*), es urgente

   que (yo) _____ uno de tiempo parcial (*part-time*), por lo menos.

B. **Consejos y opiniones.** Complete las oraciones con la forma apropiada del verbo indicado. Use complementos pronominales cuando sea posible. **¡OJO!** No se usa el subjuntivo en todas las oraciones.

MODELOS: Isabel piensa *escribirles otra carta* a sus primos mañana, pero es importante

escribírsela hoy.

Isabel piensa *escribirles otra carta* a sus primos mañana, pero es importante que

se la escriba hoy.

1. Tienes que *mandarles el cheque* a los muchachos. Es urgente que _____ hoy.

2. No olvides *pedirle el aumento* al jefe. Es necesario _____ pronto.

3. Ellos *buscan un taxi* delante del cine, pero es mejor _____ en la esquina (*corner*).

4. Manuel no quiere *empezar su trabajo* hasta el lunes. Su jefe prefiere que _____ mañana.

5. José dice que va a *traerme el cheque* esta noche, pero no es necesario que _____ hasta mañana.

C. **¿Qué quieres que haga (yo)?** Imagine que Ud. quiere ayudar a un amigo que va a dar una fiesta. Hágale las siguientes preguntas en español.

MODELO: *What do you want me to buy?* → ¿Qué quieres que compre?

1. *What do you want me to bring?* _____

2. *What do you want me to prepare?* _____

3. *What do you want me to look for?* _____

4. *What do you want me to cook?* _____

D. **¿Qué recomienda el nuevo jefe?** Imagine que Ud. tiene un nuevo jefe y que él quiere hacer algunos cambios en la oficina. Cuando oiga el número correspondiente, diga lo que recomienda el nuevo jefe con las frases que se dan. Luego escuche la respuesta correcta y repítala.

MODELO: (Ud. oye) Uno.

(Ud. ve) **1.** El jefe: recomienda… / Ud. buscar otro trabajo

(Ud. dice) El jefe recomienda que Ud. busque otro trabajo.

(Ud. oye y repite) El jefe recomienda que Ud. busque otro trabajo.

2. El jefe: recomienda… / yo copiar el contrato
3. El jefe: insiste en… / todos trabajar hasta muy tarde
4. El jefe: prohíbe… / Federico dormir en la oficina
5. El jefe: sugiere… / tú escribir el blog de la empresa (*company*)

E. **Antes del viaje: ¿Qué quiere Ud. que hagan estas personas?** Imagine que Ud. viaja al extranjero con un grupo de estudiantes. Con las frases que se dan, dígales a los estudiantes lo que Ud. quiere que ellos o ellas hagan. Empiece cada oración con **Quiero que…**

MODELO: (Ud. oye) hacer las maletas

(Ud. ve) Uds.

(Ud. dice) Quiero que Uds. hagan las maletas.

1. Toño   2. tú   3. Ana y Teresa   4. todos   5. todos

F. ¿Hermanito o hermanita?

Paso 1. Va a escuchar una conversación entre Manolo, su esposa Lola, que está embarazada, y su hija Marta. Primero, escuche el **Vocabulario útil.** Luego escuche la conversación y escriba los dos verbos que Ud. oye en la conversación que están en el presente de subjuntivo. (Uno de ellos se usa dos veces.)

Vocabulario útil

la tertulia	una reunión social donde se habla de cosas interesantes
echar de menos	to miss (a person)
ojalá que pudiera	I wish I could
me pidió que escribiera	asked me to write
no me queda...	I don't have any . . . left
cuidar	to take care of
vale	OK

1. _____   2. _____

Paso 2. Ahora complete las siguientes oraciones sobre lo que quieren las siguientes personas.

1. Manolo quiere que Lola _____ a la tertulia con los amigos.

2. Javier quiere que Lola _____ una crítica de un artículo.

3. Lola quiere _____ bien al bebé.

4. Marta y Manolo quieren que el nuevo bebé _____ una niña.

Un poco de todo

A. La familia Rosales. Complete la siguiente narración con la forma apropiada de los verbos o la palabra correcta entre paréntesis.

La familia Rosales acaba de _____[1] (mudarse) a un apartamento en el centro de la

ciudad. El apartamento _____[2] (le/les) gusta a todos porque

_____[3] (es/está) cerca de las escuelas, las tiendas y las paradas del metro y del

autobús. También, hay un mercado donde venden toda clase de verduras, carnes y pescado.

Aunque[a] tienen coche, el Sr. Rosales prefiere _____[4] (usar) el metro porque es más

rápido y barato _____[5] (que/qué) usar el coche. Como la señora también trabaja,

es necesario que _____[6] (su/sus) hijos la _____[7] (ayudar) con los

quehaceres domésticos. Por eso, _____[8] (les/los) dice:

—Chicos, _____[9] (venir) aquí. Necesito _____[10] (enseñarles) cómo

_____[11] (funcionar) la nueva lavadora.

—Y Pepe, quiero que _____[12] (ir) al mercado porque necesitamos más leche y pan.

Pero, por favor, _____[13] (ir) a tu cuarto primero y _____[14]

(ponerse) una camisa limpia.

—Y María, no _____[15] (olvidarse) de llevar este paquete[b] a tu tía Consuelo. Pero,

por favor, no _____[16] (quedarse) mucho tiempo. Vamos a cenar temprano.

[a]Although [b]package

B. *Listening Passage:* **Las redes sociales en Colombia**

❖ **Antes de escuchar.** Before listening, do the following prelistening activity.

Answer these questions to see how much you already know about this topic.

1. ¿Cuál es la capital de Colombia?

_____

2. Aparte de Facebook y Twitter, ¿sabe Ud. el nombre de otra red social?

_____

3. ¿Cuántos usuarios (*users*) de Facebook piensa Ud. que hay en Colombia?

_____

4. ¿Qué sabe Ud. del uso de las redes sociales cuando ocurre un desastre mundial (*global*)?

_____

Listening Passage. Now you will hear a passage about social networking in Colombia and the Spanish-speaking world. First, listen to the **Vocabulario útil** and read the statements in **Después de escuchar** to know what information to listen for. Then listen to the passage.

Vocabulario útil

he conocido	I have met
diariamente	daily
por medio de	by means of
los usuarios	users
no parecen nada	don't seem like anything
el terremoto	earthquake
devastador	devastating
los supervivientes	survivors
han sido	have been

Después de escuchar. Check all the statements that are true, according to the passage.

1. ☐ Alberto Morales estudia en una universidad de Brasil.
2. ☐ Los colombianos tienen mucho interés en las redes sociales.
3. ☐ Bogotá es la única ciudad latinoamericana con un gran número de usuarios de Facebook.
4. ☐ Hubo un terremoto devastador en Buenos Aires en 2010.
5. ☐ Alberto menciona que tiene muchos amigos en varios países.

C. Decisiones sobre la vivienda

Paso 1. Ud. va a volver a escuchar la misma entrevista de la actividad C, en **Vocabulario: Preparación: La ciudad y el barrio,** con unas oraciones más al final. Primero, escuche la entrevista. Luego escriba los <u>cuatro</u> verbos en el presente de subjuntivo. No todos los contextos para usar el subjuntivo son contextos que Ud. conoce, pero de todas formas (*anyway*) va a poder identificar los verbos.

1. _____ **2.** _____ **3.** _____ **4.** _____

Paso 2. Ahora va a participar en una conversación telefónica con un agente de bienes raíces en la cual (*in which*) Ud. hace el papel (*you play the role*) de un cliente que busca vivienda. Primero, complete el diálogo con las siguientes oraciones. Segundo, haga la conversación en voz alta. Después de oír lo que el agente dice, lea su respuesta. Luego escuche la pronunciación correcta y repítala. Verifique las repuestas correctas en el Apéndice antes de hacer la conversación en voz alta.

Pues, no tengo coche. Por eso es necesario que yo encuentre un apartamento en el centro.
A mi celular, por favor.
Sí, muy bien. Gracias. Hasta luego.
Busco un apartamento amueblado con dos cuartos.
Sí, claro. Cuanto antes, mejor. (*The sooner, the better.*)
Necesito que el apartamento esté cerca de la universidad.

EL AGENTE: ¿Qué tipo de vivienda busca Ud.?

UD.: _____

_____ 1

EL AGENTE: Eso no es ningún problema, porque hay muchos. A ver, ¿quiere Ud. vivir en el centro
o en las afueras?

UD.: _____

_____ 2

EL AGENTE: Muy bien. ¿Tiene alguna preferencia de barrio o zona?

UD.: _____

_____ 3

EL AGENTE: Ya.[a] Déjeme que mire la lista de apartamentos disponibles[b] con esas características y
hablamos esta tarde. ¿Quiere Ud. que salgamos a ver algunos apartamentos mañana
mismo[c]?

UD.: _____ 4
_____

EL AGENTE: Perfecto. Voy a hacer una lista de posibles apartamentos y algunas citas para ver
apartamentos mañana. Y esta tarde volvemos a hablar. ¿Quiere que lo llame a su
celular o a su casa?

UD.: _____ 5
_____

EL AGENTE: Pues, hablamos más tarde.

UD.: _____ 6
_____

EL AGENTE: De nada. Hasta luego.

[a]*OK* [b]*available* [c]*mañana… as soon as tomorrow*

CULTURA

Colombia

A. Mapa. En el siguiente mapa, identifique Colombia, la capital del país y las siguientes ciudades: Cartagena y Medellín.

B. Comprensión. Complete las oraciones con información de la **Lectura cultural: Colombia** de la página 376 del libro de texto.

a. Los vecinos de un barrio colombiano se _____[1] bien y hasta organizan _____[2] para celebraciones especiales. Es común saber los _____[3] de todos los vecinos del barrio, no solo de los que viven en su edificio de apartamentos. El barrio es un lugar de mucha vida _____,[4] especialmente para los que no _____[5] fuera de casa y para las personas _____.[6]

b. En todas las ciudades hispanas la _____[7] es un lugar central para la organización social y cívica.

c. El _____[8] de Buenos Aires es el más antiguo del Hemisferio

_____,[9] y el de _____[10] es el segundo de Norteamérica en

longitud. Para ayudar a las personas analfabetas, usan un sistema de palabras y dibujos muy

coloridos para identificar las diferentes _____.[11]

d. El baile típico de Colombia es la _____,[12] y la _____[13] es la

flor nacional. _____,[14] un hombre ficticio, representa a todos los campesinos

colombianos que trabajan en los campos cafeteros (*coffee planations*).

PÓNGASE A PRUEBA

A. *Tú* **Commands.** Complete la siguiente tabla.

INFINITIVO	AFIRMATIVO	NEGATIVO	INFINITIVO	AFIRMATIVO	NEGATIVO
decir		*no digas*	salir		
escribir	*escribe*		ser		
hacer			tener	*ten*	
ir			trabajar		*no trabajes*

B. **Present Subjunctive: An Introduction**

1. Escriba el modo subjuntivo de la tercera persona singular (**él/ella**) de los siguientes verbos.

   a. buscar: que _____
   b. dar: que _____
   c. escribir: que _____
   d. estar: que _____
   e. estudiar: que _____
   f. ir: que _____
   g. oír: que _____
   h. poder: que _____
   i. saber: que _____
   j. ser: que _____
   k. traer: que _____
   l. vivir: que _____

2. Complete la siguiente tabla.

comenzar	que yo	que nosotros
dormir	que yo *duerma*	que nosotros
perder	que yo	que nosotros *perdamos*
sentirse	que yo me	que nosotros nos

C. **Use of the Subjunctive: Influence.** Subraye la forma apropiada del verbo.

1. Juan (prefiere / prefiera) que ellos (vienen / vengan) a casa.
2. (Es / Sea) urgente que Ricardo (comience / comienza) a trabajar.
3. El profesor (prohíba / prohíbe) que (entramos / entremos) tarde.
4. Mis padres (insisten / insistan) en que sus amigos (se quedan / se queden) a comer.
5. (Sea / Es) mejor que tú (traes / traigas) el vino.

PRUEBA CORTA

A. **Mandatos.** Use el verbo entre paréntesis para pedirle a su compañero/a de cuarto que haga las cosas indicadas.

1. _____ (Venir) a mirar este programa.

2. No _____ (apagar: *to turn off*) la computadora; necesito trabajar más tarde.

3. _____ (Llamar) al portero y _____ (decirle) que la luz (*light*) se apagó.

4. No _____ (poner) la televisión ahora; _____ (ponerla) después.

5. No _____ (preocuparse: *to worry*) por el trabajo; _____ (descansar) un poco.

B. **¿El infinitivo o el subjuntivo?** Complete las siguientes oraciones con el infinitivo o con el subjuntivo del verbo entre paréntesis.

1. Sugiero que _____ (*tú:* buscar) otro modelo con más memoria.

2. Todos queremos _____ (comprar) una computadora nueva.

3. Un amigo recomienda que _____ (*nosotros:* ir) a Compulandia.

4. Insistimos en _____ (hablar) con el director. Es necesario que _____ (*nosotros:* hablar) primero con él.

5. ¿Es tan importante que tú _____ (comprar) una plasma?

    Francamente, prefiero que no _____ (perder) tu dinero.

C. **Una oficina con problemas.** Ud. es el jefe o la jefa de una oficina con muchos problemas. Ud. va a oír lo que los empleados no quieren hacer. Con los verbos que se dan y las palabras que se escuchan, dígales lo que Ud. quiere que hagan. Use pronombres de complemento directo. Luego escuche la respuesta correcta y repítala.

MODELO: (Ud. oye) **1.** No queremos mandar los documentos.
              (Ud. ve) querer
              (Ud. dice) Pues, yo quiero que Uds. los manden.
        (Ud. oye y repite) Pues, yo quiero que Uds. los manden.

2. recomendar
3. querer
4. sugerir
5. mandar

D. Los mandatos de la niñera (*baby-sitter*). Imagine que Ud. es la niñera de Tito. Dígale a Tito con las frases que oiga lo que debe o no debe hacer. **¡OJO!** Va a usar mandatos informales en sus respuestas. Luego escuche la respuesta correcta y repítala.

MODELO: (Ud. oye)   sentarse en el sofá

(Ud. dice)   Tito, siéntate en el sofá.

(Ud. oye y repite)   Tito, siéntate en el sofá.

1. …   **2.** …   **3.** …   **4.** …   **5.** …   **6.** …

PUNTOS PERSONALES

A. Lo que tengo y lo que quiero. Exprese su situación o deseo, según el modelo.

MODELO: un iPod nuevo →

Ya tengo uno. (Me encantaría [*I would love*] tener uno.

[No] Me interesa tener uno.)

1. un coche descapotable _____

2. un casco nuevo _____

3. una motocicleta _____

4. un apartamento de alquiler barato _____

5. una computadora portátil _____

6. un apartamento con vista al parque _____

7. una impresora _____

8. un teléfono celular _____

B. Sus mandatos. Escriba dos mandatos afirmativos y dos negativos dirigidos (*directed*) a sus compañeros de clase o a miembros de su familia. Indique el nombre de la persona a quien se los dirige.

MODELO: Mamá, no seas tan impaciente.

AFIRMATIVO:

1. _____

2. _____

NEGATIVO:

3. _____

4. _____

C. ¿Qué quiere Ud. que hagan los otros? Escriba tres cosas que Ud. quiere que hagan sus profesores o su jefe. Use cualquiera (*any*) de las siguientes expresiones: **Quiero que... , Insisto en que... , Sugiero que... , Le pido que... , Prefiero que...**

_____

_____

_____

D. Encuesta sobre la tecnología. Va a oír algunas oraciones sobre la tecnología. Primero, escuche el **Vocabulario útil.** Luego escoja la respuesta que corresponde a su propia (*own*) opinión.

Vocabulario útil

cara a cara	face-to-face
reemplazar	to replace
en línea	online

1. ☐ Estoy de acuerdo.   ☐ No estoy de acuerdo.   ☐ No tengo opinión.
2. ☐ Estoy de acuerdo.   ☐ No estoy de acuerdo.   ☐ No tengo opinión.
3. ☐ Estoy de acuerdo.   ☐ No estoy de acuerdo.   ☐ No tengo opinión.
4. ☐ Estoy de acuerdo.   ☐ No estoy de acuerdo.   ☐ No tengo opinión.
5. ☐ Estoy de acuerdo.   ☐ No estoy de acuerdo.   ☐ No tengo opinión.
6. ☐ Estoy de acuerdo.   ☐ No estoy de acuerdo.   ☐ No tengo opinión.
7. ☐ Estoy de acuerdo.   ☐ No estoy de acuerdo.   ☐ No tengo opinión.

E. Guided Composition. En una hoja aparte, escriba una composición de tres párrafos sobre el barrio donde vive Ud.

Primer párrafo: Descripción

- ¿Es un barrio nuevo o bien establecido (*well-established*)?
- ¿Hay casas o apartamentos? ¿Los vecinos son dueños de sus residencias o inquilinos?
- ¿Hay jardines privados (*private*) o parques públicos?

Segundo párrafo: Relaciones con los vecinos

- ¿Se ayudan los unos a los otros?
- Cuando los vecinos están de vacaciones, ¿vigilan (*watch over*) Uds. sus casas?
- ¿Se visitan los vecinos o se reúnen para organizar fiestas?
- En general, ¿las relaciones sociales son buenas o malas? ¿Hay alguna familia que cause problemas?

Tercer párrafo: Ventajas (*Advantages*) y desventajas (*disadvantages*) de vivir en ese barrio

- ¿Hay mercados, tiendas, restaurantes, etcétera, en su barrio?
- ¿Está cerca de la universidad o de su trabajo?
- ¿Cómo es el tráfico? ¿Hay mucho ruido?
- ¿Hay paradas cercanas (*close by*) del metro y del autobús?

Recuerde usar palabras conectivas como, por ejemplo, **por eso, Como...** (*Since . . .*), **porque** y **aunque** (*although*).

F. Mi diario

Antes de escribir en su diario, lea la siguiente nota curiosa sobre un invento muy popular.

El invento del teléfono por Alexander Graham Bell en 1876 ciertamente ha cambiado[a] la rapidez de las comunicaciones en todo el mundo, pero se dice que el inventor mismo,[b] hasta el día de su muerte en 1922, no permitió tener un teléfono dentro de su oficina porque lo consideraba una distracción. «Cuando estoy pensando, no quiero que me molesten por ninguna razón. Los mensajes pueden esperar; las ideas no.»

[a]ha... *has changed*   [b]*himself*

¿Qué cree Ud.? ¿El teléfono interrumpe o facilita (*interrupts or facilitates*) el proceso creativo? ¿Y los demás aparatos «modernos»? Piense en todos los aparatos que usa Ud. y haga una lista de ellos.

Vocabulario útil

la computadora (portátil)
el iPod
la lavadora
el lavaplatos
el secador de pelo (*hair dryer*)
la secadora
el teléfono celular

Ahora escriba en su diario cuáles son los aparatos más importantes para Ud. y diga por qué. Explique cómo afectan su vida.

G. Intercambios. Escuche las siguientes preguntas y contéstelas por escrito.

1. _____
_____

2. _____
_____

3. _____
_____

4. _____
_____

5. _____
_____

Capítulo 13 El arte y la cultura

VOCABULARIO Preparación

Las artes

A. Identificaciones

Paso 1. Identifique la profesión de cada persona. **Nota:** No se usa el artículo indefinido al identificar (*when identifying*) la profesión de una persona.

MODELO: **1.**

La mujer es bailarina.

2. La mujer es _____.

3. La mujer es _____.

4. La mujer es _____.

5.  El hombre es _____.

(Continúa.)

6.    La mujer es _____.

7.    El hombre es _____.

8.    El hombre es _____.

 Paso 2. Cuando oiga el número correspondiente, identifique cada dibujo. Empiece cada una de sus respuestas con **Es un…** o **Es una…** Luego escuche una respuesta posible y repítala.

MODELO: (Ud. oye)   Uno.

(Ud. ve)   **1.**

(Ud. dice)   Es un escenario.
(Ud. oye y repite)   Es un escenario.

2.    **3.**

4.    **5.**

2. …   **3.** …   **4.** …   **5.** …

B. Definiciones

Paso 1. Escriba la profesión o la cosa que corresponde a cada definición.

1. Una mujer que escribe una novela: _____ o _____

2. Un hombre que saca fotos profesionalmente: _____

3. Una mujer que escribe obras de teatro: _____

4. Lo que leen los actores cuando ensayan (*rehearse*) para una película: _____

5. Un hombre que compone música: _____

6. Un hombre que escribe poesía: _____

7. Una mujer que toca un instrumento en una orquesta: _____

8. La mejor obra de un artista: _____

Paso 2. Ud. va a oír algunas definiciones. Escoja la letra de la palabra definida.

1. **a.** el bailarín   **b.** el cantante
2. **a.** la arquitecta   **b.** la aficionada
3. **a.** el director   **b.** la ópera
4. **a.** la escultora   **b.** el dramaturgo
5. **a.** la actriz   **b.** el guía
6. **a.** el espectador   **b.** el artista

Paso 3. Ahora va a oír algunas preguntas. Contéstelas con las palabras que escogió en el **Paso 2.** Empiece cada una de sus respuestas con **Es el...** o **Es la...** Luego escuche la respuesta correcta y repítala.

MODELO: (Ud. oye)   Uno. ¿Quién es la persona que baila?
                 (Ud. ve)   **a.** el bailarín
                 (Ud. dice)   Es el bailarín.
       (Ud. oye y repite)   Es el bailarín.

2. ...   3. ...   4. ...   5. ...   6. ...

C. ¿Qué hicieron? Empareje el nombre del / de la artista con lo que hizo. Use el verbo en el pretérito.

1. Gabriel García Márquez	cantar	*El laberinto del fauno* (Pan's Labyrinth)
2. Diego Rivera	dirigir	óperas italianas
3. Plácido Domingo	diseñar	murales
4. Guillermo del Toro	escribir	casas y museos muy modernos
5. Frank Gehry	pintar	*Cien años de soledad*

1. _____

   _____

2. _____

   _____

3. _____

   _____

(Continúa.)

4. _____

_____

5. _____

_____

D. Preguntas y respuestas

Paso 1. En esta entrevista, Tané, Miguel René y Karina hablan de los artistas más famosos de su país de origen. Primero, escuche el **Vocabulario útil.** Luego escuche la entrevista y escriba la letra inicial del nombre de la persona que menciona a cada artista: **T** (Tané), **MR** (Miguel René) o **K** (Karina).

Vocabulario útil

el/la ensayista	essayist
exponer	to exhibit (art)
el alma llanera	soul of the plains

Tané   Miguel René   Karina

ARTISTAS

1. Rómulo Gallegos: _____

2. Wifredo Lam: _____

3. Jaime Sabines: _____

4. Simón Díaz: _____

5. José Martí: _____

Paso 2. Escuche la entrevista otra vez y escriba la profesión de los artistas mencionados.

1. Rómulo Gallegos: _____

2. Wifredo Lam: _____

3. Jaime Sabines: _____

4. Simón Díaz: _____

5. José Martí: _____

Ranking Things: Ordinals

A. **¿Sabía Ud. eso?** Use el número ordinal indicado para completar las siguientes oraciones.

1. Miguel de Cervantes escribió *Don Quijote de la Mancha*, considerada como la

   _____ (1ª) novela moderna.

2. El estudio de Pablo Picasso estaba en el _____ (4º) piso del edificio.

3. La catedral «La Sagrada Familia» de Antoni Gaudí, en Barcelona, está en su

   _____ (2º) siglo (*century*) de construcción.

4. El rey Carlos _____ (1º) de España fue al mismo tiempo Carlos

   _____ (5º) de Alemania.

5. Francisco de Goya pintó retratos (*portraits*) muy realistas de los reyes Carlos

   _____ (3º) y Carlos _____ (4º) de España.

6. Enrique _____ (8º) de Inglaterra hizo decapitar a sus esposas

   _____ (2ª) y _____ (5ª), Ana Bolena y Catalina Howard,

   respectivamente.

7. El papa (*Pope*) León _____ (10º), Juan de Médicis, fue un gran protector de

   las artes, las letras y las ciencias en el siglo XV.

8. El _____ (1er) escritor centroamericano que ganó el Premio Nóbel de Literatura

   fue Miguel Ángel Asturias, de Guatemala.

9. El _____ (9º) presidente de los Estados Unidos fue William Henry Harrison,

   pero gobernó solamente por treinta y un días. Se resfrió (*He caught a cold*) durante la

   inauguración y nunca se recuperó.

B. **¿En qué piso?** Ud. va a oír algunas preguntas sobre el piso en el que (*on which*) viven algunas familias o el piso en el que está un negocio (*business*). Primero, mire el dibujo. Luego conteste las preguntas, según el dibujo. Después escuche la respuesta correcta y repítala.

1. ...   **2.** ...   **3.** ...   **4.** ...   **5.** ...

C. El orden correcto

Paso 1. Ud. va a oír una serie de preguntas. Indique la respuesta correcta.

1. febrero	enero	junio	abril
2. julio	agosto	octubre	diciembre
3. lunes	jueves	sábado	martes
4. Michael Jordan	Conan O'Brian	Neil Armstrong	Antonio Banderas

Paso 2. Ahora escriba una oración sobre las respuestas correctas del **Paso 1.** Use números ordinales en sus oraciones. La oración número cuatro ya está hecha.

1. _____

2. _____

3. _____

4. *La primera persona que caminó en la luna fue Neil Armstrong.*

PRONUNCIACIÓN   y and ll

At the beginning of a word or syllable, the Spanish sound [y], written as **y** or **ll,** is pronounced somewhat like the letter *y* in English *yo-yo* or *papaya*. However, there is no exact English equivalent for this sound. In addition, there are variants of the sound, depending on the country of origin of the speaker. Listen to these differences.

　　el Caribe:　Yolanda lleva una blusa llamativa. Yo no.
　　España:　Yolanda lleva una blusa llamativa. Yo no.
la Argentina:　Yolanda lleva una blusa llamativa. Yo no.

- Although **y** and **ll** are pronounced exactly the same by most Spanish speakers, in some regions of Spain **ll** is pronounced like the [ly] sound in *million,* except that it is one single sound. Listen to these differences.

　　　España:　Guillermo es de Castilla.
　Sudamérica:　Guillermo es de Castilla.

- Recall that the letter **y** alone or at the end of a word has the same sound as the vowel **i.**

　　i:　　y　　hay　　hoy

A. Repeticiones. Repita las siguientes palabras, imitando al hablante.

1. llamo	lluvia	yogurt	yate	yanqui		yoga
2. ellas	tortilla	millón	mayo	destruyo (*I destroy*)		tuya

Ahora cuando oiga el número correspondiente, lea las siguientes palabras, frases y oraciones. Luego escuche la pronunciación correcta y repítala.

3. botella
4. mayor
5. llamar
6. aquellas pantallas
7. aquellos camellos (*camels*)
8. Ella va a montar a caballo.
9. Mirella llegó ayer para ayudarnos.

B. **¿*Ll* o *l*?** Ud. va a oír algunas palabras. Escoja la letra que se usa para escribir cada una.

   1. ll   l   **2.** ll   l   **3.** ll   l   **4.** ll   l   **5.** ll   l   **6.** ll   l

C. **Repaso:** *ñ, l, ll, y.* Ud. va a oír algunas oraciones. Escriba lo que oye.

   1. _____

   2. _____

   3. _____

   4. _____

GRAMÁTICA

¿Recuerda Ud.?

El indicativo frente al (*opposite*) **subjuntivo.** Complete los siguientes ejemplos del uso del infinitivo o del subjuntivo después de verbos de influencia.

   MODELOS: **a.** un sujeto, una cláusula: Prefiero __*llegar*__ temprano. (llegar)

   b. dos sujetos, dos cláusulas: Prefiero __*que*__ Uds. __*lleguen*__ temprano. (llegar)

1. **a.** un sujeto, una cláusula: Quiero _____ aquí. (sentarme)

   b. dos sujetos, dos cláusulas: Quiero _____ Uds. _____ aquí. (sentarse)

2. **a.** un sujeto, una cláusula: (Yo) Insisto en _____ aquí. (estar)

   b. dos sujetos, dos cláusulas: (Yo) Insisto en _____ tú _____ aquí. (estar)

3. **a.** un sujeto, dos cláusulas: Él prefiere _____ al concierto con nosotros. (venir)

   b. dos sujetos, dos cláusulas: Él prefiere _____ su amigo _____ al concierto con nosotros. (venir)

36. Expressing Feelings • Use of the Subjunctive (Part 3): Emotion

A. **Una visita al museo.** Escriba oraciones completas, según el modelo.

   MODELO: es mejor que / (nosotros): salir pronto → Es mejor que salgamos pronto.

1. me alegro de que / (nosotros): ir al museo esta tarde

   _____

2. espero que / (ellos): vender entradas (*tickets*) con precios rebajados para estudiantes

   _____

3. siento que / tus amigos: no poder venir

_____

4. es una lástima que / el museo: no mostrar más obras de Frida Kahlo

_____

5. es extraño que / (ellos): no exhibir más esculturas indígenas

_____

B. **Reacciones.** Escriba oraciones completas, según el modelo.

   MODELO: es increíble / la gente: no ir más al teatro →
   Es increíble que la gente no vaya más al teatro.

1. es una lástima / mis amigos: no poder salir con nosotros

_____

2. me sorprende / ellos: no ir nunca al teatro

_____

3. espero / (tú): saber dónde está el teatro

_____

4. temo / hay mucho tráfico a estas horas

_____

5. me molesta / estas entradas: ser tan caras

_____

C. **El día del espectáculo.** Diga cómo se sienten las personas, según las siguientes oraciones y las frases que se oyen. Luego escuche la respuesta correcta y repítala.

   MODELO: (Ud. ve)   Los actores olvidan sus líneas.
           (Ud. oye)   el director teme
           (Ud. dice)   El director teme que los actores olviden sus líneas.
   (Ud. oye y repite)   El director teme que los actores olviden sus líneas.

1. Los actores no se enferman.
2. La actriz está muy nerviosa.
3. Los otros actores no llegan a tiempo.
4. El musical es bueno.
5. La obra es muy larga.

D. Esperanzas (*Hopes*) **y temores** (*fears*). Ud. va a oír dos preguntas que corresponden a cada dibujo. Contéstelas, según los dibujos y las frases que se dan. Luego escuche la respuesta correcta y repítala.

1. su equipo ganar / su equipo perder

2. su celular funcionar /
   su celular no funcionar

3. su hija tener fiebre / su hija estar bien

E. Sentimientos. Exprese su reacción a las siguientes circunstancias y complete las oraciones con las palabras que se dan. Haga todos los cambios necesarios. **¡OJO!** Recuerde que, en general, se usa el infinitivo cuando no hay un cambio (*change*) de sujeto.

MODELOS: siento / Uds.: no poder venir →

Siento que Uds. no puedan venir. (*two clauses*)

siento: (yo) no poder ir →

Siento no poder ir. (*infinitive phrase*)

1. es una lástima / Juanes: no cantar esta noche

   _____

2. es terrible / pagar tanto por las entradas al espectáculo

   _____

3. me sorprende / tú: no conocer las novelas de García Márquez

   _____

4. sentimos / (nosotros): no poder ayudarlos a Uds.

   _____

5. me molesta / haber tanta gente que habla durante una película

   _____

6. es absurdo / algunos actores y atletas: ganar tanto dinero

   _____

37. Expressing Uncertainty • Use of the Subjunctive (Part 4): Doubt and Denial

A. ¿Indicativo o subjuntivo? En cada caso, indique si se usa el indicativo (**I**) o el subjuntivo (**S**).

1. Es obvio que + _____   5. No es cierto que + _____

2. Dudan que + _____   6. Es verdad que + _____

3. Es posible que + _____   7. Niega que + _____

4. Creo que + _____   8. Es imposible que + _____

B. ¿Lo cree Ud. o lo duda? Vuelva a escribir las oraciones de la derecha combinándolas con las frases de la izquierda. **¡OJO!** No todas las oraciones requieren el subjuntivo.

1. Dudo que...   A mis amigos les encanta el *jazz.*

   _____

2. Creo que...   El museo está abierto los domingos.

   _____

3. No estoy seguro/a de que...   Todos los niños tienen talento artístico.

   _____

4. No es cierto que...   Mi profesor va al teatro todas las semanas.

   _____

5. No creo que...   Mi profesor siempre expresa su opinión personal.

   _____

C. **En el Museo del Prado.** Haga oraciones completas, según las indicaciones. Añada (*Add*) palabras cuando sea necesario.

1. creo que hoy / (nosotros): ir a visitar el Museo del Prado.

   _____

2. es probable que / (nosotros): llegar temprano

   _____

3. estoy seguro/a de que / hay precios especiales para estudiantes

   _____

4. es probable que / (nosotros): tener que dejar nuestras mochilas en la entrada del museo

   _____

5. dudo que / (nosotros): poder ver todas las obras de Velázquez

   _____

6. creo que / los guardias: ir a prohibir que / (nosotros): sacar fotos

   _____

7. ¿es posible que / (nosotros): volver a visitar el museo mañana?

   _____

D. **Los gustos** (*likes*) **artísticos de Belén.** Ud. va a oír una breve narración en la que (*in which*) Belén habla de sus gustos y preferencias con respecto al arte. Primero, escuche el **Vocabulario útil** y la narración. Luego en voz alta complete las siguientes oraciones con el indicativo o el subjuntivo del verbo que oiga. Después escuche la respuesta correcta y repítala.

Vocabulario útil

aunque	although
apreciar	to appreciate
la habilidad	ability
de hecho	in fact
de vez en cuando	every now and then
la gracia	grace

MODELO: (Ud. oye) Uno: encantar

(Ud. ve) 1. (No) Es cierto que a Belén le _____ la ópera.

(Ud. dice) Es cierto que a Belén le encanta la ópera.

(Ud. oye y repite) Es cierto que a Belén le encanta la ópera.

2. (No) Es cierto que Belén _____ talento artístico.

3. (No) Es cierto que Belén _____ el cine al teatro.

4. (No) Es cierto que Belén _____ a un director de teatro.

5. (No) Es cierto que Belén _____ aficionada al ballet.

E. **Observaciones.** Ud. va a oír algunas oraciones sobre los siguientes dibujos. Exprese su reacción a cada oración. Empiece cada una de sus respuestas con **Es verdad que...** o **No es verdad que...**

MODELO: (Ud. oye) Carlos tiene un coche blanco.

(Ud. ve)

(Ud. dice) No es verdad que Carlos tenga un coche blanco.

(Ud. oye y repite) No es verdad que Carlos tenga un coche blanco.

1.

2.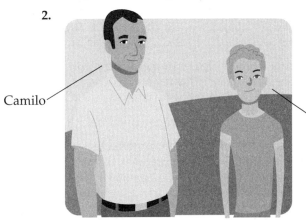

Camilo

Quique

3.

4.

5.

1. ... **2.** ... **3.** ... **4.** ... **5.** ...

F. Entrevista con un artista

Paso 1. En esta entrevista, Juan Prudencio contesta preguntas sobre su arte. Primero, escuche el **Vocabulario útil.** Luego escuche la entrevista y complete las siguientes oraciones.

Vocabulario útil

mejor dicho	that is, rather
actual	current
preferirían	they would prefer
pintara	that I paint
el paisaje	landscape
el retrato	portrait
apreciar	to appreciate

1. Juan es _____.

2. Es de _____.

3. Pinta cuadros _____ que representan sus _____.

4. Sus _____ no entienden sus obras. Ellos prefieren los cuadros de paisajes o retratos.

5. Pero sus _____ sí aprecian su arte.

Paso 2. Ahora cuando oiga el número correspondiente, exprese su reacción a las siguientes oraciones. Empiece cada una de sus respuestas con una frase de la lista. Luego escuche una respuesta posible y repítala.

(No) Es cierto que… (No) Me sorprende que… Me alegro de que…

1. El arte abstracto es difícil de comprender.
2. Los padres de Juan no comprenden sus cuadros.
3. A los hermanos de Juan les gusta su pintura.

38. Expressing Influence, Emotion, Doubt, and Denial • The Subjunctive (Part 5): A Summary

A. En la galería de arte. Complete las oraciones con el presente de subjuntivo de los verbos entre paréntesis. Luego escriba a cuál de los usos del subjuntivo pertenece (*it belongs*): influencia, emoción, duda o negación (*denial*).

MODELO: Me encanta que la galería ___*venda*___ (vender) copias de cuadros famosos. (___*Emoción*___)

1. No creo que la galería _____ (ofrecer) buenos precios. (_____)

2. Temo que aquí los precios _____ (ser) muy altos. (_____)

3. Me alegro de que _____ (*tú:* saber) tanto de la pintura. (_____)

4. El vendedor (*salesperson*) duda que _____ (haber) una copia mejor que esta. (_____)

5. ¡Qué bueno que _____ (*ellos:* permitir) que _____ (*nosotros:* pagar) con tarjeta de crédito! (_____, _____)

6. Quiero que ellos la _____ (empaquetar: *to pack*) bien para llevarla en el avión. (_____)

B. Situaciones. Complete las oraciones con el subjuntivo, el indicativo o el infinitivo del verbo entre paréntesis.

1. Es mejor que _____ (*tú:* apagar) la televisión al salir (*upon leaving*) del cuarto.

   Nuestra última cuenta fue altísima y no me gusta _____ (pagar) tanto.

2. Es verdad que David _____ (ser) inteligente, pero dudo que _____

   (saber) resolver este problema con la computadora. Dice que el problema no _____

   (ser) tan complicado.

3. Siento que _____ (*tú:* estar) enfermo. Ojalá que _____ (sentirte)

   mejor mañana.

4. Nuestro profesor nos prohíbe que _____ (hablar) en inglés en esta clase.

   Insiste en que _____ (tratar) de expresarnos en español, pero a veces es difícil

   _____ (hacerlo).

5. Pablo, es imposible que _____ (*tú:* estudiar) con tanto ruido. ¿Cómo es posible

   que te _____ (gustar) escuchar esa música tan fuerte? Además, temo que te

   _____ (hacer) daño en los oídos.

6. Prefiero que _____ (*tú:* estacionar [*to park*]) cerca del cine. Prefiero no

   _____ (caminar) mucho porque me duelen los pies.

7. Creo que la película _____ (empezar) a las seis y media, pero es posible que

   yo no _____ (recordar) la hora exacta.

C. Problemas con los hijos. Los Sres. Castillo son muy conservadores y a veces no están de acuerdo con lo que hacen sus hijos, Carlitos, Jaime y Luisa. Exprese esto, según el modelo.

   MODELO: Jaime fuma delante de ellos. → No les gusta que fume delante de ellos.

1. Luisa desea estudiar para ser bailarina.

   Les sorprende que _____

2. Jaime y Luisa vuelven tarde de las fiestas.

   Les molesta que _____

3. Carlitos juega en la calle con sus amigos.

   Le prohíben a Carlitos que _____

4. Jaime va de viaje con su novia y otros amigos.

   No les gusta que _____

5. Luisa busca un apartamento para vivir con otra amiga.

   Se oponen (*They oppose*) a que _____

6. Carlitos quiere ser músico.

   Temen que _____

7. Los amigos de sus hijos son una influencia positiva.

   Dudan que _____

D. Se venden coches nuevos y usados

Paso 1. Ud. va a oír cuatro anuncios (*ads*) para cuatro coches diferentes. Primero, lea las siguientes oraciones. Luego escuche el **Vocabulario útil** y los anuncios. Después escriba el número del anuncio en el espacio correspondiente.

Vocabulario útil

la maravilla   wonder

a. Dudo que el coche de anuncio número _____ sea una ganga.

b. Es verdad que el coche del anuncio número _____ es pequeño y económico.

c. Es probable que el coche del anuncio número _____ gaste mucha gasolina.

d. Es cierto que el coche del anuncio número _____ no necesita gasolina.

Paso 2. Ahora va a oír algunas preguntas sobre los anuncios que oyó. Contéstelas con información del **Paso 1.** Luego escuche la respuesta correcta y repítala.

1. …   **2.** …   **3.** …   **4.** …

E. ¿Qué quiere Ud.? Ud. va a oír algunas preguntas. Contéstelas con una respuesta apropiada. Empiece cada respuesta con **Quiero que…** Use las frases apropiadas de abajo en sus respuestas. Luego escuche la respuesta correcta y repítala.

MODELO: (Ud. oye)   ¿Qué quiere Ud. que haga el profesor?

          (Ud. dice)   Quiero que no nos dé un examen.

(Ud. oye y repite)   Quiero que no nos dé un examen.

aceptar (*to accept*) mi solicitud de amistad (*friendship request*) en Facebook
explicarme las obras de arte
no darnos un examen
tomarme la temperatura
traerme la ensalada

1. …   **2.** …   **3.** …   **4.** …

F. ¡Estoy nervioso por el examen! En esta conversación, Lupe y Diego hablan sobre Frida Kahlo y del examen que tiene Diego. Primero, escuche el **Vocabulario útil.** Luego escuche la conversación y complete las siguientes oraciones.

Vocabulario útil

sufrir	to suffer
la belleza	beauty
me gustaría	I would like
sacar	to get, to receive (a grade)
la calificación	grade (academic)

1. A Lupe le _____ el arte de Frida Kahlo.

2. Lupe quiere _____ al Museo de Arte Moderno con Diego.

3. Diego no cree que _____ ir.

4. Diego teme que el tercer examen _____ difícil.

5. Lupe espera que Diego _____ bien.

Un poco de todo

A. La antropología y la cultura

Paso 1. Lea la inscripción que se encuentra en la entrada del Museo de Antropología de la Ciudad de México. Luego complete las siguientes oraciones, según la inscripción.

El hombre creador[a] de la cultura ha dejado[b] sus huellas[c] en todos los lugares por donde ha pasado.[d] La antropología, ciencia del hombre que investiga e interpreta esas huellas... nos enseña la evolución biológica del hombre, sus características y su lucha por el dominio de la naturaleza.[e] Las cuatro ramas[f] de esa ciencia única —antropología física, lingüística, arqueología y etnología— nos dicen que... todos los hombres tienen la misma capacidad para enfrentarse a[g] la naturaleza, que todas las razas[h] son iguales, que todas las culturas son respetables y que todos los pueblos[i] pueden vivir en paz.[j]

[a]*creator* [b]ha... *has left* [c]*traces* [d]ha... *he has passed* [e]dominio... *control of nature* [f]*branches* [g]enfrentarse... *confront* [h]*races* [i]*peoples* [j]*peace*

1. Las cuatro ramas de la antropología son _____, _____, _____ y la etnología.

2. La antropología _____ e interpreta la cultura del hombre.

3. Todos los hombres tienen la misma _____ para enfrentarse a la naturaleza.

4. Todas las razas son _____.

5. Todas las _____ son respetables.

6. Todos los pueblos pueden _____ en paz.

❖ **Paso 2.** Ahora comente sobre tres de los puntos de esta inscripción con algunas de las siguientes frases:

Dudo que...   (No) Es posible que...   Ojalá que...

Es cierto que...   Espero que...   Quiero que...

1. _____

2. _____

3. _____

B. *Listening Passage:* El arte de tejer en Bolivia

❖ **Antes de escuchar.** Before listening, do the following prelistening activity.

Answer these questions to see how much you already know about this topic.

1. ¿Qué idiomas se hablan en Bolivia?

_____

2. ¿Cómo pueden los artesanos conseguir buenos precios por sus productos?

_____

3. ¿Qué materiales se usan para fabricar o hacer artesanías en Bolivia?

_____

(Continúa.)

4. ¿Quiénes se encargan de (*are in charge of*) hacer o fabricar la mayoría de los tejidos bolivianos, los hombres o las mujeres?

_____

5. ¿Cómo aprenden los artesanos a hacer o fabricar sus artesanías? ¿Asisten a una escuela especial o aprenden su arte de alguien en su familia?

_____

 Listening Passage. Now you will hear a passage about Chaska Morales's work as an artisan weaver in Bolivia and how she learned this important Bolivian tradition from her mother. First, listen to the **Vocabulario útil** and read the true/false statements in **Después de escuchar** to know what information to listen for. Then listen to the passage.

Vocabulario útil

la alpaca	Andean animal whose wool is used for weaving
la vicuña	Andean animal whose wool is used for weaving
el/la tejedor(a)	weaver
la cooperativa artesana	artisan cooperative
el tejer	weaving
el oficio	trade
la bufanda	scarf
la feria	fair
ya que	since
la calidad	quality
la belleza	beauty
justo/a	fair, just
el diseño	design
reflejar	to reflect
apreciar	to appreciate

Después de escuchar. Circle **C** if the statement is true or **F** if it is false, based on the passage. If the information is not contained in the passage, circle **ND (No lo dice).** Correct the statements that are false.

1. C   F   ND   En Bolivia se hablan otros idiomas además del (*besides*) español.

_____

2. C   F   ND   Las cooperativas artesanas ayudan a las tejedoras a conseguir bufandas buenas.

_____

3. C   F   ND   Chaska vendió mucho por el Internet el año pasado.

_____

4. C   F   ND   Chaska y las otras tejedoras usan lana para hacer zapatos y pantalones.

_____

5. C   F   ND   El tejer es un oficio principalmente de los hombres.

_____

6. C   F   ND   Chaska espera que su hija pueda apreciar la tradición que ella aprendió de su madre.

_____

C. ¿Vamos a... ?

Paso 1. En este diálogo, Diego invita a Lupe a ir al Museo de Arte Moderno, que está en el Bosque de Chapultepec, un parque grande de la Ciudad de México. Primero, escuche el **Vocabulario útil.** Luego escuche el diálogo y conteste las siguientes preguntas por escrito.

Vocabulario útil

el bosque	forest
el siglo	century
agradable	pleasant
la exposición	show, exhibit
el castillo	castle
el D.F.	**el Distrito Federal (la Ciudad de México)**
la gracia	charm

1. ¿Cuándo van a ir al Museo de Arte Moderno Diego y Lupe?

   _____

2. ¿Qué tipo de artistas están representados en el museo?

   _____

3. ¿Qué hay en el jardín del museo?

   _____

4. ¿Qué hay en el Castillo de Chapultepec?

   _____

5. ¿Por qué está segura Lupe de que va a haber mucha gente el sábado?

   _____

6. ¿Qué desea Lupe que no ocurra el sábado?

   _____

Paso 2. Ahora va a participar en una conversación similar. Primero, complete el diálogo con las siguientes frases. **¡OJO!** Las frases que se dan no están en el orden correcto y tiene que conjugar los verbos. Segundo, haga la conversación en voz alta. Después de oír lo que dice su amiga, lea su respuesta. Luego escuche la pronunciación correcta y repítala. Verifique las repuestas correctas en el Apéndice antes de hacer la conversación en voz alta.

haber entradas (*tickets*)

ir (nosotros) a un concierto de música clásica

ser más emocionante (*exciting*)

SU AMIGA: ¿Qué tal si vamos a un concierto este fin de semana? Hace tiempo que no vamos.

UD.: Está bien, pero esta vez prefiero que _____.[1]

SU AMIGA: Bueno, si insistes. Pero, ¿por qué te gusta tanto ese tipo de música?

UD.: Me gusta porque creo que _____[2] que otros tipos de música.

SU AMIGA: Bueno, hay un concierto de Beethoven el sábado a las ocho. ¿Qué te parece (*What do you think*)?

UD.: ¡Perfecto! Ojalá que todavía _____.[3]

El Ecuador y Bolivia

A. Mapa. Identifique el Ecuador, Bolivia y sus respectivas capitales en el siguiente mapa.

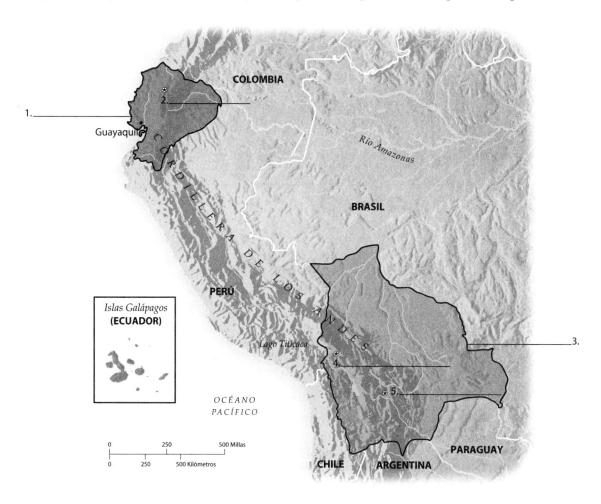

B. Comprensión. Complete las oraciones con información de la **Lectura cultural: El Ecuador y Bolivia** de la página 406 del libro de texto.

1. La Casa de la Cultura Ecuatoriana Benjamín Carrión promueve (*promotes*) la

   _____ ecuatoriana. Esta institución es una red nacional de lugares culturales

   con su centro en _____.

   La Capilla del Hombre es un _____ dedicado a las obras de un solo

   _____: Oswaldo Guayasamín.

2. En Bolivia, la editorial Yerba Mala Cartonera, _____ libros de

   _____ locales a un precio baratísimo.

3. El Museo del _____ en Madrid contiene obras de Velázquez, Goya y otros

_____ anteriores al siglo XX. El Museo Nacional de _____, en

México D.F., muestra ejemplos de las mejores obras de _____ y arquitectura de

los pueblos mesoamericanos.

4. El gran porcentaje de la población _____, tanto en el Ecuador como en Bolivia,

es el orgullo (*pride*) de ambos países. La _____ geográfica del Ecuador y

Bolivia es espectacular, desde los Andes hasta la selva amazónica, desde el Lago Titicaca en

_____ hasta las _____ Galápagos en el _____.

PÓNGASE A PRUEBA

A. Use of the Subjunctive: Emoción. Cambie los infinitivos a la forma apropiada del subjuntivo.

1. Me sorprende que _____ (*tú:* llegar) temprano.

2. Me alegro de que Uds. _____ (estar) aquí.

3. Es extraño que nosotros no _____ (ver) a nadie.

4. Esperamos que Uds. _____ (poder) venir al teatro.

5. Ojalá que los chicos no _____ (aburrirse) en el concierto.

B. Use of the Subjunctive: Doubt and Denial. Escriba la forma apropiada del verbo: indicativo o subjuntivo.

1. Dudo que la obra _____ (ser) de Rivera.

2. Creo que _____ (ser) de Siqueiros.

3. No creo que _____ (*tú:* saber) apreciar el arte moderno.

4. ¿Cómo es posible que a la gente le _____ (gustar) este tipo de arte?

5. Es verdad que muchos _____ (decir) que el arte moderno es incomprensible, pero a mí me gusta.

C. ¿Subjuntivo o indicativo? Escriba la forma apropiada del verbo: indicativo, subjuntivo o infinitivo. Luego subraye la expresión que motiva su selección de la forma del verbo.

MODELO: Es urgente que _____ (*nosotros:* comprar) las entradas pronto. →
Es urgente que compremos las entradas pronto.

1. Es cierto que a mí no me _____ (atraer) este tipo de música.

2. Me alegro de que _____ (haber) grupos folclóricos que siguen tocando la

música tradicional.

3. Dudamos que Carmen y Pablo _____ (ir) al Ecuador este verano.

(Continúa.)

4. Los padres quieren que sus hijos _____ (estudiar) en el extranjero.

5. Es una lástima que no _____ (*nosotros:* conseguir) boletos para ese concierto.

6. Les recomiendo que _____ (llegar) un poco temprano.

7. Mi padre no cree que _____ (*yo:* cocinar) bien.

PRUEBA CORTA

A. **Una visita al mercado de Otavalo, Ecuador.** Escriba oraciones completas, según las indicaciones. Haga todos los cambios necesarios.

1. Espero: (Uds.) poder / acompañarnos al mercado esta tarde

   _____

2. Quiero: (yo) comprar / alguno recuerdos de nuestro viaje

   _____

3. Es probable: Julia / no ir con nosotros

   _____

   _____

4. Es una lástima: Julia / perder esta oportunidad de visitar este mercado.

   _____

5. No creo: el mercado / estar abierto los domingos

   _____

6. Me sorprende: Marcos / no estar aquí

   _____

7. Es posible: (nosotros) encontrar / Marcos luego

   _____

8. Es obvio: este mercado / tener los mejor precios para comprar tejidos indígenas

   _____

B. **Los números ordinales.** Escriba la forma apropiada del número ordinal indicado.

1. el _____ (*third*) hombre

2. la _____ (*first*) vez

3. su _____ (*second*) novela

4. el _____ (*seventh*) día

5. el _____ (*fifth*) grado

C. Se buscan bailarines. El coreógrafo (*choreographer*) Joaquín Cortés busca bailarines para su nueva compañía de baile. Cuando oiga el número correspondiente, haga oraciones con las palabras dadas (*given*) y en el orden dado (*given*) para hablar de su búsqueda (*search*). Use el presente de indicativo o subjuntivo de los verbos, según el contexto. Si el sujeto está entre paréntesis, no lo use. Haga todos los cambios necesarios. Luego escuche la respuesta correcta y repítala.

    MODELO: (Ud. ve)   **1.** Joaquín quiere / los bailarines: tener mucha experiencia

                       (Ud. oye)   Uno.

                       (Ud. dice)   Joaquín quiere que los bailarines tengan mucha experiencia.

          (Ud. oye y repite)   Joaquín quiere que los bailarines tengan mucha experiencia.

  2. (Joaquín) insiste en / los bailarines: ser muy atléticos
  3. también es necesario / (ellos): saber cantar música flamenca
  4. es cierto / Joaquín: ser muy exigente (*demanding*)
  5. Joaquín teme / no poder encontrarlos pronto
  6. (Joaquín) espera / los bailarines: ser los mejores de todos

PUNTOS PERSONALES

❖ **A. Preferencias artísticas.** Complete con oraciones completas.

  1. ¿Cuál de las artes mencionadas en este capítulo le interesa más? ¿O le aburren todas las artes?

    _____

  2. ¿Le gustan los dramas o prefiere las comedias? Dé ejemplos.

    _____

  3. Cuando visita un museo, ¿qué tipo de pintura o escultura le atrae más? ¿La pintura impresionista? ¿Clásica? ¿Contemporánea? ¿Surrealista?

    _____

    _____

  4. ¿Qué actividad artística le aburre más a Ud.?

    _____

    _____

  5. ¿Hay un(a) novelista o poeta que Ud. prefiere? ¿Cuándo leyó una de sus obras por primera vez?

    _____

❖ **B. Sentimientos.** Crea oraciones con elementos de las dos columnas.

(no) creo	a mucha gente / gustarle el *jazz*
dudo	las entradas de los grandes conciertos / ser tan caras
es increíble	el ballet / interesar a tan poca gente
es una lástima	Shakira / ser tan famosa
estoy seguro/a	yo / sacar «A» en el próximo examen
me molesta	el profesor (la profesora) / olvidarse de venir a clase
(no) me sorprende	nosotros / no tener tarea para mañana
siento	nosotros / divertirse mucho

1. _____
2. _____
3. _____
4. _____
5. _____
6. _____
7. _____
8. _____

❖ **C. ¿Cierto o falso?** Ud. va a oír algunas oraciones. Indique si las oraciones son ciertas o falsas para Ud.

1. ☐ No es cierto que me encante.　　☐ Es cierto que me encanta.

2. ☐ No es cierto que lo tenga.　　☐ Es cierto que lo tengo.

3. ☐ No es cierto que lo prefiera.　　☐ Es cierto que lo prefiero.

4. ☐ No es cierto que conozca a uno.　　☐ Es cierto que conozco a uno.

5. ☐ No es cierto que sea aficionado/a.　　☐ Es cierto que soy aficionado/a.

D. Apuntes. Ud. va a oír un breve anuncio sobre la apertura (*opening*) de un nuevo museo. Primero, lea la siguiente información que va a tener que rellenar (*fill out*). Segundo, escuche el **Vocabulario útil.** Luego escuche el anuncio. Mientras escucha el anuncio, escriba la información que falta (*is missing*).

Vocabulario útil

el placer	pleasure
anunciar	to announce
se exhibirán	will exhibit
abrirá	will open
el ciudadano	citizen
se dará	will be given
para que	so that

1. El nombre del museo: _____

2. El tipo de arte que se va a exhibir: _____

3. La fecha en que se va a abrir el museo: _____

4. El nombre del director del museo: _____

5. La hora de la recepción: _____

6. ¿Es necesario hacer reservaciones?: _____

7. ¿Va a ser posible hablar con algunos de los artistas?: _____

❖ **E. Guided Composition.** En una hoja aparte, conteste las siguientes preguntas sobre el estudio de las artes en la escuela secundaria. Luego organice y combine sus respuestas en una composición de dos párrafos. Recuerde usar palabras conectivas como, por ejemplo, **por eso, Como...** (*Since . . .*), **porque, aunque** (*although*) y **luego.**

1. Cuando estaba en la escuela secundaria, ¿tomaba Ud. clases de música, canto (*singing*), dibujo o pintura? ¿Fue una experiencia positiva o negativa? Dé Ud. un ejemplo de una experiencia positiva o negativa. ¿Tenía un maestro (una maestra) en particular que le ayudaba en cuanto a (*with respect to*) sus inclinaciones artísticas? ¿Descubrió Ud. que tenía habilidades (*abilities*) que no sospechaba (*suspected*)? Si nunca tomó ninguna clase de arte, explique por qué.

2. ¿Le parece (*seem*) bueno que las clases de arte sean parte del programa oficial de la escuela secundaria? Explique por qué sí o por qué no.

❖ **F. Mi diario.** Describa una experiencia cultural que tuvo; por ejemplo: una visita a un museo, una galería de arte, un teatro o su asistencia a un recital de poesía o a un concierto de música. Mencione dónde y cuándo fue, qué vio u oyó y qué efecto tuvo ese evento en Ud. Al final, mencione si le gustaría (*would like*) o no repetir esa experiencia y por qué.

G. Intercambios. Escuche las siguientes preguntas y contéstelas por escrito.

1. _____

2. _____

3. _____

4. _____

5. _____

Capítulo 14 Las presiones de la vida moderna

VOCABULARIO — Preparación

Las presiones de la vida académica

A. Acciones. Empareje un verbo con un sustantivo de manera lógica.

1. _____ estar bajo
2. _____ pedir
3. _____ acordarse de
4. _____ estacionar
5. _____ entregar
6. _____ tomar
7. _____ devolver
8. _____ sacar

a. apuntes
b. buenas/malas notas
c. la tarea
d. muchas presiones
e. el informe
f. disculpas
g. el coche
h. el plazo

B. Situaciones. Empareje las preguntas o comentarios con las respuestas apropiadas.

1. _____ Les recomiendo que preparen este informe con mucho cuidado y que no se olviden de incluir la bibliografía.

2. _____ Esta es la tercera vez que llega tarde para la clase.

3. _____ ¿Me puedes prestar tus apuntes sobre la vida de Pizarro?

4. _____ ¿Por qué tienes que ir a la oficina del profesor Martínez?

5. _____ ¿Oíste? Van a subir el costo de la matrícula el próximo semestre.

6. _____ ¿Qué tal saliste en el último examen?

a. —Bastante bien, considerando que empecé un nuevo trabajo de tiempo parcial esta semana y solo tuve un día para estudiar.

b. —¡No me digas! Si las cosas siguen así, voy a tener que buscar trabajo de tiempo completo.

c. —No los tengo aquí, pero te los puedo traer pasado mañana.

d. —¿Cuántos días de plazo tenemos para entregárselo?

e. —Discúlpeme. No encontré estacionamiento cerca y tuve que dejar el coche lejos del campus.

f. —Dice que se olvidó de traer mi informe y quiere hablar conmigo antes de devolvérmelo.

C. ¡Qué día más terrible!

Paso 1. Ud. va a oír algunas oraciones sobre el día terrible de algunas personas. Primero, mire los dibujos y escuche el **Vocabulario útil.** Luego escuche las oraciones y escriba la letra de cada oración que oye al lado del dibujo correspondiente.

Vocabulario útil

llenar el tanque   to fill the gas tank

MODELO: (Ud. oye) **a.**   A Patricio le dolió la cabeza durante el examen.

(Ud. ve)

5. _____

(Ud. escribe) **5.** a_____

Violeta

Emesto

1. _____   **2.** _____

Lisa

Julia

3. _____   **4.** _____

Patricio

5. _____

Paso 2. Describa cada dibujo, según lo que oye y lo que ve en los dibujos. **Nota:** Haga todos los cambios necesarios. Siga el modelo.

MODELO: (Ud. oye) Uno. doler la cabeza durante el examen

        (Ud. ve)

        (Ud. dice) A Patricio le dolió la cabeza durante el examen.

   (Ud. oye y repite) A Patricio le dolió la cabeza durante el examen.

2. ... **3.** ... **4.** ... **5.** ...

D. Causas de estrés. En esta entrevista, Karina, Miguel René y Tané hablan de los momentos de la vida en que sufren de más estrés. Primero, escuche el **Vocabulario útil** y la entrevista. Luego empareje las ideas con las personas que las mencionan: **K** (Karina), **MR** (Miguel René) o **T** (Tané).

Vocabulario útil

la temporada	season, time of year
se me juntan	all come together
sudar	to sweat
hacerle falta a alguien	**necesitar**
el apoyo	support
respaldar	to support

Karina

Miguel René

Tané

Causas de estrés:	los exámenes:	_____
	los trabajos de clase:	_____
	el tráfico en la ciudad:	_____
Las personas que ayudan:	los amigos:	_____
	los padres:	_____

¡Qué mala suerte!

A. Reacciones. Empareje cada situación con una reacción lógica.

1. _____ A Ud. le duele la cabeza

2. _____ Un amigo le rompe su florero (*vase*) favorito.

3. _____ Un amigo lo/la llama a Ud. para preguntarle por qué no fue a la cita con él.

4. _____ Ud. se olvida del nombre de una persona en una fiesta.

5. _____ Ud. se equivoca de abrigo y se pone uno que no es suyo (*yours*).

a. —¡Ay! Lo siento mucho. ¿No era para mañana?
b. Le doy la mano y le confieso (*confess*) que no recuerdo su nombre.
c. —Perdón. ¡Qué distraído soy! Este no es mío (*mine*).
d. Tomo dos aspirinas en seguida.
e. —No te preocupes (*Don't worry*). Yo sé que fue sin querer.

B. ¡Pobre Pedro! Exprese en español las palabras o expresiones en inglés. Pedro Peralta, un joven algo distraído, va a ver al doctor después de un accidente.

PEDRO: Doctor, ¡qué _____[1] (*clumsy*) soy! Esta mañana _____[2] (*I fell*)

en la calle y creo que _____[3] (*I injured*) en el pie. Me _____[4]

(*hurts*) mucho.

DOCTOR: Vamos a ver... Parece que no es nada serio.

PEDRO: ¿Está seguro de que _____[5] (*you're not wrong*) Ud.? Creo que me

_____[6] (*I broke*) algo. Me duele la pierna.

DOCTOR: Nada de eso... Tome dos aspirinas cada cuatro horas y vuelva a verme en dos días si no

_____[7] (*feel*) mejor. Ah, y quédese con la pierna levantada (*raised*) mañana.

PEDRO: ¡_____![8] (*What bad luck!*) Ahora _____[9] (*I remember*) que

mañana es la fiesta anual de la oficina.

C. ¡Una semana fatal!

Paso 1. Ud. va a oír algunas oraciones sobre lo que les pasó a varias personas la semana pasada. Escuche la descripción y luego complete la oración correcta con el nombre de la persona.

MODELO: (Ud. oye) **1.** Manuel chocó contra otro coche. Manuel está bien, ¡pero su coche no funciona!

(Ud. ve) **e.** _____ todavía no puede usar su coche.

(Ud. escribe) **e.** __Manuel__ todavía no puede usar su coche.

a. A _____ todavía le duele mucho la cabeza.

b. _____ no puede caminar bien.

c. _____ no puede escribir.

d. _____ no va a sacar una buena nota en el examen.

e. __Manuel__ todavía no puede usar su coche.

Paso 2. Ahora Ud. va a oír una pregunta sobre cada persona. Conteste para decir lo que le pasó. Luego escuche la respuesta correcta y repítala.

MODELO: (Ud. oye) **1.** ¿Por qué no puede usar su coche Manuel?

(Ud. ve) Porque _____ otro coche.

(Ud. dice) Porque chocó contra otro coche.

(Ud. oye y repite) Porque chocó contra otro coche.

2. Porque _____ en los dedos de la mano.

3. Porque _____ en todas las respuestas del examen.

4. Porque _____ por las escaleras y _____ la pierna.

5. Porque _____ la cabeza contra la puerta.

D. Supersticiones comunes

Paso 1. Tres estudiantes hispanas van a hablar de algunas supersticiones que existen en sus países respectivos. Primero, escuche el **Vocabulario útil** y la narración. Mientras hablan, tome apuntes. Luego indique las oraciones que son ciertas, según la narración.

Vocabulario útil

evitar	to avoid
la escalera	ladder
cruzarse	to cross paths
matar	to kill
la maldición	curse
derramar	to spill
la uva	grape
la campanada	toll (of a bell)

(Continúa.)

APUNTES

_____

_____

_____

_____

_____

_____

¿CIERTO?

1. ☐ En los tres países, el gato hace un papel (*plays a role*) en las supersticiones.
2. ☐ En Colombia, es buena suerte derramar sal para el Año Nuevo.
3. ☐ El martes trece es un día de mala suerte en uno de los países hispanos.
4. ☐ Muchas de estas supersticiones son semejantes (*similar*) a las supersticiones estadounidenses.

Paso 2. Ahora describa las supersticiones de la narración, según las indicaciones que oye y ve. Siga el modelo.

MODELO: (Ud. oye) pasar por debajo de una escalera
                      (Ud. ve) **1.** la Argentina, Colombia y Honduras / tipo de suerte
                    (Ud. dice) En la Argentina, Colombia y Honduras, es mala suerte pasar por debajo de una escalera.
        (Ud. oye y repite) En la Argentina, Colombia y Honduras, es mala suerte pasar por debajo de una escalera.

2. la Argentina y Colombia / tipo de suerte
3. Colombia / tipo de suerte
4. Colombia / tipo de suerte

Nota comunicativa: Más sobre los adverbios: *adjetivo* + −mente

A. Adjetivos → adverbios

Paso 1. Convierta los adjetivos en adverbios. **Nota:** Use la forma femenina del adjetivo y añada **-mente**.

1. fácil _____
2. inmediato _____
3. impaciente _____
4. lógico _____
5. total _____
6. rápido _____
7. directo _____

Nota: Vea las respuestas al **Paso 1** en el Apéndice antes de empezar el **Paso 2**.

Paso 2. Ahora va a oír algunas preguntas. Use los adverbios del **Paso 1** para contestarlas lógicamente. Luego escuche la respuesta correcta y repítala.

MODELO: (Ud. oye) ¿Cómo escriben ellos?
                      (Ud. ve) **1.** fácilmente
                    (Ud. dice) Escriben fácilmente.
        (Ud. oye y repite) Escriben fácilmente.

2. … **3.** … **4.** … **5.** … **6.** … **7.** …

B. **Mas adverbios.** Complete las oraciones con adverbios derivados de los siguientes adjetivos. Use cada adjetivo solo una vez.

aproximado   final   posible   sincero   solo   tranquilo

1. Después de jugar todo el día, los niños están durmiendo _____.

2. Después de esperar casi una hora, _____ vamos a subir al avión.

3. No sé cuándo llegan mis amigos. _____ mañana.

4. Creo que son _____ las dos y media.

5. Te digo _____ que no me gusta esa clase.

6. Juan tiene cien pesos, pero yo tengo _____ cincuenta.

PRONUNCIACIÓN   *x* and *n*

The letter *x*

The letter **x*** is usually pronounced [**ks**], as in English. Before a consonant, however, it is often pronounced [**s**]. Listen to the pronunciation of the following words.

[ks] *sound:*   éxodo   exigente   exagerado   excelente

[s] *sound:*   extremadamente   expectativa   exterior   explicar

The letter *n*

Before the letters **p, b, v,** and **m,** the letter **n** is pronounced [**m**]. Before the sounds [**k**], [**g**], and [**x**], **n** is pronounced like the [**ng**] sound in the English word *sing*. In all other positions, **n** is pronounced as it is in English. Listen to the pronunciation of the following words and phrases.

before **p, b, v, m:**	en Panamá	ten paciencia	en Bolivia	en vez	conmigo
before [k], [g], [x]:	encontrar	en casa	engordar	en Granada	con Juana
in other positions:	nada	nunca	anuncio	naturalmente	tenemos

A. **Repeticiones.** Escuche las siguientes palabras y repita lo que oye.

1. léxico   sexo   axial   existen   examen
2. explican   extraordinario   extremo   sexto   extraterrestre

Ahora cuando oiga el número correspondiente, lea las siguientes oraciones. Luego escuche la pronunciación correcta y repítala.

3. ¿Piensas que existen los extraterrestres?
4. ¡Nos explican que es algo extraordinario!
5. No me gustan las temperaturas extremas.
6. La medicina no es una ciencia exacta.

B. **Más repeticiones.** Escuche las siguientes palabras y frases y repita lo que oye.

1. convence   un beso   un peso   con Manuel   con Pablo   en Venezuela
2. encontrar   conjugar   son generosos   en Quito   en Granada   en Jalisco

---

*It can also represent the Spanish **j** and the sound of the consonant **g** in Spanish **ge** and **gi.**

(Continúa.)

Ahora cuando oiga el número correspondiente, lea las siguientes frases y oraciones. Luego escuche la pronunciación correcta y repítala.

3. en Perú
4. son jóvenes
5. con Gloria
6. Los museos están en Caracas.
7. En general, sus poemas son buenos.
8. Tuvieron una conversación en privado.

GRAMÁTICA

¿Recuerda Ud.?

El verbo **hacer** se usa para hablar de varias cosas. Conjugue **hacer** de manera apropiada, según el contexto.

1. hacer tiempo:
   What's the weather like?
   It's very windy.
   ¿Qué tiempo _____?
   _____ mucho viento.

2. hacer un viaje:
   I suggest you take a trip
   to the Caribbean.
   Sugiero que (Ud.) _____ un
   viaje al Caribe.

3. hacer las maletas:
   Did you pack yet?
   ¿Ya _____ tus maletas?

4. hacer escala(s):
   The plane makes one stop.
   El avión _____ una escala.

5. hacer la cama:
   Make your bed.
   ¡_____ tu cama!

6. hacerse daño (en):
   Did you hurt your finger?
   ¿Te _____ daño en el dedo?

39. Telling How Long Something Has Been Happening or How Long Ago Something Happened • *Hace... que:* Another Use of *hacer*

A. **Tabla.** Complete la tabla con la forma apropiada de **hacer** y los verbos indicados.

PRESENTE	**hace** + *time* + **que** + *present tense verb*	*present tense verb* + **desde hace** + *time*
1. I've lived (been living) here *for* two years.	_____ dos años que _____ aquí.	_____ aquí desde _____ dos años.
2. I've studied (been studying) Spanish *for* one year.	_____ un año que _____ español.	_____ español desde _____ un año.
PRETÉRITO	**hace** + *time* + **que** + *preterite tense verb*	*preterite tense verb* + **hace** + *time*
3. I met my best friend ten years *ago*.	_____ diez años que _____ a mi mejor amigo.	_____ a mi mejor amigo _____ diez años.

B. Momentos históricos. ¿Cuánto tiempo hace que pasó lo siguiente? Escriba oraciones completas con las palabras indicadas.

1. Pizarro: fundar (*to found*) la ciudad de Lima (más de 450 años)

   _____

2. los Estados Unidos: declarar su independencia de Inglaterra (más de 230 años)

   _____

3. el primer hombre: pisar (*to step on*) la luna (más de cuarenta años)

   _____

4. los terroristas: atacar a los Estados Unidos (más de diez años)

   _____

5. el Canal de Panamá: abrirse (casi cien años)

   _____

C. ¡A Ud. le toca hacer las preguntas! Forme preguntas que podría (*you could*) hacerle a un compañero (una compañera) de clase para saber la siguiente información.

How long he or she has been . . .

1. *studying Spanish*

   _____

2. *attending this university*

   _____

3. *living in the same place*

   _____

How long he or she has not . . .

   MODELO: *had a car* → ¿Cuánto tiempo hace que no tienes coche?

4. *gone to the movies*

   _____

5. *received money from his/her family*

   _____

D. ¿Cuánto tiempo hace... ? Los siguientes dibujos muestran cuánto tiempo hace que pasa algo. Primero, mire los dibujos. Luego escuche cada una de las preguntas sobre los dibujos y contéstela, según los años y las horas que se dan. Después escuche la respuesta correcta y repítala.

1. ...

2. ...

3. ...

4. ...

E. Un estudiante en el Perú

Paso 1. Imagine que después de estudiar español durante un semestre, Ud. hace un viaje al Perú. Durante las últimas dos semanas Ud. ha estado conociendo el país. Hace una semana que Ud. está en Lima en donde está haciendo un curso intensivo de español, empezó que hace cinco días. Ud. recibió noticias de sus padres hace una semana. Un estudiante le hace las siguientes preguntas. Contéstelas por escrito. Use **hace... que.**

1. ¿Cuánto tiempo hace que estudias español?

   _____

2. ¿Cuánto tiempo hace que estás en el Perú?

   _____

3. ¿Cuánto tiempo hace que estás en Lima?

   _____

4. ¿Cuánto tiempo hace que empezaste el curso intensivo de español?

_____

5. ¿Cuánto tiempo hace que recibiste noticias de tus padres?

_____

Nota: Verifique las respuestas correctas al **Paso 1** antes de empezar el **Paso 2**.

Paso 2. Ahora va a oír las preguntas del **Paso 1**. Contéstelas con la información que escribió. Luego escuche una respuesta posible y repítala.

1. ... 2. ... 3. ... 4. ... 5. ... 6. ...

¿Recuerda Ud.?

A. Verbos como *gustar, doler, molestar.* Subraye la forma correcta del verbo.

1. Me duele / duelen los ojos.
2. ¿No te gusta / gustan cantar?
3. No me gusta / gustan estas canciones.
4. Espero que no les moleste / molesten esta música.

B. Usos de *se.* Empareje cada uso de **se** con la oración apropiada.

1. _____ Las hermanas se llaman por teléfono cada semana.

2. _____ ¿El informe? Se lo entregué al profesor Díaz hoy.

3. _____ No se permite fumar aquí.

4. _____ El niño se cepilló los dientes.

    a. to express *one* or *you*
    b. to express a reflexive action
    c. to express a reciprocal action
    d. to replace the indirect object pronoun **le** or **les** before **lo/la/los/las**

---

40. Expressing Unplanned or Unexpected Events • Another Use of *se*

A. ¡Problemas, problemas! Empareje las situaciones con las explicaciones.

1. _____ Necesito comprarme otros lentes porque...

2. _____ Tengo que volver a casa porque...

3. _____ Necesito hablar con un policía porque...

4. _____ Tengo que ir a la tienda porque...

5. _____ Rompí la ventana del coche porque...

    a. se me perdió la bolsa con 200 dólares adentro.
    b. se me rompieron los que tenía.
    c. se me acabó el papel.
    d. se me olvidó la cartera.
    e. se me quedaron las llaves adentro.

B. Accidentes. Describa lo que les pasó a estas personas, seleccionando los verbos apropiados.

1.

A la mujer se le olvidó / olvidaron los lentes.

2.

Al chico se le cayó / cayeron los libros.

3.

Al hombre se le acabó / acabaron
la gasolina.

4.

A la chica se le rompió / rompieron el
el espejo (*mirror*).

C. Conversación. Ud. y su amigo tienen problemas en entenderse, y cada vez Ud. tiene que repetirle la información. Conteste las preguntas según la información dada (*given*).

MODELO: A Marta se le olvidaron los boletos en casa.

    a. ¿Qué se le olvidó a Marta? → Se le olvidaron los boletos.

    b. ¿Se le olvidó la cartera? → No, se le olvidaron los boletos.

    c. ¿A quién se le olvidaron los boletos? → Se le olvidaron a Marta.

1. A Pablo se le quedó el libro en casa.

    a. ¿Dónde se le quedó el libro? _____

    b. ¿Se le quedaron los papeles en casa? _____

    c. ¿Se te quedó a ti el libro en casa? _____

2. Se me olvidaron los papeles en la biblioteca.

    a. ¿Qué se te olvidó? _____

    b. ¿Dónde se te olvidaron? _____

    c. ¿Se te olvidó la tarjeta en la biblioteca? _____

3. A Carla se le perdió ayer el paraguas (*umbrella*) en el cine.

    a. ¿Qué se le perdió? _____

    b. ¿Cuándo se le perdió? _____

    c. ¿Dónde se le perdió? _____

    d. ¿A quién se le perdió el paraguas? _____

D. Oraciones incompletas. Ud. va a oír las siguientes oraciones. Escriba las palabras que faltan.

    1. A ellos _____ el número de teléfono de Beatriz.

    2. A Juan _____ los lentes.

    3. Durante nuestro último viaje _____ el equipaje en la estación del tren.

    4. A los niños _____ los juguetes (*toys*).

E. ¡Qué distraído!

Paso 1. Ud. va a oír una descripción de Luis. Luego va a oír algunas oraciones sobre lo que a Luis se le olvidó hacer esta mañana. Escriba el número de cada una de las oraciones que oye al lado del resultado lógico.

    a. _____ Va a llegar tarde al trabajo.

    b. _____ No va a poder arrancar (*start*) el coche.

    c. _____ Es posible que se le queme (*burn*) el apartamento.

    d. _____ Le van a robar la computadora.

    e. _____ Lo van a echar (*evict*) de su apartamento.

Nota: Verifique las respuestas al **Paso 1** en el Apéndice antes de empezar el **Paso 2.**

Paso 2. Ahora va a oír algunas preguntas sobre cada resultado lógico. Conteste cada pregunta, según sus respuestas al **Paso 1** y las siguientes palabras y frases. Luego escuche la respuesta correcta y repítala.

    1. el despertador   **4.** las llaves del coche
    2. el alquiler   **5.** la estufa
    3. la puerta de su apartamento

41. *¿Por o para?* • A Summary of Their Uses

A. *¿Por o para?* Complete las oraciones con **por** o **para**. Luego empareje cada oración con el uso apropiado de **por** o **para** de la lista a la derecha.

    1. _____ Volvieron _____ recoger sus libros.

    2. _____ Quieren $300.000 dólares _____ la casa.

    3. _____ Hay que entregar el informe _____ el lunes.

    4. _____ No te pongas nervioso _____ el examen.

    5. _____ Ese niño es muy inteligente _____ un niño de 5 años.

    6. _____ Mi padre trabaja _____ el banco.

    7. _____ Vamos a caminar _____ el parque.

    a. *for, in the employ of*
    b. *because of, due to*
    c. *through, along*
    d. *in order to* + infinitive
    e. *for, in exchange for*
    f. *for, in comparison with*
    g. *for, by, deadline*

B. Expresiones con *por*. Complete las oraciones con **por** o con una expresión o frase con **por**.

1. ¡_____! No debes manejar tan rápidamente _____ esta calle.

2. ¿Dónde está Inés? No está en clase _____ vez este semestre.

3. Elena no se cuida mucho; _____ se enferma frecuentemente. Debe comer

   más frutas y verduras ricas en vitamina C, como _____, naranjas y

   pimientos (*peppers*).

4. Creo que tenemos bastante leche en casa, pero voy a comprar otra botella,

   _____ .

5. _____ , las madres recogen a sus niños en la escuela, pero también

   hay algunos padres que los recogen.

6. Tu hija no debe caminar sola _____ ese parque; es peligroso (*dangerous*).

7. Necesito _____ treinta dólares para pagar este libro.

8. Carmen está muy contenta _____ los resultados del examen. ¡_____ sacó

   una «A»!

C. Un viaje al Perú. Exprese en español las siguientes oraciones. Use **por** o expresiones con **por**.

1. My brother and I went to Perú for the first time in the summer of 2009.

   _____

2. We went to Perú for (*because of*) the celebration of the Inti Raymi* in Cusco.

   _____

3. We traveled from San Francisco to Lima by plane.

   _____

4. We went through Miami.

   _____

5. We spent (**pasar**) at least twelve hours on the plane.

   _____

D. La maravillosa María Rosa. Dos hermanos hablan de la visita de una amiga de la familia.
Complete el diálogo usando **para,** según las indicaciones.

   MODELO: ¿Cuándo necesita papá el coche? (jueves) → Lo necesita para el jueves.

1. ¿Por qué lo necesita él? (ir a recoger a María Rosa)

   _____

2. ¿Por qué viene ella a Reno ahora? (esquiar)

   _____

_____
*an indigenous celebration in honor of the sun

3. Y esos esquís, ¿son para mí? (no, ella)

_____

4. ¿Es verdad que ella solo tiene 17 años y ya está en la universidad? (sí, lista, edad [*age*])

_____

5. ¿Qué carrera (*major*) estudia ella en la universidad? (sicóloga)

_____

6. ¿Trabaja también? (sí, compañía de teléfonos)

_____

E. **De viaje por Europa.** Complete las oraciones con **por** o **para.**

Los Sres. García fueron a Madrid _____[1] avión y se quedaron allí _____[2] un mes. Antes de llegar a Madrid pasaron _____[3] Portugal y después fueron a Italia _____[4] ver a su hija Cecilia. La chica estudia _____[5] actriz y _____[6] la noche trabaja _____[7] el Cine Paradiso. Dicen que la muchacha va a pasar sus vacaciones en Francia. Viaja mucho _____[8] ser tan joven.

En Italia, los García fueron _____[9] varias ciudades de la costa en un pequeño Fiat _____[10] no gastar mucho dinero en trenes o aviones. El papá de Cecilia le mandó dinero a ella _____[11] pagar el alquiler, pero ella lo gastó en regalos _____[12] su familia y sus amigos. Sus padres se molestaron _____[13] lo que hizo con el dinero.

F. **¿Qué hacen estas personas?** Cuando oiga el número correspondiente, diga lo que hacen estas personas. Use **por.**

MODELO: (Ud. oye) Uno.
(Ud. ve)

Agustín — Clara

1. hablar / teléfono
(Ud. dice) Agustín y Clara se hablan por teléfono.
(Ud. oye y repite) Agustín y Clara se hablan por teléfono.

(Continúa.)

Héctor

Blanca

2. caminar / el parque

3. pagar 150 dólares / los libros

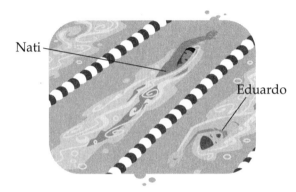

Nati

Eduardo

los pasajeros

4. nadar / la mañana

5. viajar / avión

 G. **¿Para qué están Uds. aquí?** Varias personas están en un lugar dado (*given*) por una razón específica. Primero, escuche la lista de razones. Cuando oiga una pregunta, conteste usando una de las razones de la lista. Siga el modelo. Después escuche la respuesta correcta y repítala.

celebrar nuestro aniversario
descansar y divertirse
hablar con el médico
hacer reservaciones para un viaje a Lima
preparar la comida

MODELO: (Ud. ve) Armando: Está allí...
(Ud. oye) ¿Para qué está Armando en la cocina?
(Ud. dice) Está allí para preparar la comida.
(Ud. oye y repite) Está allí para preparar la comida.

1. Diana: Está allí...
2. el Sr. Alba: Está allí...
3. mi esposo/a y yo: Estamos aquí...
4. la familia Aragón: Está allí...

H. La vida diaria. Ud. va a oír algunas oraciones. Después de cada oración, va a oír una frase. Extienda cada oración con **por** o **para** y la frase que oye. Siga el modelo.

MODELO: (Ud. ve y oye)   Tengo que mandar los cheques.
          (Ud. oye)   el miércoles
          (Ud. dice)   Tengo que mandar los cheques para el miércoles.
          (Ud. oye y repite)   Tengo que mandar los cheques para el miércoles.

1. Salen el próximo mes.
2. Fueron al cine.
3. Estuvo en el Perú.
4. Habla muy bien el inglés.
5. A las ocho vamos a salir.
6. Vendieron su coche viejo.

Un poco de todo

A. Un perrito perdido (*lost puppy*). Complete el diálogo entre Ricardo y su amiga Patricia con las palabras necesarias. Use la forma apropiada de los verbos indicados en el presente o el pretérito, según el significado.

RICARDO: Acabo de ver _____[1] tu hermano Tito y _____[2] (estar) muy triste.

¿Qué _____[3] pasa?

PATRICIA: _____[4] (Perderse) el perrito que le _____[5] (*nosotros:* dar) para

_____[6] cumpleaños.

RICARDO: ¡Pobrecito! ¿Cuándo lo _____[7] (saber) él?

PATRICIA: Anteayer. Parece que el perro _____[8] (escaparse) del patio y cuando Tito

_____[9] (despertarse) el perrito no estaba allí. Tito _____[10] (vestirse)

y _____[11] (salir) a buscarlo, pero no lo _____[12] (encontrar).

RICARDO: Hace tres semanas que el perro _____[13] (hacer) lo mismo, ¿no? ¿Cómo

_____[14] (poder) escaparse esta vez?

PATRICIA: Parece que Tito _____[15] (olvidarse) de cerrar bien la puerta del corral[a] y el

perrito se escapó _____[16] (por / para) allí. Tito _____[17] (sentirse)

tan preocupado que no _____[18] (dormir) toda la noche.

RICARDO: Si no lo encuentran, cómprenle otro _____[19] (por / para) Navidad.

PATRICIA: ¡Ay, Ricardo! ¡Qué buena idea!

[a]*yard*

B. *Listening Passage:* **Viajar por el Perú como estudiante**

❖ **Antes de escuchar.** Before listening, do the following prelistening activity.

Answer these questions to see how much you already know about this topic.

1. ¿Ha estudiado (*Have you studied*) en el extranjero? Si no, ¿le gustaría hacerlo? ¿Adónde le gustaría ir?

_____

2. ¿Ha viajado al Perú? Si no, ¿le gustaría visitar ese país?

_____

3. ¿Cuál es la capital del Perú?

_____

4. ¿Sabe Ud. de algunos lugares famosos del Perú?

_____

5. ¿Sabe Ud. algo de la comida peruana?

_____

Listening Passage. Now you will hear a passage in which Liliana Marcos talks about her experiences in Perú, where she is an exchange student (**una estudiante de intercambio**). First listen to the **Vocabulario útil**. Then listen to the passage.

Vocabulario útil

en fin	well
el quechua	**lengua indígena que se habla en el Perú, Bolivia y otros países sudamericanos**
el idioma	**la lengua**
ir de excursión	**ir de viaje**
maravilloso/a	marvelous
la altura	height
a mediados	in the middle of
el siglo	century
he tenido	I have had
hasta	even

Después de escuchar. You will hear several questions. Write down your answers.

1. _____
2. _____
3. _____
4. _____
5. _____
6. _____

C. Un día fatal

Paso 1. Ud. va a escuchar una conversación entre José Miguel, su madre Elisa y su abuela María. Primero, escuche el **Vocabulario útil**. Después de escuchar la conversación, lea cada una de las oraciones e indique la persona descrita: **José Miguel, la madre** o **la abuela**. Si no se describe a ninguno de ellos, indique **nadie**.

José Miguel, su abuela María y su madre Elisa

Vocabulario útil

tener cuidado	be careful
¡Qué lata!	What a pain!
no vale la pena	it's not worth it

1. Se le cayeron las compras.
   a. José Miguel   **b.** la madre   **c.** la abuela   **d.** nadie
2. Se le perdieron los lentes.
   a. José Miguel   **b.** la madre   **c.** la abuela   **d.** nadie
3. Se le ocurre (*occurs*) que hay algo bueno en todo.
   a. José Miguel   **b.** la madre   **c.** la abuela   **d.** nadie
4. Acepta las disculpas que se le pide.
   a. José Miguel   **b.** la madre   **c.** la abuela   **d.** nadie
5. Se chocó con otra persona.
   a. José Miguel   **b.** la madre   **c.** la abuela   **d.** nadie
6. Se levantó con el pie izquierdo.
   a. José Miguel   **b.** la madre   **c.** la abuela   **d.** nadie

Paso 2. Ahora Ud. va a participar en dos conversaciones en las que hace el papel de **Ud.** Primero, complete las conversaciones con las siguientes frases y verifique sus respuestas en el Apéndice. Segundo, haga las conversaciones en voz alta. Luego escuche la respuesta correcta y repítala.

Discúlpeme.   No se preocupe.   ¡Lo siento! Fue sin querer.

1. *En la farmacia:* Ud. se da contra (*bump into*) una señora y a ella se le cae el frasco (*jar*) de medicina que llevaba.

   SEÑORA: ¡Ay, no!... ¡el frasco!

   UD.:   _____[1]

   SEÑORA: ¿Qué voy a hacer? Era una medicina para mi hijito, que está enfermo.

   UD.:   _____[2] Yo le compro otro frasco.

   (Continúa.)

2. *En el avión:* Ud. se equivoca y toma el asiento de otro pasajero. Cuando la persona vuelve, quiere que Ud. le dé su puesto.

SEÑOR: Perdón, pero ese es mi asiento.

UD.: _____³ Aquí lo tiene.

SEÑOR: Muchas gracias.

El Perú

A. Mapa. Identifique el Perú y la capital de ese país en el siguiente mapa.

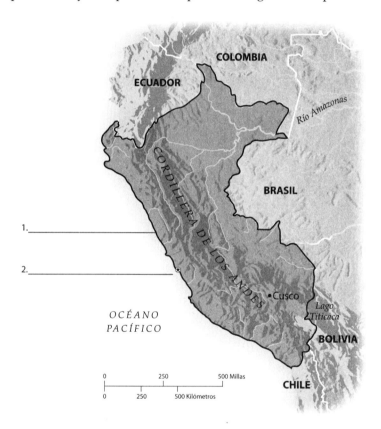

B. Comprensión. Complete las siguientes oraciones con información de la **Lectura cultural: El Perú** de la página 436 del libro de texto.

1. La _____ pública es un tema que causa mucha discusión en el Perú. Se necesita

   más _____ para que el sistema sea más efectivo y sirva a todos. El problema

   con el _____ mínimo es que no permite que el trabajador gane lo suficiente

   para cubrir (*cover*) sus _____.

2. En las ciudades hispánicas dos problemas que causan _____ son el

_____ y el estacionamiento. Afortunadamente, el sistema de

_____ público alivia (*alleviates*) este problema, especialmente en ciudades como

Madrid, México, D.F., y Buenos Aires.

3. Muchas _____ forman parte del folclore popular. Por ejemplo,

_____ un espejo trae siete años de _____ _____;

cuando el 13 del mes cae en martes, hay que tener mucho cuidado con los accidentes. En los

Estados Unidos ese día es el _____ 13.

4. El _____ es un instrumento de percusión creado por los descendientes de los

esclavos _____. El pisco es una bebida alcohólica de _____ que

se fabrica desde _____ más de 300 _____. La _____,

la danza nacional del Perú, es un baile de cortejo entre el hombre y su pareja.

PÓNGASE A PRUEBA

A. *Hace… que:* **Otro uso de *hacer*.** Complete las oraciones.

1. *How long has the following been happening?*

   a. (*nosotros:* vivir) _____ diez años _____ en esta casa.

   b. (*tú:* estudiar) ¿Cuánto tiempo _____ español?

2. *How long ago did the following happen?*

   a. (*yo:* entregar) _____ dos días _____ mi trabajo.

   b. (*ellos:* recoger) _____ una hora _____ los documentos.

B. **Otro uso de *se*.** Exprese las siguientes oraciones usando construcciones con el reflexivo **se**.

1. Perdí mi cartera. _____ la cartera.

2. Perdimos la llave. _____ la llave.

3. Juan rompió los lentes. (A Juan) _____

   los lentes.

4. Olvidaron poner el despertador. _____

   el despertador.

C. **¿Por o para?** Escriba el número del ejemplo apropiado para cada uso de la lista de la izquierda.

1. Usos de *para*

   a. _____ destination (in time or in space)

   b. _____ "in order to" + *infinitive*

   c. _____ compared with others

   d. _____ in the employ of

   1. Ella lee muy bien para una niña de 7 años.
   2. Todos trabajamos para Microsoft.
   3. Salimos para París el 14 de junio.
   4. Hay que estudiar para sacar buenas notas.

2. Usos de *por*

   a. _____ by means of

   b. _____ through, along

   c. _____ in exchange for

   d. _____ during

   1. Lo vi caminando por la playa.
   2. Gracias por ayudarme.
   3. Preferimos viajar por tren.
   4. Siempre estudia por la noche.

PRUEBA CORTA

A. **En español, por favor.** Use una expresión de tiempo con **hacer.**

1. *I went to see the doctor a week ago.*

   _____

2. *I took my pills an hour ago.*

   _____

3. *I've been sick for three weeks.*

   _____

4. *I've been feeling better for two days.*

   _____

B. **Un uso de *se*.** Seleccione la forma que expresa mejor el significado (*meaning*) del verbo en cursiva (*italics*).

1. *Olvidé* la tarea en casa.
   a. Se le olvidó
   b. Se me olvidó
2. Josefina *perdió* veinte dólares.
   a. (A Josefina) Se le perdió
   b. (A Josefina) Se le perdieron
3. Mis libros *cayeron* de la mochila.
   a. se me cayeron
   b. se me cayó
4. ¿Cómo *rompiste* tu bicicleta?
   a. se te rompió
   b. se me rompió
5. Julio *acabó* toda la leche.
   a. (A Julio) Se le acabó
   b. (A Julio) Se me acabó

C. **¿*Por* o *para*?** Llena los espacios en blanco con **por** o **para**.

1. Marta fue a Dallas _____ la enfermedad de su madre.

2. Picasso pintaba _____ ganarse la vida (*earn a living*).

3. En la universidad estudio _____ ser arquitecto.

4. Fueron a París en avión _____ la ruta del Polo Norte.

5. Habla muy bien el francés, _____ estadounidense.

6. Mi hermano trabaja _____ Teléfonos de México.

D. **¿Cuánto tiempo hace que... ?** Ud. va a oír algunas preguntas sobre varias personas. Primero, mire la siguiente tabla. Después conteste las preguntas que oye con información de la tabla. **¡OJO!** Suponga (*Assume*) que el año actual es 2012. Luego escuche una respuesta posible y repítala.

PERSONA(S)	ACTIVIDAD	AÑO EN QUE EMPEZÓ (EMPEZARON) LA ACTIVIDAD
Silvia	trabajar para la universidad	2010
Ernesto	vivir en California	1988
Samuel y Ana	casarse	2000
Laura y su hermana	hacer ejercicios aeróbicos	2006
el Sr. Alvarado	llegar a los Estados Unidos	2007

1. ...   2. ...   3. ...   4. ...   5. ...

E. **Recuerdos.** Cuando oiga el número correspondiente, forme oraciones sobre Benito con las siguientes palabras y frases y en el orden dado (*given*). Haga todos los cambios necesarios. **¡OJO!** Use los verbos en el pretérito o el imperfecto, según el contexto. Si el sujeto está entre paréntesis, no lo use. Luego escuche la respuesta correcta y repítala.

MODELO: (Ud. ve) **1.** de niño / Benito / ser muy torpe
                (Ud. oye) Uno.
                (Ud. dice) De niño, Benito era muy torpe.
      (Ud. oye y repite) De niño, Benito era muy torpe.

2. (él) / lastimarse con frecuencia
3. Benito / también ir muy distraído
4. frecuentemente / (él) olvidarse de poner el despertador
5. casi siempre / quedársele la tarea en casa
6. muchas veces / perdérsele las llaves
7. una vez / (él) caerse y romperse el brazo
8. el médico / ponerle un yeso (*cast*)

PUNTOS PERSONALES

❖ **A. En la escuela secundaria y ahora.** Conteste las preguntas comparando su vida de antes con su vida universitaria.

1. En la escuela secundaria, ¿en qué clases sacaba Ud. buenas notas?

   _____

2. ¿Siempre tomaba Ud. muchos apuntes en clase y mientras estudiaba?

   _____

3. ¿Con frecuencia se le olvidaba el plazo para entregar un informe o siempre lo entregaba a tiempo?

   _____

4. ¿Tenía más presiones que ahora o menos? ¿Por qué?

   _____

5. ¿Se le perdían o se le olvidaban las cosas con frecuencia? Dé ejemplos.

   _____

   _____

6. ¿Alguna vez se le rompió un brazo u otra parte del cuerpo en algún accidente? Explique cómo ocurrió.

   _____

   _____

7. ¿Tenía Ud. un trabajo de tiempo completo o parcial? ¿Y ahora?

   _____

   _____

❖ **B. ¿Cuánto tiempo hace que... ?** Conteste las siguientes preguntas sobre su vida.

1. ¿Cuánto tiempo hace que vive en la ciudad donde vive ahora?

   _____

   _____

2. ¿Cuánto tiempo hace que asiste a esta universidad?

   _____

   _____

3. ¿Cuánto tiempo hace que estudia español?

   _____

   _____

4. ¿Cuánto tiempo hace que habló con su mejor amigo/a?

_____

_____

5. ¿Cuánto tiempo hace que fue al doctor? ¿Lo vio por algún problema específico o fue por un examen anual? Explique.

_____

_____

❖ **C. Cosas inesperadas** (*unexpected*). Describa lo que le pasó alguna vez. Después indique las consecuencias.

MODELO: Una vez se me (*olvidó*)/ *olvidaron* guardar un trabajo en la computadora y lo perdí todo.

1. Una vez se me *cayó* / *cayeron* _____

_____

2. Una vez se me *olvidó* / *olvidaron* _____

_____

3. Una vez se me *rompió* / *rompieron* _____

_____

4. Una vez se me *quedó* / *quedaron* en casa _____

_____

D. ¿Qué tipo de presiones tiene en la universidad?

Paso 1. En esta entrevista, Antonio Carlos Solórzano, un estudiante universitario, habla de las presiones que tiene en la universidad. Primero, escuche el **Vocabulario útil** y la entrevista. Luego complete el párrafo con información de la entrevista.

Vocabulario útil

el recinto el *campus* (Puerto Rico)
aliviar to relieve

Antonio Carlos Solórzano estudia _____[1] en la _____,[2] que está cerca

de _____,[3] la capital de _____.[4] En un día típico, Antonio

_____[5] temprano, _____[6] a la universidad, _____[7] por

la tarde y _____[8] ejercicio por la noche.

Antonio tiene _____[9] como la mayoría de los _____,[10] a causa de[a] los

_____,[11] los proyectos, las _____[12] y la familia.

Para aliviar el estrés, Antonio _____[13] _____[14] y _____[15]

a bailar con sus amigos.

[a]a... *due to*

❖ **Paso 2.** Ahora, conteste en voz alta las mismas preguntas que contestó Antonio.

    1. ...   **2.** ...   **3.** ...   **4.** ...   **5.** ...   **6.** ...

❖ **E. Guided Composition.** En una hoja aparte, escriba una composición sobre un día horrible que tuvo alguna vez. Si Ud. es una de esas personas a quienes siempre todo les sale bien, ¡invente algo!

Recuerde usar:

el imperfecto para describir:
- el día que era
- el tiempo que hacía
- dónde estaba Ud.
- si había otras personas con Ud. o si estaba solo/a

el pretérito para hablar de:
- las cosas inesperadas (*unexpected*) que le pasaron a Ud.
- cómo reaccionó Ud. y/o las otras personas que estaban allí
- lo que le pasó al final

Puede usar las siguientes palabras y otras para conectar las ideas de su composición y hacerla más interesante: **por eso, y, aunque** (*although*), **también, como, luego** y **porque.**

❖ **F. Mi diario.** Describa lo que le pasó cuando tuvo que faltar a (*miss*) clase por un accidente o una enfermedad que tuvo.

¿Dónde estaba y qué hacía Ud. cuando le ocurrió el accidente? ¿Iba distraído/a? ¿Se levantó con el pie izquierdo? ¿Alguien le ayudó? ¿Tuvo que ir al doctor o al hospital? ¿Se hizo daño en la rodilla (*knee*), el brazo, la cara (*face*) o en otra parte del cuerpo? ¿Cuántos días de clase perdió? Si estuvo enfermo/a, ¿tenía fiebre? ¿le dolía el cuerpo? ¿tosía mucho? ¿O tenía otros síntomas? ¿Qué hizo para mejorarse? ¿Le dieron antibióticos? ¿Cuántos días de clase perdió?

❖ **G. Intercambios.** Escuche las siguientes preguntas y contéstelas por escrito.

    1. _____

         _____

    2. _____

         _____

         _____

    3. _____

         _____

    4. _____

         _____

    5. _____

         _____

Capítulo 15 — La naturaleza y el medio ambiente

VOCABULARIO — Preparación

La ciudad y el campo

A. Definiciones. Empareje las definiciones con las palabras de la lista siguiente.

bello   desarrollar   la naturaleza   salvaje
conservar   destruir   proteger
contaminar   la finca   el rascacielos
el delito   el medio ambiente reciclar

1. usar más de una vez   _____

2. lo contrario de *feo*   _____

3. guardar   _____

4. lo contrario de *domesticado*   _____

5. hacer sucio, ensuciar   _____

6. un edificio muy, muy alto   _____

7. hacer más grande (mejor)   _____

8. arruinar, deshacer   _____

9. la propiedad en el campo   _____

10. cuidar   _____

11. todo lo que nos rodea (*surround*)   _____

12. lo que crece naturalmente   _____

13. el crimen   _____

B. ¿La ciudad o el campo? A Guillermo le parece que la vida en la ciudad causa muchos problemas. Por eso se ha mudado (*he has moved*) al campo. Para él es un lugar casi ideal. Complete las opiniones de Guillermo con la forma apropiada de las palabras de la lista.

bello	falta	puro
desarrollar	medio ambiente	ritmo de la vida
destruir	población	transporte
fábrica	proteger	

1. A mí me gusta el campo. Aquí en mi finca el aire es más _____ y la naturaleza más _____.

2. El gran número de personas, coches y _____ en los centros urbanos contamina el _____.

3. Prefiero el _____ tranquilo del campo a la vida agitada de la ciudad.

4. La _____ de viviendas adecuadas para los pobres es un problema serio en las ciudades. Casi siempre hay más violencia en los barrios de _____ densa.

5. Los _____ públicos en la ciudad no son muy buenos; los trenes llegan atrasados y se necesitan más autobuses.

6. Cada año, en la ciudad se _____ edificios históricos para construir más rascacielos.

7. Es importante que cada generación _____ los recursos naturales para que no se acaben. Al mismo tiempo es necesario buscar y _____ nuevos métodos de energía.

C. Los animales

Paso 1. Cuando oiga el número correspondiente, identifique los siguientes animales. Empiece cada una de sus respuestas con **Es un...** , **Es una...** o **Son...**

1.

2.

3.

4.

5.   **6.**

7.

Paso 2. Ud. va a oír algunas preguntas. Contéstelas dando los nombres de los animales que se ven en el **Paso 1.** Luego escuche la respuesta correcta y repítala.

1. ...   **2.** ...   **3.** ...   **4.** ...   **5.** ...

 D. Ciudades

Paso 1. Ud. va a oír algunas respuestas que tres estudiantes hispanos dieron a esta pregunta: ¿Cuáles son las semejanzas (*similarities*) y diferencias más grandes entre las ciudades hispanas y las estadounidenses? Primero, escuche el **Vocabulario útil.** Luego indique cuáles de estas oraciones describen las ciudades hispanas y cuáles describen las ciudades estadounidenses, según lo que Ud. oye.

Vocabulario útil

recorrer un gran trecho	to travel a great distance
el comercio	stores
no hace falta	**no es necesario**
la fuente	fountain
como no sea	unless it is (unless we are talking about)
hecho/a	made
parecido/a	similar
el calor	warmth
seguro/a	safe

	LAS CIUDADES HISPANAS	LAS CIUDADES ESTADOUNIDENSES
1. Las ciudades grandes están contaminadas.	☐	☐
2. Tienen más vida.	☐	☐
3. Son menos seguras.	☐	☐
4. La gente vive en la ciudad misma (*proper*).	☐	☐
5. Las tiendas están en los barrios.	☐	☐
6. Hay mas árboles, vegetación y parques.	☐	☐

Nota: Verifique las respuestas correctas al **Paso 1** en el Apéndice antes de empezar el **Paso 2.**

Paso 2. Ahora va a oír algunas oraciones del **Paso 1.** Diga si estas oraciones describen las ciudades hispanas o las ciudades estadounidenses. Siga el modelo.

MODELO: (Ud. oye)   La gente vive en la ciudad misma.

              (Ud. dice)   En las ciudades hispanas la gente vive en la ciudad misma.

        (Ud. oye y repite)   En las ciudades hispanas la gente vive en la ciudad misma.

1. ...   **2.** ...   **3.** ...

E. Gustos y preferencias. Ud. va a oír las descripciones de dos personas: Nicolás y Susana. Después va a oír algunas oraciones. Escriba el número de cada oración al lado del nombre de la persona correspondiente. Primero, escuche el **Vocabulario útil**.

Vocabulario útil

el puesto	job, position
disfrutar de	to enjoy
graduarse (me gradúo) (en)	to graduate
a pesar de	in spite of
la desventaja	disadvantage

Nicolás: _____

Susana: _____

Los autos

A. Hablando de coches. Ud. va a oír algunas definiciones. Escoja la letra de la palabra que corresponde a cada definición.

1. **a.** la batería **b.** la gasolina **c.** la licencia
2. **a.** la licencia **b.** el camino **c.** el taller
3. **a.** el parabrisas **b.** los frenos **c.** el semáforo
4. **a.** la esquina **b.** la carretera **c.** la llanta
5. **a.** el accidente **b.** el aceite **c.** el taller

B. Consejos. Déle consejos a un amigo que acaba de recibir su licencia de manejar. Llene los espacios con la forma apropiada de las palabras de la lista.

arrancar	chocar	doblar	gastar	parar
autopista	circulación	estacionar	licencia	seguir
carretera	conducir	funcionar	manejar	semáforo

1. Es muy peligroso _____ si los frenos no _____ bien porque es difícil _____ el auto.

2. Si necesitas un buen taller, tienes que _____ a la izquierda y luego _____ todo derecho hasta llegar a la gasolinera Yáñez. Allí los mecánicos son honrados y atentos.

3. Es mejor comprar un coche pequeño; es más económico porque _____ poca gasolina.

4. Se prohíbe _____ el coche en esta calle durante las horas de trabajo.

5. No conduzcas sin _____ porque es ilegal.

6. Si la batería no está cargada (*charged*), tu coche no va a _____.

7. ¡Cuidado! Si _____ en el lado izquierdo de la _____, vas a _____ con alguien.

8. Debes ir por la Segunda Avenida; allí la _____ es más rápida y no hay tantos _____ para controlar el tráfico.

9. En muchas _____ la velocidad máxima es ahora de 70 millas por hora, aproximadamente 113 kilómetros por hora. No debes manejar más rápido.

C. Servicio completo. Dígale al mecánico del taller que haga las siguientes cosas. Use mandatos formales.

cambiar	aceite
lavar	auto
limpiar	llanta
llenar	parabrisas
revisar	tanque

1. _____

2. _____

3. _____

4. _____

5. _____

D. Un accidente

Paso 1. Cuando oiga el número correspondiente, identifique los objetos correspondientes. Empiece cada una de sus respuestas con **Es un...** , **Es una...** o **Son...** Luego escuche una respuesta correcta y repítala.

(Continúa.)

Paso 2. Ahora va a oír algunas oraciones sobre el dibujo del **Paso 1.** Indique si cada oración es cierta (**C**) o falsa (**F**).

1. C F   **2.** C F   **3.** C F   **4.** C F   **5.** C F   **6.** C F

E. Problemas con el carro

Paso 1. En esta conversación, Roberto habla con su amigo Miguel sobre los problemas que tiene con su auto. Miguel es mecánico y él ha ayudado (*has helped*) a su amigo Roberto muchas veces. Primero, escuche el **Vocabulario útil** y la conversación. Luego indique todas las cosas de la siguiente lista que *no* pueden ser el problema que tiene el carro de Roberto.

Roberto y Miguel

Vocabulario útil

la lata de aluminio	aluminum can
no hace falta	**no es necesario**
meter	to insert
prenderse	to turn on
calmarse	to calm down
sencillo/a	simple

_____ **1.** las luces

_____ **2.** la batería

_____ **3.** los frenos

_____ **4.** la transmisión

_____ **5.** algo muy sencillo

Paso 2. ¿Cuáles son las reacciones de Roberto y el mecánico? Complete las siguientes oraciones con información de la conversación. **¡OJO!** Es necesario usar el subjuntivo en algunos casos.

1. Roberto cree que su carro simplemente no quiere _____.

2. Roberto quiere que el mecánico _____.

3. Roberto desea que su carro _____.

4. El mecánico le pide a Roberto que _____.

5. El mecánico cree que Roberto _____.

Nota: Verifique sus respuestas al **Paso 2** en el Apéndice antes de empezar el **Paso 3.**

Paso 3. Ahora, cuando oiga el número correspondiente, lea las respuestas del **Paso 2.** Luego escuche la respuesta correcta y repítala.

1. ...   **2.** ...   **3.** ...   **4.** ...   **5.** ...

Nota comunicativa: Frases para indicar cómo llegar a un lugar

¿Cómo se llega al Museo de Arte Moderno? Exprese en español las siguientes oraciones. Use mandatos formales.

1. *Go straight ahead on Avenida Prado until you get to the corner of Calle Ocho.*

_____

2. *Turn right on Calle Ocho and go straight ahead until you get to the second traffic light.*

_____

3. *Then turn left on Avenida Miranda and go straight until you get to the Plaza Mayor.*

_____

4. *Look to the left. The museum is next to the Plaza Mayor.*

_____

PRONUNCIACIÓN   More Cognate Practice

You were introduced to cognates in Chapter 1. As you know, English and Spanish cognates do not always share the same pronunciation or spelling. Listen to the following pairs of cognates, paying close attention to some of the typical changes in spelling patterns and pronunciation.

English → Spanish

ch → qu: *chemical* / químico
ff → f: *affirm* / afirmar
t → c: *national* / nacional
y → i: *cycle* / ciclo
ph → f: *telephone* / teléfono
qu → c: *quality* / calidad
ss → s: *professor* / profesor
ty → ad: *liberty* / libertad
ure → ura: *literature* / literatura
th → t: *theory* / teoría

A. Repeticiones. Escuche las siguientes palabras y repita lo que oye.

1. contaminación	típico	líquido	actividad	agricultura
2. artificial	natural	popular	actor	televisión

Ahora, cuando oiga el número correspondiente, lea las siguientes palabras. Luego escuche la pronunciación correcta y repítala.

3. correcto   **6.** teléfono   **9.** teoría
4. anual   **7.** patético   **10.** biología
5. físico   **8.** intención   **11.** clase

B. Palabras incompletas. Ud. va a oír algunas palabras. Escriba las letras que les faltan (*are missing*).

1. _____ os _____ ato

2. a _____ en _____ ión

3. _____ antid _____

4. _____ eología

5. o _____ osi _____ ión

6. _____ otogra _____ ía

7. co _____ ección

8. ar _____ itecta

GRAMÁTICA

¿Recuerda Ud.?

Concordancia (*Agreement*). Subraye (*Underline*) la forma apropiada del adjetivo.

1. (perder) la maleta	**a.** perdida	**b.** perdido
2. (cansar) el niño	**a.** cansada	**b.** cansado
3. (preocupar) los padres	**a.** preocupadas	**b.** preocupados
4. (contaminar) el río	**a.** contaminada	**b.** contaminado
5. (aburrir) una clase	**a.** aburrida	**b.** aburrido
6. (escribir) un trabajo	**a.** escrita	**b.** escrito
7. (abrir) las ventanas	**a.** abiertas	**b.** abiertos
8. (proteger) las especies	**a.** protegidas	**b.** protegidos

42. *Más descripciones* • Past Participle Used as an Adjective

A. Los participios pasados. Escriba el participio pasado.

1. preparar _____

2. salir _____

3. correr _____

4. romper _____

5. volver _____

6. decir _____

7. poner _____

8. morir _____

9. ver _____

10. hacer _____

B. Definiciones. Ud. va a oír algunas definiciones. Escoja la letra de la palabra que corresponde a cada definición. **¡OJO!** Puede haber más de una respuesta posible en algunos casos.

1.	**a.** el agua	**b.** el aire	**c.** la batería
2.	**a.** Stephen King	**b.** Descartes	**c.** Dan Brown
3.	**a.** la mano	**b.** los ojos	**c.** la ventana
4.	**a.** el papel	**b.** el pie	**c.** la computadora

C. Descripciones

Paso 1. Ud. va a oír algunas oraciones. Escoja la letra del dibujo descrito (*described*) por cada oración.

MODELO: (Ud. oye)   Uno. La mesa está puesta.

               (Ud. ve) **1.** poner **a.**

   **b.**

             (Ud. escoja) **1.** a

2. hacer   **a.**   **b.**

3. ocupar **a.**   **b.**

(Continúa.)

4. contaminar **a.**

b.

5. cerrar **a.**

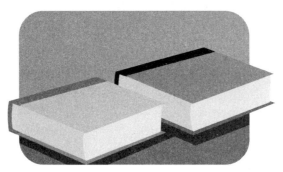

b.

Paso 2. Ahora, cuando oiga el número y la letra correspondiente, describa cada dibujo del **Paso 1** con el verbo **estar** y el participio pasado apropiado del verbo que se da. Luego escuche la respuesta correcta y repítala.

MODELO: (Ud. oye)   Uno. a.

                 (Ud. ve)   **1.** poner **a.**

                (Ud. dice)   La mesa está puesta.

  (Ud. oye y repite)   La mesa está puesta.

                 (Ud. oye)   Uno. b.

                 (Ud. ve)   **1.** poner **b.**

                (Ud. dice)   La mesa no está puesta.

  (Ud. oye y repite)   La mesa no está puesta.

2. ... **3.** ... **4.** ... **5.** ...

D. Preparativos para una fiesta. Imagine que Ud. va a dar una fiesta esta noche.

    MODELO: planes / hacer → Los planes están hechos.

1. invitaciones / escribir   _____
2. comida / preparar   _____
3. mesa / poner   _____
4. limpieza (_cleaning_) / hacer   _____
5. puerta / abrir   _____
6. ¡yo / morir de cansancio (_dead tired_)!   _____

E. Consecuencias lógicas. Ud. va a oír algunas oraciones que describen acciones que se hicieron en el pasado. Después diga el resultado de la acción, según el modelo. Luego escuche la respuesta correcta y repítala.

    MODELO: (Ud. oye) Escribí la composición.

        (Ud. dice) Ahora la composición está escrita.

        (Ud. oye y repite) Ahora la composición está escrita.

1. ...   2. ...   3. ...   4. ...   5. ...

F. Entrevista

Paso 1. En esta entrevista, Natalia de Ángelo habla del medio ambiente y de las organizaciones medioambientales en la Argentina. Primero, escuche el **Vocabulario útil** y la entrevista. Luego indique si las siguientes oraciones son ciertas (**C**) o falsas (**F**). Corrija las oraciones falsas por escrito. ¡OJO! En la lista se dan los infinitivos de algunos participios pasados que aparecen en la entrevista.

Vocabulario útil

preocuparse	to worry
crecer	to grow, increase
reflejar	to reflect
el aumento	increase
la cobertura	protection
poblar	to populate
centrar (en)	to center, focus (on)
la pesca	fishing

1. C F   Natalia aspira a ser científica.

_____

2. C F   En Buenos Aires hay un aumento de organizaciones medioambientales.

_____

3. C F   La Patagonia es una ciudad argentina.

_____

(Continúa.)

4. C F   Poca gente vive en la Patagonia.

5. C F   Pocos turistas visitan la Patagonia.

Paso 2. Ahora complete las siguientes oraciones, según la entrevista. Use la forma correcta de los participios pasados de los verbos del **Vocabulario útil** del **Paso 1.**

1. Los estudiantes están _____ por el medio ambiente.

2. La preocupación por el medio ambiente está _____ en el aumento de organizaciones.

3. La Patagonia es una región argentina que está poco _____.

4. Muchas actividades en la Patagonia están _____ en la pesca y el turismo.

43. ¿Qué has hecho? • Perfect Forms: Present Perfect Indicative and Present Perfect Subjunctive

A. Formas del presente perfecto. Complete la tabla.

INFINITIVO: SUJETO	PRESENTE PERFECTO (INDICATIVO)	PRESENTE PERFECTO (SUBJUNTIVO)
apagar: yo	*he apagado*	que *haya apagado*
beber: ellos		que *hayan bebido*
vivir: tú		que
romper: Ud.		que *haya roto*
ver: nosotros		que

B. ¿Qué han hecho? ¿Qué han hecho estas personas para ser famosas? Siga el modelo.

MODELO: George López (ser) → George López ha sido comediante por muchos años.

1. Stephen King _____ (escribir) muchos libros de horror.

2. Anderson Cooper _____ (dar) las noticias desde 1995.

3. Pau Gasol _____ (jugar) al basquetbol con los Lakers por varios años.

4. Woody Allen _____ (dirigir) más de treinta películas.

5. Frank Gehry _____ (construir) muchos edificios famosos.

6. Bill Gates _____ (hacerse: *to become*) rico vendiendo programas para computadoras.

C. ¿Qué ha pasado ya? Ud. va a oír algunas oraciones. Escoja la letra del sujeto del verbo en cada oración.

1. **a.** yo   **b.** ella
2. **a.** él   **b.** ellas
3. **a.** nosotros   **b.** tú
4. **a.** nosotros   **b.** yo
5. **a.** tú   **b.** usted
6. **a.** ellos   **b.** él

D. Las sugerencias de Raúl. Imagine que Tina lo/la llama a Ud. por teléfono para decirle lo que su amigo Raúl quiere que Ud. haga. Use complementos pronominales cuando sea posible. Siga el modelo.

> MODELO: (arreglar el auto) →   Tina: Raúl quiere que arregles el auto.
>   Ud.:   Ya lo he arreglado.

1. (ir al centro)   Tina: _____

                                 Ud.: _____

2. (hacer las compras)   Tina: _____

                                 Ud.: _____

3. (preparar la comida)   Tina: _____

                                 Ud.: _____

4. (darle nuestra dirección Tina: _____
   a Bernardo)
                                 Ud.: _____

5. (devolverle el libro   Tina: _____
   a Marta)
                                 Ud.: _____

E. ¿Te ayudo? Imagine que Ud. tiene mucho que hacer antes de una cena especial y su amigo Ernesto quiere saber si le puede ayudar. Ud. aprecia su ofrecimiento (*offer*), pero Ud. ya tiene todo hecho. Va a oír las preguntas de Ernesto. Contéstelas, según el modelo. Luego escuche la respuesta correcta y repítala. **¡OJO!** Use pronombres de complemento directo en sus respuestas.

> MODELO: (Ud. oye)   ¿Quieres que llame a los Sres. Moreno?
>   (Ud. dice)   No, gracias, ya los he llamado.
>   (Ud. oye y repite)   No, gracias, ya los he llamado.

1. …   2. …   3. …   4. …   5. …

F. Las noticias. Cuando su amigo lo/la llama a Ud. con las últimas noticias, contéstele con un comentario apropiado. Use las indicaciones dadas (*given*) y el presente perfecto de subjuntivo de los verbos en cursiva (*italics*). Además, use complementos pronominales cuando sea posible. Siga el modelo.

> MODELO: Por fin *arreglaron* la autopista 91. (Me alegro de que…) → Me alegro de que la hayan arreglado.

1. *Construyeron* un rascacielos más en el centro. (Es increíble…) _____

_____

2. *Plantaron* veinte árboles en el parque. (Es bueno…) _____ _____

_____

(Continúa.)

3. *Cerraron* el tráfico en la autopista. (Es terrible que…) _____

_____

4. Nuestros mejores amigos se *mudaron* al campo. (Es una lástima que…) _____

_____

5. Jorge Romero *perdió* su finca. (Siento que…) _____

_____

6. Su esposa *consiguió* otro trabajo bueno. (Me alegro de que…) _____

_____

G. ¿Por qué lo han hecho? Use los verbos indicados para describir la situación que se presenta en cada dibujo. En la oración **a** use el presente perfecto de indicativo y en la oración **b** comente Ud. la situación usando el presente perfecto de indicativo o subjuntivo, según el significado.

MODELO:

    a. almorzar → El niño ha almorzado.
    b. probable / tener hambre → Es probable que haya tenido hambre.

1.

    a. volver al coche

_____

    b. (ella): pensar / perder / llave

_____

2.

    a. caérsele el café

_____

    b. lástima / malgastar (*to waste*) / dinero

_____

3.

    a. comer / restaurante elegante

_____

    b. posible / no traer / suficiente dinero

_____

4.

    a. policía: ver el accidente

_____

    b. no hay duda / conducir / demasiado rápido

_____

H. **Un caso de contaminación.** Imagine que este año hubo (*there was*) un caso de contaminación en su comunidad. Forme oraciones sobre el caso con las palabras que se dan y las frases que oye para expresar lo que han dicho los habitantes de su comunidad. Luego escuche la respuesta correcta y repítala.

MODELO: (Ud. ve)   **1.** ya estudiar el problema

                      (Ud. oye)   Uno. Es probable

                      (Ud. dice)   Es probable que ya hayan estudiado el problema.

        (Ud. oye y repite)   Es probable que ya hayan estudiado el problema.

2. todavía no avisar (*to notify*) a todos los habitantes
3. ya consultar con los expertos
4. encontrar la solución todavía
5. proteger los animales de la zona
6. no haber más problemas en el futuro

I. **Antes del año pasado.** ¿Qué cosas habían ocurrido —o *no* habían ocurrido— antes del año pasado? Escriba oraciones, según las indicaciones. Haga todos los cambios necesarios.

MODELO: (nunca) yo / viajar Argentina → Antes (del año pasado), (nunca) había viajado a la Argentina.

1. construirse / tantos rascacielos _____

2. preocuparnos / el medio ambiente _____

3. mi madre / cambiar una llanta _____

4. mi hermana / ver una ballena _____

Un poco de todo

A. **Una artista preocupada por el medio ambiente.** Complete la siguiente narración con la forma apropiada de las palabras entre paréntesis.

No solo los científicos[a] sino[b] también los artistas están _____[1] (preocupar) por

los _____[2] (diverso) aspectos del medio ambiente en Latinoamérica. La pintora

_____[3] (puertorriqueño) Betsy Padín muestra _____[4] (este)

preocupación en sus cuadros. En una entrevista _____[5] (hacer) en San Juan, Puerto

Rico, nos ha _____[6] (decir) que ella ha _____[7] (pintar) algunos

cuadros sobre las urbanizaciones puertorriqueñas actuales.[c] En estos cuadros, Padín ha

_____[8] (incluir) imágenes de edificios _____[9] (construir) con

bloques de cemento, edificios que ella llama «ruinas del futuro». Ella se ha _____[10]

(inspirar) en sus visitas a las ruinas mayas e incaicas. También, motivada por su preocupación por

el medio ambiente, ha _____[11] (tratar) de _____[12] (preservar) en sus

pinturas los campos _____[13] (verde), los árboles retorcidos[d] y las costas solitarias

_____[14] (cubrir) de enormes rocas.

[a]*scientists* [b]*but* [c]*present-day* [d]*twisted*

B. *Listening Passage:* **Los coches**

❖ **Antes de escuchar.** Answer the following questions to see how much you already know about the topic.

1. ¿Qué marcas (*brands*) de autos son populares en este país? ¿Cree Ud. que las mismas marcas son populares en Latinoamérica? ¿Y en España?

_____

_____

2. ¿Cuántos autos tiene la familia típica de este país? ¿Cree Ud. que la familia típica hispana en otros países tiene más, menos o tantos autos como en este país?

_____

_____

3. ¿Cuánto cuesta la gasolina donde Ud. vive? Busque en el Internet para ver cuánto cuesta la gasolina en España y cuánto cuesta en un país latinoamericano. ¿Hay mucha diferencia entre el precio de la gasolina en su ciudad y el precio de la gasolina en España o el precio de la gasolina que encontró para un país latinoamericano?

_____

_____

4. ¿Cree Ud. que los autos grandes son muy comunes en Latinoamérica y en España? ¿Por qué sí o por qué no?

_____

_____

Listening Passage. Now you will hear a passage about the types of cars driven in the Hispanic world. First, listen to the **Vocabulario útil** and read the true/false statements in **Después de escuchar** to know what information to listen for. Then listen to the passage.

Vocabulario útil

aun más	even more	**la clase media-baja**	lower middle class
de tal forma	in such a way	**suelen ser**	are usually
la molestia	bother, hindrance	**la marca (de coche)**	make (of car)
la ayuda	help	**en cambio**	on the other hand

Después de escuchar. Circle **C** if the statement is true or **F** if it is false, based on the passage. Correct the statements that are false.

1. C   F   En general, los autos son más grandes en los países hispanos.

_____

2. C   F   Hay muchos autos japoneses en España.

_____

3. C   F   No se venden marcas europeas en Latinoamérica.

_____

4. C   F   En general, la gasolina es más cara en el resto del mundo que en los Estados Unidos.

_____

5. C   F   En México, es posible encontrar marcas que ya no se fabrican en otras partes del mundo.

_____

C. En busca de un taller

Paso 1. En esta conversación, Elisa y su hijo José Miguel ayudan a una conductora que tiene problemas con su carro. Primero, escuche el **Vocabulario útil.** Luego escuche la conversación. Después de escuchar, indique las oraciones que corresponden a lo que oye.

Elisa, su hijo José Miguel y la conductora

Vocabulario útil

podría	could you
a cuánto queda...	how far away is . . .
no se molesten	don't trouble yourselves, it's OK

1. La conductora tiene una llanta desinflada. ☐
2. Es dudoso que el pueblo que queda a diez minutos tenga un taller. ☐
3. Elisa cree que hay un pueblo no muy lejos con un taller. ☐
4. José Miguel le da direcciones a la conductora para llegar al pueblo. ☐
5. Elisa y José Miguel van a acompañar a la conductora. ☐
6. Elisa y José Miguel probablemente necesitan llenar el tanque. ☐

Paso 2. Ahora Ud. va a participar en una conversación en la que hace el papel de la conductora del **Paso 1** que ha llegado al taller. Primero, complete la conversación con las siguientes frases y conjugue los verbos, según el contexto. Segundo, verifique sus respuestas en el Apéndice. Después haga la conversación en voz alta: lea las líneas de diálogo de la conductora y luego escuche la pronunciación correcta y repítala.

muchísimas gracias   ser el motor   ser un auto nuevo
revisarle las llantas y los frenos   tener algo serio   haber comenzado

CONDUCTORA: Temo que mi auto _____.[1]

_____[2] a hacer un ruido extraño.

MECÁNICO: Es posible que sea el motor.

CONDUCTORA: Dudo que _____[3]... _____.[4]

MECÁNICO: En ese caso, le recomiendo que lo deje aquí para poder revisarlo con cuidado.

CONDUCTORA: Está bien. También quiero que _____.[5]

MECÁNICO: Por supuesto. Eso es parte de nuestro servicio normal. ¿Puede venir a buscar su auto dentro de tres horas?

CONDUCTORA: Sí, _____.[6]

La Argentina y el Uruguay

A. Mapa. Identifique en el siguiente mapa la Argentina, el Uruguay y sus respectivas capitales.

B. Comprensión. Conteste las siguientes preguntas con información de la **Lectura cultural: La Argentina y el Uruguay** de la página 464 del libro de texto.

1. ¿De qué están orgullosos los argentinos y los uruguayos?

   _____

2. ¿Cuáles son los tres países que comparten la atracción turística, las Cataratas del Iguazú?

   _____

3. ¿Qué río divide la Argentina del Uruguay?

   _____

(Continúa.)

4. ¿Cómo se llama el territorio extenso de la Argentina y el Uruguay donde hay ganado (*cattle*) y se cultivan granos?

   _____

5. ¿Qué son los Humedales de Santa Lucía y del Este en el Uruguay?

   _____

6. ¿Cuáles son las dos formas de energía renovable que está desarrollando España?

   _____

7. ¿Qué bebida es muy popular en la Argentina y el Uruguay?

   _____

8. ¿Qué baile se cree que se originó en la Argentina?

   _____

9. ¿Qué figura folclórica se asocia con la Pampa?

   _____

PÓNGASE A PRUEBA

A. Past Participle Used as an Adjective

1. Escriba el participio pasado de los siguientes verbos.

   a. decir _____   d. poner _____

   b. ir _____   e. romper _____

   c. leer _____   f. ver _____

2. Cambie el infinitivo por la forma apropiada del participio pasado como adjetivo.

   a. las puertas _____ (cerrar)   c. los delitos _____ (investigar)

   b. el libro _____ (abrir)   d. los problemas _____ (resolver)

B. Present Perfect Indicative, Present Perfect Subjunctive, and Past Perfect Indicative. Complete la tabla.

INFINITIVO: SUJETO	PRESENTE PERFECTO (INDICATIVO)	PRESENTE PERFECTO (SUBJUNTIVO)	PLUSCUAMPERFECTO (INDICATIVO)
cantar: yo	*he cantado*	que	*había cantado*
conducir: tú		que *hayas conducido*	
decir: nosotros		que	
tener: Uds.		que	

C. Pluscuamperfecto. Cambie los verbos del presente perfecto de indicativo al pluscuamperfecto de indicativo.

    MODELO: Nos hemos divertido. → Nos habíamos divertido.

1. He descubierto la causa. _____

2. Han contaminado el agua. _____

3. Luis ha hecho investigaciones. _____

4. Hemos parado en la esquina. _____

PRUEBA CORTA

A. El participio pasado como adjetivo. Escriba la forma adjetival del participio pasado para cada sustantivo.

    MODELO: pájaros / proteger → los pájaros protegidos

1. fábricas / destruir _____

2. luces / romper _____

3. energía / conservar _____

4. montañas / cubrir de nieve _____

5. flores / morir _____

B. ¿Cuál es el tiempo verbal correcto? Seleccione la forma verbal apropiada para completar cada oración lógicamente.

1. Dudo que Juan _____ en el campo toda su vida.
   a. vive   **b.** haya vivido   **c.** ha vivido

2. Estoy seguro de que _____ este libro con papel reciclado.
   a. hayan hecho   **b.** han hecho   **c.** hagan

3. Dicen que ya _____ gran parte de los bosques amazónicos.
   a. han destruido   **b.** destruían   **c.** hayan destruido

4. Tú _____ tres viajes a Europa, ¿verdad?
   a. haces   **b.** hayas hecho   **c.** has hecho

5. No. Yo _____ a Europa solo una vez.
   a. haya ido   **b.** voy   **c.** he ido

C. ¿Por qué no... ? Ud. va a oír algunas preguntas. Contéstelas, según el modelo. Use el presente perfecto en sus respuestas. Luego escuche la respuesta correcta y repítala.

> MODELO: (Ud. oye) ¿Por qué no resuelve Ud. ese problema?
> (Ud. dice) Porque ya está resuelto.
> (Ud. oye y repite) Porque ya está resuelto.

1. ... **2.** ... **3.** ... **4.** ... **5.** ...

D. El medio ambiente. Cuando oiga el número correspondiente, forme oraciones con las siguientes palabras y frases. **¡OJO!** Use el presente perfecto de los verbos. Luego escuche la respuesta correcta y repítala. Siga el modelo.

> MODELO: (Ud. ve) **1.** el gobierno: tratar de proteger la naturaleza
> (Ud. oye) Uno.
> (Ud. dice) El gobierno ha tratado de proteger la naturaleza.
> (Ud. oye y repite) El gobierno ha tratado de proteger la naturaleza.

2. el gobierno: no resolver el problema del tránsito
3. algunas compañías: desarrollar la energía eólica
4. otras compañías: descubrir petróleo
5. el público: no conservar energía

❖ PUNTOS PERSONALES

A. Ud. y el medio ambiente. ¿Qué hace Ud. para proteger los recursos naturales?

1. ¿Recicla Ud. papel siempre, a veces, o nunca?

_____

2. ¿Recicla Ud. botellas y latas (*cans*) de aluminio con frecuencia?

_____

3. ¿Trata Ud. de limitar sus duchas (*showers*) a tres minutos o típicamente se ducha por diez minutos o más?

_____

4. ¿Va caminando a la universidad o va en bicicleta? ¿Por qué sí o por qué no?

_____

5. ¿A qué organizaciones sin fines de lucro (*non-profit*) dona Ud. dinero? ¿Dona (*Do you donate*) Ud. dinero para la protección de las ballenas y otras especies en peligro de extinción?

_____

B. Los coches y Ud. ¿Qué tipo de conductor(a) es Ud.? Si Ud. no conduce, evalúe los hábitos de otra persona.

_____ Me evalúo a mí mismo/a.   _____ Evalúo a _____

1. ¿ Se le olvida a veces llevar su licencia de manejar cuando conduce?

_____

2. ¿Sabe Ud. cambiarle el aceite a un coche? ¿Cuántas veces lo ha hecho?

_____

3. Cuando llega a una esquina y no está seguro/a por dónde ir, ¿sigue Ud. todo derecho sin preguntar?

_____

4. ¿Cuántas veces le han puesto una multa (*have you gotten a ticket*) por infracciones de tránsito?

_____

5. ¿Cuántas veces le han puesto una multa por estacionarse en zonas prohibidas?

_____

6. Cuando ve a un amigo caminando por la acera, ¿toca Ud. la bocina?

_____

C. Experiencias. ¿Ha hecho Ud. cualquiera (*any*) de estas cosas alguna vez? Si la respuesta es afirmativa, escriba cuántas veces.

MODELOS: escribir una carta a un periódico →
　　　　　　Sí, he escrito una carta a un periódico una vez.
　　　　　　Nunca he escrito una carta a un periódico.

1. tener un accidente de auto

_____

2. estar en un terremoto (*earthquake*)

_____

3. hacer un viaje al extranjero

_____

4. romper un espejo (*mirror*)

_____

D. Antes de este año. ¿Qué cosas había hecho —o *no* había hecho— Ud. antes de este año? Dé oraciones nuevas, según las indicaciones.

MODELO: (nunca) pensar en... →

Antes (de este año), (yo) (nunca) había pensado seriamente en el futuro.

1. (nunca) tener _____

2. (nunca) aprender a _____

3. (nunca) escribir _____

4. (nunca) hacer un viaje a _____

5. (nunca) estar en _____

E. ¿Qué opina sobre el medio ambiente y los autos?

Paso 1. Ud. va a oír algunas oraciones sobre el medio ambiente y los autos. Escoja la respuesta que refleja (*reflects*) sus propias (*own*) opiniones.

	SÍ ENFÁTICO	SÍ	NO TENGO OPINIÓN	NO	NO ENFÁTICO
1.	☐	☐	☐	☐	☐
2.	☐	☐	☐	☐	☐
3.	☐	☐	☐	☐	☐
4.	☐	☐	☐	☐	☐
5.	☐	☐	☐	☐	☐
6.	☐	☐	☐	☐	☐
7.	☐	☐	☐	☐	☐
8.	☐	☐	☐	☐	☐
9.	☐	☐	☐	☐	☐

Paso 2. Ahora va a oír algunas preguntas basadas en las oraciones del **Paso 1.** Contéstelas en voz alta con oraciones completas.

1. ... 2. ... 3. ... 4. ... 5. ...

F. Guided Composition. Piense en una de las cosas más interesantes que ha hecho en su vida. En una hoja aparte, escriba una composición sobre esa experiencia. O, si prefiere, puede describir cualquier (*any*) experiencia, buena o mala, que haya tenido importancia en su vida. Mencione:

- cuándo ocurrió
- dónde estaba Ud.
- con quién(es) estaba
- por qué estaba Ud. allí
- lo que pasó

Incluya todos los detalles interesantes que pueda. Al final, describa las consecuencias que esta experiencia ha tenido en su vida.

Puede usar las siguientes palabras y otras para conectar las ideas de su composición y hacerla más interesante: **por eso, y, aunque** (*although*), **también, como, luego** y **porque.**

G. Mi diario. Describa un viaje que ha hecho Ud. solo/a o con su familia o amigos. Mencione:

- el motivo del viaje
- adónde fue (fueron)
- qué medio de transporte usó (usaron)
- lugares interesantes que visitó (visitaron)
- lo que hizo (hicieron) allí

Al final escriba sobre lo que más le gustó del viaje.

H. Intercambios. Escuche las siguientes preguntas y contéstelas por escrito.

1. _____

   _____

2. _____

   _____

   _____

3. _____

   _____

4. _____

   _____

5. _____

   _____

6. _____

   _____

Capítulo 16 La vida social y afectiva

VOCABULARIO Preparación

Las relaciones sentimentales

A. La vida social. Complete las oraciones con las palabras apropiadas del vocabulario.

1. La _____ es una ceremonia religiosa o civil por la que se casan dos personas.

2. El color tradicional del vestido de la _____ es el blanco.

3. Muchas personas creen que los _____ deben ser largos para evitar problemas

   después del _____. Después de la boda los novios son _____.

4. Una persona que no demuestra cariño no es _____.

5. Una mujer _____ es una persona que no se ha casado.

6. Cuando una pareja no se _____ bien, debe tratar de solucionar sus problemas

   antes de separarse y _____.

7. Entre los novios hay amor; entre los amigos hay _____.

8. En los Estados Unidos, Hawai y las Cataratas del Niágara son dos de los lugares favoritos

   para pasar la _____.

9. Un hombre _____ es un hombre cuya (*whose*) esposa ha muerto.

B. Definiciones

Paso 1. Ud. va a oír algunas definiciones. Escoja la letra de la palabra que se define.

1. **a.** la amistad   **b.** el corazón   **c.** el divorcio
2. **a.** la separación   **b.** el amor   **c.** cariñoso
3. **a.** la luna de miel   **b.** la cita   **c.** la pareja
4. **a.** el noviazgo   **b.** la boda   **c.** una visita al consejero matrimonial
5. **a.** la dueña   **b.** la consejera   **c.** la novia

Paso 2. Ahora recree las definiciones que escuchó en el **Paso 1** con las indicaciones que oye y las respuestas correctas del **Paso 1**. Luego escuche la respuesta correcta y repítala.

> MODELO: (Ud. oye) **1.** Es una relación cariñosa entre personas.
>   (Ud. ve) **1.** (a.) la amistad
>   (Ud. dice) La amistad es una relación cariñosa entre personas.
> (Ud. oye y repite) La amistad es una relación cariñosa entre personas.

2. … **3.** … **4.** … **5.** …

C. Querida María Auxilio. Lea la siguiente carta de «Indignada» y la respuesta de la sicóloga María Auxilio. Luego conteste las preguntas.

Querida María Auxilio:

 Hace poco, mi novio decidió acabar con nuestro noviazgo y yo tuve que cancelar los planes para la boda, a la cual[a] ya habíamos invitado a muchas personas. Por supuesto, mis padres perdieron una buena cantidad de dinero en contratos con el Country Club, la florista, etcétera. Pero lo peor para mí es que mi ex novio demanda que le devuelva el anillo de compromiso[b] que me dio hace dos años.

 Yo se lo devolvería[c] sin protestar, pero mis padres insisten en que el anillo es mío,[d] y que me debo quedar con él. En verdad, es un anillo precioso, con un brillante de casi un quilate.[e] ¿Qué me aconseja Ud. que haga?

Indignada

Querida «Indignada»:

Sus padres tienen razón. Legalmente, el anillo es de Ud. Yo también le recomiendo que no se lo devuelva, y si él insiste, le puede decir que Ud. consideraría[f] hacerlo si él les reembolsara[g] a sus padres todos los gastos que ellos hicieron en los preparativos para la boda.

María Auxilio

[a]*la… which* [b]*anillo… engagement ring* [c]*would give back* [d]*mine* [e]*brillante… diamond of almost one carat*
[f]*would consider* [g]*repaid*

Comprensión

1. ¿Cuándo rompió el novio con «Indignada»?

_____

2. ¿Qué preparativos habían hecho ya la novia y sus padres?

_____

3. ¿Qué pide el novio que haga ahora «Indignada»?

_____

4. Según María Auxilio, ¿debe «Indignada» guardar el anillo o devolverlo?

_____

5. Según la sicóloga,

a. legalmente, el anillo es de _____.

b. el ex novio les debe reembolsar a _____ los _____.

D. Relaciones sentimentales

Paso 1. En esta entrevista, Miguel René, Karina, Tané y Rubén contestan preguntas sobre sus relaciones sentimentales. Primero, escuche el **Vocabulario útil** y la entrevista. Luego complete la tabla con información de los entrevistados (*interviewees*).

Vocabulario útil

chaparrito/a	short
morenito/a	a little dark, tanned
grandotes	**grandes**
el sueño	dream
cualquier	any
chico/a	young
solventar	to support economically; to sustain
el soporte	support
aunque	although
estaré	I will be
reinar	to reign
la alegría	happiness
grato/a	pleasant
sanguíneo/a	blood

	Miguel René	Karina	Tané	Rubén
1. ¿Tiene novio/a?				
2. ¿Cómo es el novio o la novia (el ex novio o la ex novia)?				
3. ¿Quiere casarse?				
4. ¿Quiere tener hijos?				

Paso 2. Ahora indique a cuál de los entrevistados se refieren las siguientes oraciones: **MR** (Miguel René), **K** (Karina), **T** (Tané) o **R** (Rubén).

1. Cree que es demasiado joven para casarse. _____

2. Dice que su novio/a es superatractivo/a. _____

3. Se preocupa por el aspecto económico del matrimonio. _____

4. Quiere casarse y tener hijos porque ha habido (*there has been*) mucha alegría en su familia.

   _____

5. Quiere tener hijos porque es la experiencia más grata que no se debe perder en la vida.

   _____

6. Cree que los hijos son el soporte de una relación. _____

Nota: Verifique sus respuestas al **Paso 2** antes de empezar el **Paso 3**.

Paso 3. Ahora Ud. va a oír algunas preguntas. Contéstelas con sus respuestas al **Paso 2.** Luego escuche la respuesta correcta y repítala.

1. ... **2.** ... **3.** ... **4.** ... **5.** ... **6.** ...

Las etapas de la vida

A. Familias de palabras. Complete las oraciones con el sustantivo sugerido por la palabra indicada.

1. Los *jóvenes* sufren de problemas sentimentales durante su _____.

2. Los *adolescentes* pueden causarles muchos dolores de cabeza a sus padres durante la

_____.

3. El _____ (acto de *nacer*) y la _____ (acto de *morir*) forman parte del círculo de la vida.

4. Durante su _____, el *infante* depende de sus padres para todo.

5. Se cree que una persona *madura* tiene mejor juicio (*judgment*) en la _____ que en la juventud.

6. Muchos *viejos* se quejan de dolores y problemas de salud cuando llegan a la

_____.

7. Es importante que los *niños* tengan una _____ segura.

B. Oraciones incompletas

Paso 1. Ud. va a oír algunas oraciones incompletas. Primero, escuche el **Vocabulario útil.** Luego indique la letra de la frase que completa mejor cada oración.

Vocabulario útil

lo opuesto   the opposite

1. a. está en la infancia	**b.** está en la niñez	**c.** está en la adolescencia
2. a. está en la vejez	**b.** está en la juventud	**c.** acaba de nacer
3. a. está en la madurez	**b.** está en la adolescencia	**c.** está en la infancia
4. a. está en la infancia	**b.** está en la vejez	**c.** está en la adolescencia
5. a. es la vejez	**b.** es el juguete	**c.** es la muerte
6. a. es divorciarse	**b.** es nacer	**c.** es crecer

Paso 2. Ahora haga oraciones completas con las indicaciones que oye y las respuestas correctas del **Paso 1.** Luego escuche la respuesta correcta y repítala.

MODELO: (Ud. oye)   Un chico de 8 años...
                 (Ud. ve)   **1.** (**b.**) está en la niñez.
                 (Ud. dice)   Un chico de 8 años está en la niñez.
        (Ud. oye y repite)   Un chico de 8 años está en la niñez.

2. ... **3.** ... **4.** ... **5.** ... **6.** ...

PRONUNCIACIÓN · More Cognate Practice

Amigos falsos. Unlike true cognates, false cognates do not have the same meaning in English as they do in Spanish. For example, the verb **atender** looks very similar to the English verb *to attend*. However, their meanings are quite different. **Atender** means *to attend to* (as in *to take care of, to assist*). The word **fábrica** may seem very similar to the English word *fabric*. However, **una fábrica** is a factory. The Spanish word for *fabric* is **la tela**. **Largo** means *long* (in length). The word for *large* is **grande**.

A. Repeticiones. Repita las siguientes palabras, imitando lo que oye. También, fíjese en las diferencias de significado (*meaning*) entre el español y el inglés.

la carta	letter	**el pie**	foot
dime	tell me	**actual**	current, present-day
emocionante	exciting	**actualmente**	nowadays
asistir	to attend	**embarazada**	pregnant
el pan	bread	**el pariente**	relative
el éxito	success	**dice**	he/she says; you (formal, sing.) say
sin	without	**la Red**	Internet

B. Un satélite español

Paso 1. El siguiente artículo apareció en un periódico español. Primero, deje de escuchar y subraye (*underline*) todas las palabras que son cognados.

Un satélite español El ministro de Transportes y Comunicaciones, Abel Caballero, ha declarado que el gobierno está dando los primeros pasos para la construcción de un satélite español de telecomunicaciones que, de tomarse[a] la decisión final, comenzará[b] a ser operativo el año que viene. Muchos de los componentes del satélite tendrían[c] que ser importados, pero al menos el 36 por ciento los podría[d] construir la industria española.

[a]*de... when making*   [b]*will begin*   [c]*would have*   [d]*could*

Nota: Verifique sus respuestas al **Paso 1** antes de empezar el **Paso 2**.

Paso 2. Ahora va a oír el artículo del **Paso 1**. Preste (*Pay*) atención a la pronunciación de los cognados.

Paso 3. Ahora lea el artículo en voz alta, imitando lo que oyó en el **Paso 2**.

GRAMÁTICA

¿Recuerda Ud.?

Usos del subjuntivo que ya han estudiado. Cambie los infinitivos por el presente de subjuntivo.

Influencia:

1. Quiero que Uds. _____ (ir) hoy.

2. Insisten en que (nosotros) _____ (volver) mañana.

3. Es importante que (tú) _____ (llamar) a tu papá.

Emoción:

4. Espero que (Ud.) _____ (saber) hablar francés.

5. Me alegro de que (Uds.) _____ (estar) aquí.

6. Sentimos que (tú) no _____ (poder) acompañarnos.

Duda o Negación

7. Dudo que (ella) _____ (tener) tiempo para ir al cine.

8. No es cierto que María _____ (casarse) con Pedro.

9. No creo que (ellos) _____ (ser) novios.

¡OJO! Recuerde que cuando *no* hay cambio de sujeto, se usa el infinitivo:

(Yo) Siento que **(Uds) no puedan** ir.   pero,   **(Yo) Siento no poder** ir.

(Yo) Me alegro de que **(tú) termines** hoy.   pero,   **(Yo) Me alegro** de **terminar** hoy.

44. ¿Hay alguien que... ? ¿Hay un lugar donde... ? • The Subjunctive (Part 6): The Subjunctive After Nonexistent and Indefinite Antecedents

A. La boda. Empareje las frases de las dos columnas para describir la siguiente escena.

_____ **1.** Hay dos niñas que   **a.** se portan mal

_____ **2.** Hay un hombre que   **b.** llora de felicidad

                                  c. sonríen de felicidad

_____ **3.** No hay nadie que   **d.** está tirando (*throwing*) arroz

_____ **4.** Hay varias personas que   **e.** está sacando fotos

                                    f. trate de interrumpir (*interrupt*) la ceremonia

_____ **5.** Hay una mujer mayor que

_____ **6.** Hay una mujer que

B. Todos buscan lo que no tienen. Complete las oraciones con la forma apropiada del subjuntivo de los verbos entre paréntesis.

     a. Los Vásquez viven en un apartamento en el centro. Quieren una casa que _____[1] (ser) más grande, que _____[2] (estar) en la costa, que _____[3] (tener) vista a la playa y que no _____[4] (costar) un millón de dólares. Francamente, dudo que la _____[5] (encontrar).

     b. En nuestra oficina necesitamos un secretario que _____[1] (saber) lenguas extranjeras, que _____[2] (llevarse) bien con la gente, que no _____[3] (fumar), que no _____[4] (pasar) todo el día hablando por teléfono, que _____[5] (llegar) a tiempo, que no _____[6] (ponerse) irritado con los clientes y que no _____[7] (enfermarse) cada lunes.

     c. No conozco a nadie en esta universidad. Busco amigos que _____[1] (practicar) deportes, que _____[2] (jugar) al ajedrez, que _____[3] (escuchar) *jazz*, que _____[4] (hacer) *camping* y a quienes les _____[5] (gustar) ir al cine.

C. Situaciones. Complete las oraciones, según las indicaciones. Use el subjuntivo o el indicativo, según sea necesario. **¡OJO!** ¡Cuidado con la concordancia (*agreement*) de los adjetivos y con las preposiciones!

     1. Tenemos unos amigos que _____ (vivir / playa), pero no conocemos a nadie que _____ (vivir / montañas).

     2. Luisa quiere conocer a alguien que _____ (enseñarle / hablar) francés porque tiene un primo francés que _____ (venir / visitar) a su familia durante el verano.

     3. Elena tiene unos zapatos que _____ (ser / bonito), pero que _____ (hacerle) daño en los pies. Por eso está buscando unos que _____ (ser / cómodo), que _____ (estar / de moda) y que _____ (ir bien / falda / rosado). Aquí no ve nada que _____ (gustarle).

(Continúa.)

4. Tenemos dos amigos que _____ (acabar / divorciarse), pero ninguno

de ellos _____ (querer) volver a casarse pronto. ¿Conoces a alguien

que _____ (ser / soltero) y que _____

(buscar) un compañero / una compañera de la vida?

D. Casas y vecinos. Ud. y su pareja buscan una nueva casa y vecinos diferentes. Conteste las siguientes oraciones, según el modelo. Luego escuche la respuesta correcta y repítala.

MODELO: (Ud. oye)   Uno–a. ¿Qué tipo de casa buscan Uds.?

                (Ud. ve)   **1.** **a.** una casa / estar en el campo

            (Ud. dice)   Buscamos una casa que esté en el campo.

    (Ud. oye y repite)   Buscamos una casa que esté en el campo.

1. **b.** una casa / tener piscina
    c. una casa / ser grande
2. **a.** vecinos / ser simpáticos
    b. vecinos / tener niños
    c. vecinos / saber divertirse

E. En la oficina. Ud. va a oír algunas oraciones. Responda a cada oración, según las indicaciones. Siga el modelo.

MODELO: (Ud. oye)   Necesitamos un secretario que hable español.

                (Ud. ve)   Pues, yo conozco…

            (Ud. dice)   Pues, yo conozco a un secretario que habla español.

    (Ud. oye y repite)   Pues, yo conozco a un secretario que habla español.

1. Yo tengo…
2. Lo siento, pero no hay nadie aquí…
3. Pues, yo busco…
4. Pues, yo también quiero…
5. En mi compañía hay un puesto (*job*)…

F. ¿Qué quieren? Ud. va a oír lo que tienen las siguientes personas. Diga lo que cada persona quiere, según las indicaciones. Luego escuche la respuesta correcta y repítala.

MODELO: (Ud. oye)   Arturo tiene amigos que son antipáticos.

                (Ud. ve)   Arturo: amigos / ser simpáticos

            (Ud. dice)   Quiere amigos que sean simpáticos.

    (Ud. oye y repite)   Quiere amigos que sean simpáticos.

1. Mirna: un novio / ser más cariñoso
2. Laura: hijos / llevarse bien
3. Damián: jefe / ser más flexible
4. los Sres. Jurado: vecinos / no hacer tanto ruido
5. Martín: perro / ser más obediente
6. Catalina: apartamento / tener vista

45. *Lo hago para que tú...* • The Subjunctive (Part 7): The Subjunctive After Conjunctions of Purpose and Contingency

A. La luna de miel. Mario y su esposa acaban de casarse y van de vacaciones para su luna de miel. Vuelva a escribir lo que dicen, reemplazando la frase preposicional por una cláusula con el subjuntivo del verbo indicado.

1. Llama a tus padres antes de *salir*.

   Llama a tus padres antes de que (nosotros) _____.

2. Cierra bien los grifos (*faucets*) para no *malgastar* (*to not waste*) el agua.

   Cierra bien los grifos para que (nosotros) no _____ el agua.

3. Escribamos el teléfono del hotel en caso de no *recordarlo*.

   Escribamos el teléfono del hotel en caso de que (tú) no _____

4. Hagamos este viaje sin *decírselo* a todo el mundo (*everybody*).

   Hagamos este viaje sin que tú _____ a todo el mundo.

B. «¡Antes que te cases, mira lo que haces!»* Un amigo está pensando en casarse. Recomiéndele a su amigo que haga algunas cosas antes de tomar esa decisión. Complete las oraciones con la forma apropiada de las palabras de la lista. Use cada frase solo una vez.

amarse y llevarse bien   enfermarse o haber una emergencia
casarse   tener un buen trabajo
conocerse

1. No te cases a menos que _____

   _____

2. Debes tener ahorros (*savings*) suficientes en caso de que _____

   _____

3. Debes hacer que las dos familias se reúnan para que los padres de las dos familias _____

   _____

4. No te preocupes si todos los parientes no se llevan bien, con tal de que tú y tu novia _____

   _____

5. Si hay algún problema serio, habla con un consejero matrimonial (*marriage counselor*) antes de que

   Uds. _____

---

*Popular saying (**dicho**) *that is equivalent to "Look before you leap."*

C. ¿Quién lo dijo? Cuando oiga el número correspondiente, lea las siguientes oraciones usando el presente de subjuntivo de los verbos entre paréntesis. Luego escuche la respuesta correcta y repítala. Después indique quién dijo cada oración.

1. No les doy los paquetes a los clientes antes de que me _____ (pagar).
   a. un aficionado a los deportes
   b. un dependiente en un almacén

2. Voy a revisar las llantas en caso de que _____ (necesitar) aire.
   a. un mecánico
   b. un camarero

3. No compro esa computadora a menos que _____ (ser) fácil de manejar.
   a. una tenista
   b. una profesora

4. Voy a tomarle la temperatura al paciente antes de que lo _____ (ver) la doctora.
   a. un doctor
   b. un enfermero

5. No tomo ese vuelo a menos que no _____ (hacer) escalas.
   a. un niño pequeño
   b. un pasajero

6. Pago el alquiler con tal de que me _____ (*ellos:* arreglar) la calefacción.
   a. una inquilina
   b. la dueña de un edificio de apartamentos

D. Antes del viaje

Paso 1. Ud. va a oír la conversación entre Francisco y Araceli, quienes están a punto de (*about to*) salir para el aeropuerto. Después va a oír algunas oraciones. Indique si son ciertas (**C**) o falsas (**F**). Si la información no se da, escoja **ND** (No lo dice).

1. C   F   ND   4. C   F   ND
2. C   F   ND   5. C   F   ND
3. C   F   ND

Paso 2. Ahora va a ver un par (*pair*) de oraciones basadas en el diálogo del **Paso 1.** Después va a oír una conjunción. Una (*Join*) las dos oraciones con la conjunción que oye. Cambie el verbo de la segunda oración en cada par por el presente de subjuntivo. Luego escuche la respuesta correcta y repítala. Siga el modelo.

MODELO: (Ud. ve)   Hacen el viaje. No olvidan los boletos.
         (Ud. oye)   con tal que
         (Ud. dice)   Hacen el viaje con tal que no olviden los boletos.
         (Ud. oye y repite)   Hacen el viaje con tal que no olviden los boletos.

1. Tienen cuatro horas. Sale el vuelo.
2. Ponen las maletas en el coche. Pueden salir pronto.
3. Tienen que estar bien organizados. No llegan tarde al aeropuerto.
4. No van a perder el vuelo. Algo inesperado pasa.
5. Llaman un taxi. El coche no arranca.

E. La relación ideal

Paso 1. En esta entrevista, Tané, Rubén, Miguel René y Karina contestan una pregunta sobre cómo mantener una buena relación entre una pareja. Primero, escuche el **Vocabulario útil** y la entrevista. Luego complete las oraciones con la forma correcta de los verbos entre paréntesis.

Miguel René, Karina, Rubén y Tané

Vocabulario útil

mantener	to maintain, sustain
el apoyo	support
la comprensión	understanding
hacia adelante	ahead
rodeado/a de	surrounded by
adecuarse	to adapt oneself
la confianza	trust

☐ **1.** Para que una relación _____ (funcionar), es necesario que _____ (haber) respeto entre los dos en todas las cosas. Este ingrediente es básico para todos los tipos de relaciones, no solo las románticas.

☐ **2.** No puede haber una relación estable sin que _____ (existir) cariño (*affection*) y confianza.

☐ **3.** Las relaciones son estables con tal de que la pareja _____ (compartir) creencias religiosas y espirituales.

☐ **4.** Con tal de que las dos personas _____ (tener) credibilidad, amor y respeto, se puede esperar una buena pareja.

☐ **5.** No se puede mantener una buena relación de pareja a menos que los dos _____ (sentir) amor y respeto mutuos.

☐ **6.** Para que las relaciones _____ (durar: *to last*), es importante que la pareja _____ (planear) aventuras divertidas y románticas.

Paso 2. En la columna izquierda con casillas (*checkboxes*) de la tabla del **Paso 1,** indique las ideas que se mencionan en la entrevista.

Un poco de todo

A. ¡Otra versión de Romeo y Julieta! Complete esta versión nueva de la historia. Use el presente de indicativo o subjuntivo de los verbos entre paréntesis, según sea necesario. Cuando vea *PP:* con el verbo, dé el participio pasado. Cuando se presenten dos posibilidades, escoja la palabra correcta.

En Sevilla, nadie sabe por qué, las familias de Romeo y Julieta no _____^{1} (llevarse)

bien. En verdad, _____^{2} (odiarse) y (por / para) _____^{3} eso viven

en barrios diferentes, separados por el río Guadalquivir. No hay nadie que no

_____^{4} (saber) que la mala sangre _____^{5} (haber) existido entre las

dos familias (por / para) _____^{6} mucho tiempo. Las dos familias han

_____^{7} (*PP:* hacer) todo lo posible para que sus hijos no _____^{8}

(conocerse). A pesar de todo,^{a} un día los dos jóvenes _____^{9} (encontrarse) en la

universidad, se hacen^b amigos y luego _____^{10} (enamorarse) locamente.

Para que sus padres no _____^{11} (verlos), ellos _____^{12}

(encontrarse) en secreto en la biblioteca, en el parque y ¡hasta^c en la catedral! (Por / Para)

_____^{13} fin, las familias lo _____^{14} (descubrir) todo e insisten en que

los novios _____^{15} (romper) sus relaciones. El padre de Julieta, enojadísimo, le dice

que en caso de que ella no _____^{16} (obedecerlo), él la va a sacar de la universidad

y la _____^{17} (ir) a mandar a vivir con su abuela a las Islas Canarias.

Confrontados con la terrible realidad de sus vidas, los enamorados dejan la universidad antes

de que _____^{18} (terminarse) el curso y _____^{19} (escaparse) a Santan-

der, (lejos / cerca) _____^{20} de la tiranía de las dos familias. Cuando los padres des-

cubren lo que _____^{21} (haber) hecho, les piden que _____^{22} (volver)

a Sevilla y les prometen que van a permitirles que se casen con tal de que _____^{23}

(acabar) sus estudios universitarios.

^{a}A... *In spite of everything* ^{b}se... *they become* ^{c}*even*

B. *Listening Passage:* **Semejanzas** (*Similarities*) **y diferencias**

❖ **Antes de escuchar.** Before listening, do the following prelistening activity. Answer the following questions to see how much you know about the similarities and differences between young people of the United States and Spain and the educational systems of these countries.

1. ¿Cómo pagan los jóvenes estadounidenses su educación universitaria? ¿Sacan préstamos? ¿Reciben becas? ¿Trabajan?

_____

_____

_____

2. ¿Cómo cree Ud. que los jóvenes españoles pagan su educación universitaria?

_____

_____

_____

3. ¿Es normal que los jóvenes estadounidenses mayores de 18 años vivan con sus padres?

_____

_____

4. Normalmente, ¿a qué edad se independizan los jóvenes estadounidenses? Y los jóvenes españoles, ¿a qué edad cree Ud. que se independizan ellos?

_____

_____

_____

_____

5. ¿Cuántos años dura (*lasts*) la universidad en los Estados Unidos?

_____

6. ¿Cuántos años cree Ud. que dura la universidad en España?

_____

Listening Passage. Now you will hear a conversation, already in progress, between two students: Gustavo, who is from Spain, and Mike, who is from the United States. Mike spent some time living in Chile. They are talking about the similarities and differences between people of their age group in the United States and Spain. Note that Gustavo, who is from Spain, uses the **vosotros** forms of verbs, pronouns, and possessive adjectives instead of the **Uds.** forms. Although the **vosotros** forms are not frequently used in *Puntos de partida,* you should be able to understand them in context. Listen to the **Vocabulario útil** and read the statements in the **Después de escuchar** to know what information to listen for. Then listen to the passage.

Vocabulario útil

independizarse	to become independent
darse cuenta de que	to realize
no se ve tan mal	it is not looked down upon (considered odd, viewed as bad)
durar	to last
los préstamos	loans
las becas	scholarships, grants
los ingresos	earnings
subvencionado/a	subsidized

Después de escuchar. Indicate the country to which the following sentences refer, based on the conversation that you just heard.

	ESPAÑA	LOS ESTADOS UNIDOS
1. La mayoría de las universidades públicas están subvencionadas por el gobierno.	☐	☐
2. Es normal obtener un préstamo para asistir a la universidad.	☐	☐
3. Es normal que una persona mayor de 18 años viva con sus padres	☐	☐
4. Se ve mal que los hijos vivan con la familia después de cumplir 18 años.	☐	☐
5. La universidad dura cinco años, generalmente.	☐	☐
6. A los jóvenes les gusta llevar *jeans* y escuchar música *rock*.	☐	☐

C. Una invitación

Paso 1. En esta conversación, Lola y su amiga Eva hacen planes para el fin de semana. Primero, escuche el **Vocabulario útil.** Luego escuche la conversación y fíjese en el uso de **vosotros.** Mientras escucha, indique a quién se refiere cada una de las oraciones: Lola o Eva.

Vocabulario útil

¿vale?   OK?

	LOLA	EVA
1. Vamos a una fiesta de cumpleaños.	☐	☐
2. Vamos a una boda.	☐	☐
3. Voy a estar en Sevilla.	☐	☐
4. Voy a estar en Cádiz.	☐	☐
5. No tengo planes para el domingo.	☐	☐
6. Mi prima se casa.	☐	☐

Paso 2. Ahora Ud. va a participar en una conversación en la que hace el papel de **Ud.** Primero, complete la conversación con las siguientes frases y conjugue los verbos si es necesario. Segundo, verifique sus respuestas en el Apéndice. Después haga la conversación en voz alta: Lea las líneas de **Ud.** en el diálogo y luego escuche la pronunciación correcta y repítala.

venir conmigo a tomar un café   estar libre esta tarde

UD.:   ¡Hola, Yolanda! ¡Hace tiempo que no te veo! ¿———————————?[1]

YOLANDA: ¡Qué coincidencia! Te iba a llamar anoche. Resulta que no tengo que trabajar esta tarde.

UD.:   ¡Magnífico! ¿Quieres ———————————[2]?

YOLANDA: Pues, ¡claro! Tengo mucho que contarte...

El Paraguay

A. Mapa. Identifique en el siguiente mapa el Paraguay y la capital de ese país.

B. Comprensión. Complete las siguientes oraciones con información de la **Lectura cultural: El Paraguay** de la página 488 del libro de texto.

1. Tener novio/a significa que la relación es _____ y _____.

2. Se usa el término novio/novia para referirse a la persona que _____ o

_____.

3. Cuando la relación entre dos personas es informal, se dice que _____ juntos.

4. Se usa la palabra _____ para referirse a una persona que vive con otra sin

_____.

5. Los jóvenes hispanos no tienen muchas oportunidades de demostrar su afecto excepto en los

_____, plazas y otros lugares públicos.

6. En España y otros países, en vez de salir en parejas, los jóvenes prefieren salir en

_____.

7. El Gran Chaco, compartido principalmente por el Paraguay y Bolivia, ocupa el 60 por ciento

del _____.

8. El _____ es la lengua indígena del Paraguay, y es hablada por el 80 por ciento de

la población.

PÓNGASE A PRUEBA

A. Use of Subjunctive After Nonexistent and Indefinite Antecedents. Complete las oraciones con el presente de indicativo o subjuntivo, según sea necesario.

1. Tengo un amigo que _____ (ser) de Bolivia.

2. Busco a alguien que _____ (saber) hablar guaraní.

3. Aquí hay alguien que _____ (conocer) la ciudad.

4. No veo a nadie que _____ (hacer) ejercicio.

5. ¿Hay alguien que _____ (pensar) conducir al centro?

B. Subjunctive After Conjunctions of Purpose and Contingency

1. Escriba la conjunción apropiada para completar cada oración.

a menos que	con tal (de) que	sin que
antes (de) que	para que	

   a. No voy a invitar a Juan _____ se disculpe.

   b. Luis reserva una mesa _____ tú y él cenen juntos.

   c. Voy adonde tú quieras, _____ me acompañes.

   d. Vamos a comer _____ sea muy tarde.

   e. Quiero comprar este perfume para Marta _____ ella lo sepa.

2. Complete las oraciones con el presente de subjuntivo o el infinitivo del verbo indicado, según sea necesario.

   a. Vamos a salir ahora para _____ (poder) llegar a tiempo.

   b. Llama a Elena antes de que _____ (*ella*: salir).

   c. Lleva dinero extra en caso de que _____ (*tú*: tener) algún problema.

   d. No te vayas sin _____ (llamarme) primero.

   e. Podemos ir al cine con tal de que no _____ (ser) muy tarde.

PRUEBA CORTA

A. Antecedentes definidos y existentes o no. Complete las oraciones con la forma apropiada del indicativo o del subjuntivo del verbo entre paréntesis, según el contexto.

1. Estoy buscando a alguien que _____ (querer) viajar a Europa.

2. No conozco a nadie que _____ (ir) de vacaciones en invierno, pero tengo varios

   amigos que siempre _____ (viajar) en verano.

3. Hoy día hay pocos bebés que _____ (nacer) en casa.

4. Conozco a alguien que _____ (acabar) de tener una boda grande.

5. Algunos muchachos solo quieren encontrar una novia que _____ (ser) rica y bonita.

B. **Conjunciones de propósito y contingencia.** Complete las oraciones con la forma apropiada del subjuntivo o con el infinitivo, según el contexto.

1. Uds. deben conocerse bien antes de _____ (casarse).

2. Los recién casados tienen que trabajar para _____ (poder) comprar una casa.

3. En caso de que me _____ (*tú*: necesitar), llámame.

4. No debes salir a menos que _____ (haber) estudiado para el examen.

5. Voy contigo a la ópera con tal que (tú) me _____ (conseguir) una entrada.

6. Por favor, dales dinero antes de que _____ (*ellos*: irse).

C. **En busca de los amigos perfectos.** Cuando oiga el número correspondiente, haga oraciones según las indicaciones. Empiece cada oración con **Quiero...** Haga todos los cambios necesarios. Siga el modelo.

> MODELO: (Ud. oye) Uno.
>
> (Ud. ve) **1.** un amigo / ser simpático
>
> (Ud. dice) Quiero un amigo que sea simpático.
>
> (Ud. oye y repite) Quiero un amigo que sea simpático.

2. una amiga / ser amable
3. unos amigos / ser flexibles
4. unas amigas / vivir cerca de mí
5. un amigo / tener coche
6. una amiga / saber mucho de computadoras

D. **La boda de Mireya y Alonso.** Ahora, va a ver dos oraciones. Después va a oír una conjunción. Una (*Join*) las dos oraciones con la conjunción que oye. Cambie el verbo de la segunda oración en cada par (*pair*) por el presente de subjuntivo. Luego escuche la respuesta correcta y repítala. Siga el modelo.

> MODELO: (Ud. ve) **1.** No deben casarse. Se llevan bien.
>
> (Ud. oye) Uno. a menos que
>
> (Ud. dice) No deben casarse a menos que se lleven bien.
>
> (Ud. oye y repite) No deben casarse a menos que se lleven bien.

2. Deben casarse. Están enamorados.
3. Van a confirmar la fecha. Sus padres mandan las invitaciones.
4. Van a alquilar una sala de recepciones. Vienen muchas personas.
5. Los padres les regalan dinero. Los novios empiezan a ahorrar.
6. Van a Cancún para su luna de miel. Encuentran un hotel barato.

❖ PUNTOS PERSONALES

A. El amor y el matrimonio. Dé su opinión sobre las siguientes ideas relacionadas con el amor, el noviazgo y el matrimonio.

1. ¿Conoce Ud. a alguien que haya tenido problemas en su vida matrimonial? Explique uno de esos problemas. _____

   _____

2. ¿Cree Ud. que es justo que la familia de la novia pague todos los gastos de la boda?

   _____

   _____

3. ¿Quiere Ud. tener una boda grande o cree que las bodas grandes son una tontería (*silly thing*)?

   _____

   _____

4. Si Ud. está casado/a, ¿qué tipo de boda tuvo? ¿Invitó a mucha gente? ¿Tuvo una recepción grande? ¿Dónde fue la recepción? ¿Quién preparó la comida? (Si no está casado/a, describe una boda a la que [*that*] asistió.)

   _____

   _____

5. ¿Cree Ud. que el hombre debe ser el responsable de los asuntos económicos de la pareja?

   Explique por qué sí o por qué no. _____

   _____

6. ¿Si una mujer rompe con su novio, debe ella devolverle el anillo de compromiso (*engagement ring*)? Justifique su respuesta. _____

   _____

B. Los deseos. Complete las siguientes oraciones de acuerdo con (*in accordance with*) su vida real y sus deseos.

1. Quiero conocer a alguien que _____

2. Acabo de conocer a alguien que _____

3. Nunca he conocido a nadie que _____

4. Este verano quiero _____

5. No quiero vivir nunca en un lugar que _____

C. **Situaciones.** Complete las siguientes oraciones de acuerdo con su vida real y sus deseos.

1. Quiero terminar mis estudios antes que _____

2. Después de graduarme, espero encontrar un trabajo para que _____

3. Me gusta salir con mis amigos sin que _____

4. No quiero casarme a menos que _____

5. Quiero comprar una casa con tal que _____

D. **Ingredientes de una vida feliz**

Paso 1. Complete la tabla con los «ingredientes», es decir, las condiciones y circunstancias que, en su opinión, hacen feliz cada etapa de la vida.

ETAPA DE LA VIDA	INGREDIENTES
la infancia y la niñez	*buena salud* *padres cariñosos*
la adolescencia y la juventud	
la madurez	
la vejez	

Paso 2. Ahora escuche las siguientes preguntas y contéstelas por escrito con la información que escribió en la tabla del **Paso 1.**

1. _____
   _____

2. _____
   _____
   _____

3. _____
   _____

4. _____
   _____

5. _____
   _____

6. _____
   _____

E. **Guided Composition.** En una hoja aparte, escriba una composición sobre lo que Ud. considera necesario para que una pareja funcione bien. ¿Cuáles son los «ingredientes» de una pareja feliz?

Puede mencionar:

- la personalidad de cada una de las personas
- cómo se llevan / «la química» entre las dos personas
- la apariencia física
- la atracción física entre las dos personas
- las cualidades que debe tener cada una de las dos personas
- la educación
- el trabajo
- el apoyo (*support*) de las dos familias

Puede dar ejemplos de sus propias (*own*) experiencias, de una pareja que Ud. ya conoce o de una pareja ideal. También, puede usar las siguientes palabras y otras para conectar las ideas de su composición y hacerla más interesante: **por eso, y, aunque** (*although*)**, también, como, luego, pero** y **porque.**

F. **Mi diario.** Primero describa Ud. cómo era su vida social en la escuela secundaria. (Use el imperfecto de indicativo.) Luego, escriba sobre sus actividades sociales como estudiante universitario. (Use el presente de indicativo o subjuntivo.) Haga referencias a las amistades, noviazgos, diversiones y problemas que tenía / tiene con sus compañeros. Finalmente, haga una comparación entre las dos etapas de su vida social. Puede usar la siguiente lista de **Vocabulario útil.**

Vocabulario útil

a diferencia de	unlike
a pesar de	in spite of
en cambio	on the other hand

G. **Intercambios.** Escuche las siguientes preguntas y contéstelas por escrito.

1. _____
_____

2. _____
_____
_____

3. _____
_____

4. _____
_____

5. _____
_____

6. _____
_____

Capítulo 17 ¿Trabajar para vivir o vivir para trabajar?

VOCABULARIO — Preparación

Las profesiones y los oficios

A. ¿Qué oficio o profesión tienen? Empareje cada uno de los oficios o profesiones con la definición correspondiente.

abogado/a
bibliotecario/a
enfermero/a

hombre/mujer de negocios
ingeniero/a
maestro/a
médico/a

obrero/a
periodista
plomero/a
siquiatra

1. Es dueño/a de una compañía que produce y vende ciertos productos o servicios.

   _____

2. Es un trabajador (una trabajadora) sin especialización.

   _____

3. Va a las casas para hacer instalaciones o reparaciones en el servicio del agua.

   _____

4. Ayuda al doctor en el consultorio o en el hospital. _____

5. Prepara documentos legales para sus clientes. _____

6. Es un médico que ayuda a las personas que tienen problemas mentales o sicológicos.

   _____

7. Enseña en una escuela primaria o secundaria. _____

8. Dirige la construcción de casas, edificios, calles, etcétera. Debe ser buen matemático (buena matemática).

   _____

9. Trabaja en un hospital o en su consultorio privado. Generalmente, gana mucho dinero.

   _____

10. Escribe las noticias que se publican en el periódico. _____

11. Trabaja en una biblioteca. _____

B. **¿Quiénes son?** Ud. va a identificar a las personas de los siguientes dibujos. Primero, escuche la lista de profesiones. Cuando oiga el número correspondiente, identifique a las personas. Empiece cada oración con **Es un...** o **Es una...** Luego escuche la respuesta correcta y repítala.

obrero/a	abogado/a	cocinero/a	plomero/a
peluquero/a	veterinario/a	fotógrafo/a	hombre o mujer de negocios

1. ...　2. ...　3. ...　4. ...　5. ...　6. ...　7. ...　8. ...

C. **¿A quién necesitan en estas situaciones?**

Paso 1. Ud. va a oír algunas situaciones. Indique la letra de la persona que podría (*could*) ayudar en cada situación.

1.	**a.** un arquitecto		**b.** un periodista
2.	**a.** una dentista		**b.** un enfermero
3.	**a.** una consejera matrimonial		**b.** un policía
4.	**a.** un fotógrafo		**b.** un bibliotecario
5.	**a.** un plomero		**b.** una electricista
6.	**a.** una traductora		**b.** una técnica

Paso 2. Ahora va a oír las situaciones del **Paso 1** otra vez. Responda a cada pregunta, según las respuestas correctas del **Paso 1.** Luego escuche la respuesta correcta y repítala.

MODELO: (Ud. oye) Uno. Los Sres. Castán necesitan una persona que les ayude a diseñar su casa ideal. ¿Con quién deben consultar?

(Ud. ve) **1.** ⓐ un arquitecto

(Ud. dice) Deben consultar con un arquitecto.

(Ud. oye y repite) Deben consultar con un arquitecto.

2. ... **3.** ... **4.** ... **5.** ... **6.** ...

D. **Un trabajo interesante.** En esta entrevista, María Dioni habla de su trabajo. Primero, escuche el **Vocabulario útil** y la entrevista. Luego complete los párrafos con información de la entrevista.

Vocabulario útil

a punto de	about to
recibirse	**graduarse**
la solicitud	application

María Dioni es de _____,[1] pero ahora vive en México. Trabaja de

_____[2] de estudiantes que están a punto de _____.[3] Su trabajo consiste

en ayudar a los estudiantes en proceso de _____.[4] Esto incluye llenar[a]

_____,[5] qué decir y cómo _____[6] en las _____[7] y

cómo hacer _____.[8] A María le _____[9] su trabajo.

[a]*filling out*

El mundo laboral

A. **Consejos para encontrar empleo.** Dele consejos a su hermana menor. Complete las oraciones con la forma apropiada de las palabras de la lista. Use el mandato familiar cuando sea necesario.

currículum	empresa	mujer de negocios
dejar	entrevista	renunciar
empleos	llenar	solicitud

1. Prepara tu _____ con cuidado, incluyendo todos los empleos y la experiencia

   que has tenido.

2. Ve a la oficina de _____ de la universidad y busca anuncios en el periódico.

3. Llama a todas las oficinas que ofrezcan posibilidades; no te limites a solo una. Pide una

   _____ con el director de personal.

(Continúa.)

4. Ve a la biblioteca e infórmate sobre la _____: su historia, qué tipo de trabajo hacen, etcétera.

5. Si te llaman para entrevistarte, vístete como _____.

6. _____ la _____ con bolígrafo; no uses lápiz.

7. Si te dan el empleo, ¡magnífico! Pero, si después de algún tiempo no ves oportunidades de avanzar en la empresa, piensa en _____ al puesto, pero no lo _____ antes de conseguir otro empleo.

B. En busca de un puesto

Paso 1. Imagine que Ud. ya tiene trabajo, pero busca un nuevo puesto en una empresa grande. Primero, escuche la lista de pasos necesarios para conseguir un nuevo trabajo. Luego ponga los pasos en orden lógico. Empiece por el número 3, ya que (*since*) los pasos 1 y 2 ya se han identificado.

_____ renunciar a mi puesto actual (*current*)

_____ contestar preguntas sobre mi experiencia

_____ aceptar el nuevo puesto

__2__ pedir una solicitud de empleo

_____ ir a la entrevista

_____ llenar la solicitud

__1__ llamar a la oficina de empleos

Nota: Verifique las respuestas al **Paso 1** en el Apéndice antes de empezar el **Paso 2**.

Paso 2. Ahora cuando oiga el número correspondiente, diga el paso que Ud. va a dar para buscar el nuevo puesto. Luego escuche la respuesta correcta y repítala.

MODELO:　　　　(Ud. oye)　Uno.

　　　　　　　　(Ud. ve)　__1__ llamar a la oficina de empleos

　　　　　　　　(Ud. dice)　Llamo a la oficina de empleos.

　　　　(Ud. oye y repite)　Llamo a la oficina de empleos.

C. Solicitar un trabajo

❖ **Paso 1.** Piense en el proceso de solicitar un trabajo. ¿Qué errores o situaciones debe evitar (*to avoid*) la persona que solicita un puesto? Escriba por lo menos tres errores posibles.

1. _____

2. _____

3. _____

Paso 2. En esta entrevista, Sonia Sancho habla de su trabajo. Primero, escuche el **Vocabulario útil** y la entrevista. Después conteste las siguientes preguntas.

Vocabulario útil

los recursos humanos	human resources
encargarse de	to be in charge of
mentir (miento) (i)	to lie
grave	**serio**
agradecer	to thank
proporcionar	**dar**

1. ¿De qué se encarga Sonia Sancho en su empresa?

   _____

   _____

2. ¿Qué aspecto de su trabajo es difícil para la Sra. Sancho?

   _____

   _____

3. Según la Sra. Sancho, ¿cuáles son dos de los errores más graves en una solicitud?

   _____

   _____

Una cuestión de dinero

A. **El presupuesto mensual** (*monthly*). Roberto y su esposa, Elena, están hablando de su presupuesto mensual. Complete el diálogo con la forma apropiada de las palabras de la lista.

ahorrar	devolver	presupuesto
alquiler	factura	quejarse
corriente	gastar	

ROBERTO: En los últimos dos meses hemos _____[1] tanto dinero que no hemos

podido _____[2] nada. Debemos economizar más.

ELENA: Es cierto, pero es difícil limitarnos a nuestro _____[3] mensual con el

constante aumento de gastos.

ROBERTO: Hoy es el primero de abril, y tenemos que pagar el _____[4] de la casa.

ELENA: Si no depositamos más dinero en nuestra cuenta _____,[5] no vamos a

poder pagar nuestras _____.[6]

ROBERTO: Realmente creo que debes _____[7] esos dos vestidos de Gucci que

compraste ayer, ¿no te parece?

ELENA: ¡Tú siempre _____[8] de mis gastos, pero no dejas de manejar tu Porsche!

B. En la agencia de automóviles. Carlos está comprando un auto de segunda mano y habla con el agente. Complete el diálogo con la forma apropiada de las palabras de la lista.

a plazos   cobrar   préstamo
cajera   en efectivo   tarjeta de crédito

CARLOS: Me gustaría comprar el coche _____[1] para ahorrar los intereses, pero no tengo suficientes ahorros.

AGENTE: No hay ningún problema. Ud. puede pagarlo _____.[2] Y si necesita un _____,[3] se lo damos a buen precio.

CARLOS: ¿Y cuánto _____[4] Uds. de intereses?

AGENTE: Solamente el 11 por ciento. Es la tasa (*rate*) más baja que se ofrece.

CARLOS: A mí me parece bastante alta. Puedo usar mi _____[5] para hacer el primer pago, ¿verdad?

AGENTE: ¡Cómo no! Pase a la oficina. La _____[6] le va a dar el recibo.

C. De compras

Paso 1. Ud. va a oír algunas preguntas. Contéstelas por escrito, según el dibujo.

1. _____

2. _____

3. _____

4. _____

Nota: Verifique las respuestas al **Paso 1** en el Apéndice antes de empezar el **Paso 2.**

Paso 2. Ahora va a oír las preguntas del **Paso 1** otra vez. Contéstelas con las respuestas que escribió en el **Paso 1.** Luego escuche la respuesta correcta y repítala.

1. …   2. …   3. …   4. …

Nota comunicativa: Más pronombres posesivos

Diálogos breves. Complete los diálogos con la forma tónica (*stressed*) del posesivo.

MODELO: No encuentro mi tarjeta de crédito. ¿Y tú? → Aquí tengo la mía.

1. —Pago mis cuentas con mi tarjeta de crédito. ¿Y tú?

   —Yo pago _____ con cheque.

2. —Conseguimos nuestro préstamo del banco. ¿Y Uds.?

   —Nosotros conseguimos _____ de mis padres.

3. —Nuestro banco está cobrando el 10 por ciento de intereses. Y tu banco, ¿cuánto cobra?

   —_____ solo cobra el 8 por ciento.

4. —Este mes mis gastos son muy altos. ¿Y los de Ud.?

   —_____ son muy altos también.

PRONUNCIACIÓN — More on Stress and the Written Accent

El acento escrito y los verbos. You have learned that the written accent is an important factor in the spelling of some verbs. You know that in the case of the preterite, for example, a missing accent can change the meaning of the verb. Listen to the following pairs of words.

habló (*he, she, or you spoke*) / hablo (*I speak, I am speaking*)
hablé (*I spoke*) / hable (*speak* [formal command]; *that he, she, you, or I may speak*
[present subjunctive])

El acento escrito

- The written accent also is important in maintaining the original stress of a word to which syllables have been added. In the word **jóvenes,** for example, the written accent maintains the stress of the singular word **joven,** even though another syllable has been added. Listen to the pronunciation of the following pairs of words.
  examen / exámenes
  volumen / volúmenes

- Sometimes, the reverse will be true. A word that has a written accent will lose the accent when a syllable is added. Compare **inglés** and **ingleses.** This happens because the new word receives the stress naturally; that is, it follows the rules of stress. Listen to the pronunciation of the following pairs of words.
  portugués / portugueses
  dirección / direcciones
  alemán / alemanes

El acento diacrítico. You have probably noticed that when a pair of words is written the same but has different meanings, sometimes one of the words is accented. This accent is called a *diacritical* accent. There is no difference in pronunciation between the two words. Listen to the following pairs of words, noting the differences in meaning.

1. mi (*my*) / mí (*me*)
2. tu (*your*) / tú (*you*)
3. el (*the*) / él (*he*)
4. si (*if*) / sí (*yes*)
5. se (*oneself*) / sé (*I know; be* [informal command])
6. de (*of, from*) / dé (*give* [formal command]; *give* [present subjunctive])
7. te (*you, yourself*) / té (*tea*)
8. que (*that, which*) / ¿qué? (*what?*)

A. **Diferencias.** Cuando oiga el número correspondiente, lea los siguientes pares de palabras. Escuche la pronunciación correcta y repítala, imitando lo que oye.

1. tomo / tomó
2. ahorro / ahorró
3. pague / pagué

B. **Más diferencias.** Cuando oiga el número correspondiente, lea los siguientes pares de palabras. Escuche la pronunciación correcta y repítala, imitando lo que oye.

1. diga / dígame
2. ponga / póngase
3. escriba / escríbanos
4. depositen / depositenlos
5. almacén / almacenes
6. nación / naciones

C. **¿Con acento o sin él?** Ud. va a oír las siguientes palabras. Añádales un acento escrito si es necesario.

1. cobro
2. cobro
3. toque
4. toque
5. describe
6. describemela
7. levantate
8. levanta
9. franceses
10. frances

D. **¡A corregir!** Ud. va a oír las siguientes oraciones. Añada un acento escrito a las palabras que lo necesiten, según el contexto.

1. Creo que ese regalo es para mi.
2. Aqui esta tu te. ¿Que mas quieres?
3. El dijo que te iba a llamar a las ocho.
4. Si, mi amigo compro un auto alemán.

GRAMÁTICA

¿Recuerda Ud.?

Para expresar el futuro. Indique las oraciones que expresan el futuro. **¡OJO!** En algunos casos, hay más de una respuesta correcta.

1. I'm going to deposit the check.
   a. Deposité el cheque.
   b. Voy a depositar el cheque.
   c. Deposito el cheque.

2. We'll talk later.
   a. Hablamos más tarde.
   b. Vamos a hablar más tarde.
   c. Hablábamos más tarde.

3. Juan will earn a lot.
   a. Juan ganó mucho.
   b. Juan ganaba mucho.
   c. Juan va a ganar mucho.

4. Will you help me?
   a. ¿Me ayudas?
   b. ¿Me ayudaste?
   c. ¿Me vas a ayudar?

46. Talking About the Future • Future Verb Forms

A. Formas. Complete la tabla con las formas del futuro.

INFINITIVO	YO	TÚ	UD.	NOSOTROS	UDS.
estar	estaré				
comer		comerás			
seguir			seguirá		
decir				diremos	
hacer					harán
poder	podré				
poner		pondrás			
querer			querrá		
saber				sabremos	
salir					saldrán
venir	vendré				

B. Este verano. Complete las oraciones con el futuro de los verbos.

1. Yo _____ (buscar) otro trabajo que me pague más y _____

   (comprar) un auto nuevo.

2. _____ (*Tú:* Hacer) un viaje a Francia y _____ (vivir) con una

   familia allí.

3. Mi primo Miguel _____ (venir) a visitarnos y _____ (estar) un

   mes con nosotros.

4. _____ (*Nosotros:* Ir) de excursión y _____ (divertirse).

5. Patricia y Antonio _____ (tener) que mudarse a finales de junio y por eso no

   _____ (poder) acompañarnos.

6. _____ (*Nosotros:* Salir) para México en julio y no _____ (volver)

   hasta fines de agosto.

C. El viernes por la noche. Imagine que Ud. sabe lo que harán o no harán sus parientes y amigos el viernes por la noche. Complete las oraciones con el futuro de los verbos entre paréntesis.

1. Mi hermano _____ (cobrar) su cheque y _____ (ponerlo) todo

   en su cuenta de ahorros.

2. Mis padres no _____ (querer) hacer nada y _____ (sentarse) a

   mirar la televisión.

3. Mi hermana Julia no _____ (saber) qué hacer y también _____

   (quedarse) en casa.

4. Tito _____ (decirles) a todos que tiene que estudiar.

5. Andrés y yo _____ (tener) que trabajar, pero a las once _____

   (ir) a una discoteca y _____ (bailar) hasta las dos.

D. Especulaciones. ¿Qué harán sus compañeros de la escuela secundaria? Haga especulaciones acerca de (*about*) lo que hacen ellos *ahora*, según las indicaciones. Use el futuro de probabilidad.

MODELO: A Pepe le gustaban los coches. (trabajar / taller) →
          Ahora trabajará en un taller.

1. A Mario le gustaban las matemáticas y las ciencias. (ser / ingeniero)

   _____

2. A Bárbara le encantaban las computadoras. (ser / programadora)

   _____

3. Julio solo pensaba en casarse. (estar / casado)

   _____

4. Tito jugaba muy bien al basquetbol. (jugar con / equipo profesional)

   _____

E. Un futuro perfecto

Paso 1. Ud. va a oír un párrafo en el cual (*which*) Angélica habla de su futuro. Primero, escuche el **Vocabulario útil** y el párrafo. Después va a oír algunas oraciones. Indique si cada oración es cierta (**C**) o falsa (**F**). Si la información no se menciona en el párrafo, escoja **ND** (No lo dice).

Vocabulario útil

en cuanto   as soon as
en fin   well

1. C F ND	**4.** C F ND
2. C F ND	**5.** C F ND
3. C F ND	

Paso 2. Ahora escuche el párrafo otra vez. Después de escucharlo, complete las siguientes oraciones basándose en la información del párrafo.

1. Cuando Angélica se gradúe, _____.

2. _____ en las afueras de la ciudad.

3. Su casa será _____.

4. Su casa tendrá _____.

5. Su auto _____ de último modelo y no _____ mucha gasolina.

6. _____ sus vacaciones en las Bahamas o en Europa.

7. ¡Su vida _____ perfecta!

F. El cumpleaños de Jaime. El cumpleaños de Jaime es la semana que viene. Ud. va a oír algunas preguntas sobre su cumpleaños. Conteste cada una usando el tiempo futuro y las frases que se dan. Luego escuche la respuesta correcta y repítala.

MODELO:	(Ud. oye)	¿Cuántos años va a cumplir Jaime?
	(Ud. ve)	dieciocho
	(Ud. dice)	Cumplirá 18 años.
	(Ud. oye y repite)	Cumplirá 18 años.

1. muchos regalos	**4.** una tarjeta de cumpleaños chistosa (*funny*)
2. un iPod	**5.** «¡Feliz cumpleaños!»
3. un pastel de chocolate	

¿Recuerda Ud.?

Las preposiciones. Traduzca la frase preposicional en inglés entre paréntesis a la frase preposicional equivalente en español.

1. Comeremos _____ (*after*) terminar la tarea.

2. No diremos nada _____ (*until*) recibir más noticias.

3. Llámame _____ (*before*) salir.

4. Trabajo _____ (*in order to*) vivir bien.

---

47. Expressing Future or Pending Actions • The Subjunctive (Part 8): The Subjunctive and Indicative After Conjunctions of Time

A. ¿Cuándo? Indique si cada oración se refiere a una acción habitual (el indicativo) o a una acción futura (el subjuntivo). Luego indique la mejor manera de completar las oraciones.

		HABITUAL	FUTURO
1.	Siempre le pido un préstamo a mi hermano cuando…		
	a. me falta dinero **b.** me falte dinero	☐	☐
2.	Depositaré mi cheque en cuanto…		
	a. salgo del trabajo **b.** salga del trabajo	☐	☐
3.	Firmaré los cheques después de que…		
	a. llego al banco **b.** llegue al banco	☐	☐
4.	El cajero siempre me da un recibo después de que…		
	a. deposito mi dinero **b.** deposite mi dinero	☐	☐
5.	Pienso cobrar mi cheque tan pronto como…		
	a. se abre el banco **b.** se abra el banco	☐	☐

B. ¿Cómo se dice? Exprese las siguientes frases en español. **¡Recuerde!** El uso del subjuntivo o del indicativo después de conjunciones de tiempo depende de si se habla de una acción habitual en el presente (= presente de indicativo), una acción en el pasado (= el pretérito, el imperfecto, etcétera) o una acción futura (= el presente de subjuntivo).

MODELO: (cuando / ir)

    a. When I went (*last night*) . . .   Cuando fui

    b. When I went (*habitual, past*) . . .   Cuando iba

    c. When I go (*habitual, present*) . . .   Cuando voy

    d. When I go (*future*) . . .   Cuando vaya

1. (cuando / casarse)

    a. When I got married (*last year*) . . . _____

    b. When I get married (*future*) . . . _____

2. (tan pronto como / volver)

    a. As soon as I return (*habitual, present*) . . . _____

    b. As soon as I returned (*last night*) . . . _____

    c. As soon as I return (*future*) . . . _____

3. (hasta que / llamarnos)

    a. . . . until they call us (*habitual, present*) . . . _____

    b. . . . until they called us (*habitual, past*) . . . _____

    c. . . . until they call us (*future*) . . . _____

4. (después [de] que / irnos)

    a. After we leave (*habitual, present*) . . . _____

    b. After we left (*last night*) . . . _____

    c. After we leave (*future*) . . . _____

C. ¿Qué harán? Diga lo que harán estas personas en las siguientes circunstancias.

MODELO: yo estudiar / cuando yo / tener tiempo →
Yo estudiaré cuando tenga tiempo.

1. Elena hacer su viaje / en cuanto / (ella) recibir su pasaporte

2. ellos no casarse / hasta que / (ellos) encontrar casa

3. Roberto llamarnos / tan pronto como / (él) saber los resultados

4. Mario venir a buscarnos / después de que / su hermano: volver

5. mi hermana y yo ir a México / cuando / (nosotras) salir de clases

D. Del pasado al futuro. Cambie las siguientes oraciones del pasado al futuro. Recuerde usar el subjuntivo en la cláusula dependiente después de las conjunciones de tiempo que presentan eventos futuros.

MODELO: Salí en cuanto me llamaron. → Saldré en cuanto me llamen.

1. Cuando viajé a México, tuve que cambiar los dólares a pesos.

2. Fui a la Casa de Cambio Génova, en el Paseo de la Reforma.

3. Firmé (I signed) los cheques de viajero (traveler's checks) en cuanto entré en el banco.

4. Hice cola hasta que fue mi turno.

5. Le di mi pasaporte al cajero tan pronto como me lo pidió.

6. Después de que le di 200 dólares, él me dio un recibo.

7. Me devolvieron el pasaporte cuando me dieron el dinero.

8. Fui al restaurante La Tecla en cuanto salí de la Casa de Cambio.

E. En la oficina. Ud. va a oír los siguientes pares (*pairs*) de oraciones. Combínelas con la conjunción de tiempo que oye. Luego escuche la respuesta correcta y repítala.

> MODELO: (Ud. ve y oye) Voy a decidirlo. Hablo con la jefa.
> (Ud. oye) después de que
> (Ud. dice) Voy a decidirlo después de que hable con la jefa.
> (Ud. oye y repite) Voy a decidirlo después de que hable con la jefa.

1. Amalia va a renunciar a su puesto actual (*current*). Consigue un nuevo puesto.
2. No estaré contenta. Recibo un aumento.
3. Lilia leerá las solicitudes. Tiene tiempo.
4. Los clientes van a firmar (*sign*) el contrato. Llaman a la directora.

F. Asuntos (*Matters*) económicos. Ud. va a oír algunas oraciones incompletas. Primero, indique la frase que completa mejor cada oración. Después diga la oración completa. Luego escuche la respuesta correcta y repítala. **¡OJO!** En esta actividad tiene que escoger entre el presente de subjuntivo y el presente de indicativo.

> MODELO: (Ud. oye) Voy a depositar mi cheque cuando…
> (Ud. ve) **a.** lo reciba **b.** lo recibo
> (Ud. escoge) (**a.**) lo reciba
> (Ud. dice) **a.** Voy a depositar mi cheque cuando lo reciba.
> (Ud. oye y repite) **a.** Voy a depositar mi cheque cuando lo reciba.

1. **a.** las reciba **b.** las recibo
2. **a.** tenga más dinero **b.** tengo más dinero
3. **a.** consiga otro puesto **b.** consigo otro puesto
4. **a.** lo firme (*sign*) **b.** lo firmo

Un poco de todo

A. Los problemas financieros de los estudiantes. Complete esta narración con la forma apropiada de cada verbo entre paréntesis. Use el futuro, el presente de indicativo, presente de subjuntivo o el infinitivo, según sea necesario. Cuando se presenten dos posibilidades, escoja la correcta.

Cuando Juan era joven, no tenía que _____[1] (preocuparse) por el dinero porque vivía

con sus padres. Pero ahora que Juan está en la universidad, tiene que _____[2] (manejar[a])

sus _____[3] (propias / propios) finanzas.[b]

Necesita _____[4] (abrir) su _____[5] (propia / propio) cuenta corriente. Pero

no quiere abrir una hasta que _____[6] (ahorrar) un mínimo de 2.000 dólares. Tan pronto

como _____[7] (tener) el dinero, _____[8] (abrir) su propia cuenta corriente.

Después de abrirla, le va a _____[9] (pedir / preguntar) al banco una tarjeta de crédito

y así _____[10] (empezar) a pagar sus _____[11] (propias / propios) facturas y

establecer su buen crédito. Con tal que no _____[12] (gastar) más de lo que tenga, no

_____[13] (tener) que pagar intereses al banco.

[a]*manage* [b]*finances*

También piensa que _____¹⁴ (necesite / necesitará) conseguir un auto de

_____¹⁵ (segunda / segundo) mano, pero para eso _____¹⁶ (ser) necesario

pedirle un préstamo al banco. El problema es que Juan todavía no tiene antecedentes de buen

crédito y por eso el banco le _____¹⁷ (cobrar) cerca del 11 por ciento en intereses. Un

amigo _____¹⁸ (su / suyo) acaba de comprar un auto nuevo, pero, como ese amigo ya

había establecido su crédito, consiguió un préstamo a solo 6 por ciento.

En verdad, no es fácil vivir en este mundo sin _____¹⁹ (considerar) las cuestiones

financieras.

B. *Listening Passage*: **El sistema universitario hispano**

❖ **Antes de escuchar.** Before listening, do the following prelistening activity.

Answer the following questions to see how much you already know about this topic.

1. Típicamente, ¿cuántos años dura (*lasts*) la etapa del «*Bachelor's*» en las universidades de los Estados Unidos? ¿Cree Ud. que en el mundo hispano es más larga la etapa, más corta o más o menos igual?

_____

_____

2. ¿Hay requisitos de ciencias sociales, ciencias naturales o de humanidades en la mayoría de las universidades de los Estados Unidos? ¿Y en su universidad?

_____

_____

3. ¿Cree Ud. que existen estos requisitos en la mayoría de las universidades del mundo hispano?

_____

_____

4. ¿Cree Ud. que los estudiantes que estudian en el sistema universitario del mundo hispano tienen muchas opciones en cuanto a (*as far as*) los cursos que toman?

_____

_____

5. ¿Ya «declaró» Ud. su especialización? ¿Cuándo «declaran» normalmente los estudiantes su especialización en las universidades estadounidenses? ¿Cuándo cree Ud. que la «declaran» los estudiantes en el sistema universitario del mundo hispano?

_____

_____

_____

_____

Listening Passage. You will hear a passage about the differences between the university system in most of the Hispanic world and that of the United States. First, listen to the **Vocabulario útil** and read the statements in **Después de escuchar** to know what information to listen for. Then listen to the passage.

Vocabulario útil

durar	to last	**una vez que**	once
matricularse	to enroll	**el requisito**	requirement
por lo tanto	therefore	**la profundidad**	depth

Después de escuchar. Indicate whether the following statements refer to the Hispanic world or the United States according to the information in the passage.

	EL MUNDO HISPANO	LOS ESTADOS UNIDOS
1. La mayoría de las carreras duran menos de cinco años.	☐	☐
2. Al entrar (*Upon entering*) en la universidad, un estudiante se matricula directamente en el área de su especialización.	☐	☐
3. El estudiante tiene pocas opciones una vez que empieza sus estudios.	☐	☐
4. Hay requisitos «generales» como ciencias naturales, ciencias sociales o humanidades.	☐	☐
5. El currículo es bastante estricto.	☐	☐
6. Los estudios que se hacen para una licenciatura son bastante profundos y variados.	☐	☐
7. Por lo general, la especialización no se «declara» el primer año de estudios universitarios.	☐	☐

C. En busca de trabajo

Paso 1. En este diálogo, Lupe Carrasco se entrevista con la Sra. Ibáñez para un puesto de recepcionista en un banco. Primero, escuche el **Vocabulario útil** y el diálogo. Después Ud. va a oír algunas oraciones. Indique si cada oración es cierta (**C**) o falsa (**F**). Si la información no se menciona, escoja **ND** (No lo dice).

Vocabulario útil

la jornada completa	**el empleo de tiempo completo**
el entrenamiento	training
la sucursal	branch

1. C F ND	4. C F ND
2. C F ND	5. C F ND
3. C F ND	

Paso 2. Ahora va a participar en una conversación en la que hace el papel de **Ud.** Primero, complete la conversación con las frases siguientes. Segundo, verifique sus respuestas en el Apéndice. Después haga la conversación en voz alta: Lea en el diálogo las líneas de **Ud.** y luego escuche la pronunciación correcta y repítala.

es muy amable	ya encontraste trabajo	un puesto estupendo
fantástico	tres semanas	

AMIGA: ¡Hola! Hace tiempo que no te veo. ¿Qué tal te va en tu nuevo trabajo?

UD.: ¡_____!¹ Es _____.²

AMIGA: Y tu jefa, ¿cómo es?

UD.: _____.³ Nos llevamos muy bien.

AMIGA: Espero que te den vacaciones este año.

UD.: Sí, sí... Fíjate que me dan _____.⁴ Y tú,

¿_____?⁵

AMIGA: ¡Qué va! Todavía ando buscando...ᵃ

ᵃTodavía... *I'm still looking . . .*

CULTURA

Chile

A. Mapa. En el siguiente mapa identifique Chile y la capital de ese país.

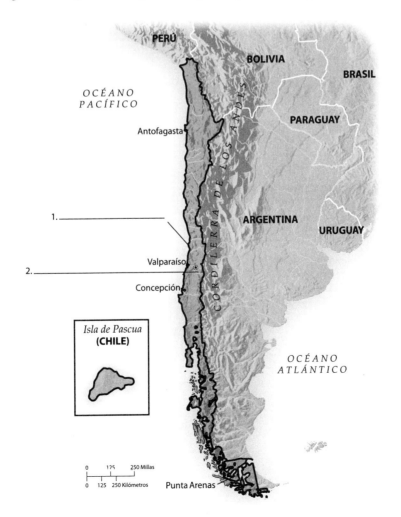

B. Comprensión. Complete las siguientes oraciones con información de la **Lectura cultural: Chile** de la página 516 del libro de texto.

1. Como en muchos países, algunos chilenos necesitan tener más de un _____ para sobrevivir.

2. Entre los que ganan más y los que ganan menos, hay una brecha (*gap*) de _____.

3. Entre los que ganan un sueldo alto están los _____, los _____, los _____, y los empresarios.

4. Entre los que reciben menos por su trabajo están los _____, los _____, los trabajadores agrícolas y los _____.

5. El adjetivo trabajólico/a se refiere a una persona que _____ mucho y que piensa que es una cualidad _____. Pero, para la mayoría de los hispanos, no se vive para trabajar sino que se trabaja para _____.

6. En España, como en gran parte de Europa, los trabajadores reciben buenos _____ establecidos por la ley. Por ejemplo, gozan de (*they enjoy*) un _____ de vacaciones al año, y cuatro meses de licencia por _____ o paternidad. También, España tiene un plan nacional de _____ que protege a casi toda la gente.

7. El cultrún es el tambor (*drum*) ceremonial de los _____, una cultura indígena muy antigua.

8. Los Andes son la frontera natural entre Chile y Bolivia y _____.

9. La gran cantautora chilena, Violeta Parra, ha dado al mundo la bella canción «_____», que glorifica los pequeños y grandes logros de los seres humanos.

PÓNGASE A PRUEBA

A. El futuro. Cambie al futuro los verbos indicados.

1. Mi padre *va a jubilarse* el año que viene. _____

2. *Voy a trabajar* este verano. _____

3. *Van a venir* cuando puedan. _____

4. ¿*Vas a poder* acompañarnos? _____

5. ¿A quién le *vas a dar* ese regalo? _____

6. ¿A qué hora *vamos a salir*? _____

B. **¿Indicativo o subjuntivo?** Escoja la forma verbal correcta.

1. Ahorraré más en cuanto _____ un aumento de sueldo.

   a. me den   **b.** me dan   **c.** me darán

2. Su madre piensa jubilarse cuando _____ 65 años.

   a. tendrá   **b.** tiene   **c.** tenga

3. Siempre cobro mi cheque cuando lo _____.

   a. recibo   **b.** recibí   **c.** reciba

4. Tan pronto como _____ a casa, te llamaremos.

   a. volvemos   **b.** volvamos   **c.** volveremos

5. No podré tener un empleo de tiempo completo hasta que _____ mis estudios.

   a. termino   **b.** terminé   **c.** termine

6. ¡Antes que _____, mira lo que haces!

   a. te casas   **b.** te cases   **c.** te casaste

PRUEBA CORTA

A. **En el futuro.** Complete las oraciones con el futuro del verbo entre paréntesis.

1. Mañana, si tengo tiempo, _____ (ir) a la biblioteca.

2. Elena va a comprar una casa y el lunes _____ (hacer) el primer pago.

3. No quiero ir a ese café. Allí _____ (haber) mucha gente.

4. Cuando reciba mi cheque, lo _____ (poner) en el banco.

5. No le prestes dinero a Enrique. No te lo _____ (devolver) nunca.

B. **¿Indicativo o subjuntivo después de conjunciones de tiempo?** Complete las oraciones con el indicativo o el subjuntivo del verbo entre paréntesis, según el contexto.

1. Pagaremos la factura tan pronto como nos la _____. (*ellos:* mandar)

2. Te daré un cheque después de que _____ (*mi padre:* depositar) dinero en mi cuenta.

3. No podré comprar un coche hasta que _____ (*mi esposo y yo:* poder) ahorrar más dinero.

4. En el banco me pidieron la licencia de manejar cuando _____ (ir) a cobrar un cheque.

5. Viajaremos a Valparaíso en cuanto se _____ (terminar) las clases.

6. El verano pasado yo siempre iba a la playa en cuanto _____ (tener) tiempo.

7. Me graduaré cuando _____ (pasar) todos mis exámenes.

C. ¿Cuándo? Ud. va a oír algunas oraciones sobre los planes de sus amigos. Usando el tiempo futuro, pregúnteles cuándo piensan hacer lo que mencionan. Use pronombres de complemento directo e indirecto cuando sea posible. Luego escuche la pregunta correcta y repítala. Después va a oír la respuesta de su amigo.

> MODELO: (Ud. oye)   Voy a pagar mis cuentas.
>
> (Ud. dice)   ¿Cuándo las pagarás?
>
> (Ud. oye y repite)   ¿Cuándo las pagarás?
>
> (Ud. oye)   Las pagaré la próxima semana.

1. ...   **2.** ...   **3.** ...   **4.** ...   **5.** ...

D. Empleos diversos. Haga oraciones sobre el trabajo que hacen o harán varias personas, según las indicaciones. **¡OJO!** Use el presente de indicativo o subjuntivo de los verbos que oye, según el contexto. Luego escuche la respuesta correcta y repítala.

> MODELO: (Ud. ve)   **1.** cuando / llegar a la oficina
>
> (Ud. oye)   **1.** la técnica arreglará las computadoras
>
> (Ud. dice)   La técnica arreglará las computadoras cuando llegue a la oficina.
>
> (Ud. oye y repite)   La técnica arreglará las computadoras cuando llegue a la oficina.

2. antes de que / la empresa publicar el artículo
3. después de que / su jefe firmarlos
4. en cuanto / leerlos
5. hasta que / (ellos) darnos un aumento

PUNTOS PERSONALES

❖ **A. Mi futuro.** Conteste las preguntas con oraciones completas.

1. ¿Tiene Ud. auto? Si tiene uno, ¿cómo lo pagó? ¿Lo pagó a plazos? ¿en efectivo?

_____

2. Cuando Ud. quiere comprar algo y no tiene suficientes fondos (*funds*) en su cuenta corriente, ¿le pide un préstamo a alguien o lo carga (*charge*) de todas maneras (*anyway*) a su tarjeta de crédito?

_____

_____

3. ¿Usa Ud. demasiado su tarjeta de crédito y casi siempre tiene que pagar intereses al final del mes? ¿O siempre tiene suficientes fondos en su cuenta corriente para pagar el balance?

_____

_____

4. ¿Qué piensa hacer después de que se gradúe?

_____

5. ¿Dónde piensa vivir? ¿Seguirá viviendo en la misma ciudad o piensa mudarse a otra parte del país? Explique sus razones.

_____

_____

6. ¿Qué tipo de trabajo quiere tener?

_____

B. Una encuesta sobre su futuro

Paso 1. Ud. va a oír algunas oraciones sobre su futuro. Escoja la respuesta que corresponde a su propia opinión o situación.

1. ☐ Sí. ☐ No.
2. ☐ Sí. ☐ No.
3. ☐ Sí. ☐ No.
4. ☐ Sí. ☐ No.
5. ☐ Sí. ☐ No.
6. ☐ Sí. ☐ No.

Paso 2. Ahora va a oír preguntas basadas en las oraciones del **Paso 1.** Contéstelas por escrito con oraciones completas.

1. _____.

2. _____.

3. _____.

4. _____.

5. _____.

6. _____.

Paso 3. Ahora va a oír las preguntas otra vez. Lea las respuestas que escribió en el **Paso 2.**

1. ... 2. ... 3. ... 4. ... 5. ... 6. ...

C. Cuestiones laborales y económicas

Paso 1. En esta entrevista, Miguel René, Tané y Rubén hablan del trabajo y del futuro. Primero, escuche el **Vocabulario útil** y la entrevista. Luego complete la tabla con información de la entrevista y con su propia información.

Vocabulario útil

de hecho	in fact
hogareño/a	home-oriented
desearía	I would hope for
encaminado/a	on track
asombrar	to amaze
ahorrativo/a	savings-minded

(Continúa.)

	Miguel René	Tané	Rubén	Ud.
1. ¿Cómo le fue en su última entrevista de trabajo?				
2. ¿Cómo ve su futuro dentro de unos diez años?				
3. ¿Qué tal lleva sus finanzas? ¿Es bueno/a para ahorrar?				

❖ **Paso 2.** Ahora, escriba un párrafo en el que habla de su vida en el futuro. Hable de lo que se relaciona con lo laboral, lo financiero y lo personal. Use lo que escribió en la columna de **Ud.** en la tabla del **Paso 1** como base para su párrafo y añada detalles.

_____

_____

_____

_____

_____

_____

_____

_____

_____

❖ **D. Guided Composition.** En una hoja aparte, escriba una composición de dos párrafos comparando sus ideas con las de sus padres. Use las siguientes preguntas como guía.

Párrafo 1

1. Cuando Ud. estaba en la escuela secundaria, ¿qué tipo de hijo/a era Ud.? (¿Era rebelde, obediente, cariñoso/a, desagradable, tranquilo/a, egoísta, comprensivo/a... ?)
2. ¿Se llevaban bien Ud. y sus padres o discutían mucho?
3. ¿En qué cosas no estaba Ud. de acuerdo con sus padres? ¿Protestaba mucho o los obedecía por lo general sin protestar?
4. ¿Era fácil o difícil hablar con sus padres?
5. ¿A quién le confesaba sus problemas más íntimos?

Párrafo 2

1. ¿Piensa Ud. casarse y tener hijos? (¿Ya se ha casado? ¿Tiene hijos?)
2. ¿Qué aspectos son importantes en las relaciones entre padres e hijos?
3. ¿Qué querrá Ud. que hagan sus hijos? (¿Qué quiere que hagan sus hijos?)
4. ¿Qué tipo de padre/madre será (es) Ud.?

❖ **E. Mi diario.** Escriba en su diario algunos párrafos sobre las ventajas y desventajas de la profesión u oficio que piensa seguir. Recuerde usar palabras conectivas.

Vocabulario útil

de todas maneras	anyway
en cambio	on the other hand
por otra parte	on the other hand
sin embargo	

Considere los siguientes puntos:

- la satisfacción personal
- las ventajas o desventajas económicas
- las horas de trabajo
- el costo del equipo profesional cuando empiece a trabajar
- la posible necesidad de mudarse para encontrar empleo o para establecer su propia oficina o negocio (*business*)

Si Ud. no ha decidido todavía qué carrera va a seguir, escriba sobre alguien que Ud. conoce (puede entrevistarlo/la), pero haga referencia a los mismos puntos.

F. Intercambios. Escuche las siguientes preguntas y contéstelas por escrito.

1. _____
_____

2. _____
_____
_____

3. _____
_____

4. _____
_____

5. _____
_____

Capítulo 18 La actualidad

VOCABULARIO — Preparación

Las noticias

A. Definiciones. Complete las definiciones con la forma apropiada de las palabras de la lista.

acontecimiento	huelga	reportera
asesinato	paz	testigo
enterarse	prensa	

1. Saber de un acontecimiento por primera vez es _____ de él.

2. La libertad de _____ es el derecho de publicar libremente periódicos, revistas y libros.

3. Una _____ consiste en dejar de trabajar para protestar por algo.

4. Un _____ es un crimen violento en el que muere la víctima.

5. Lo contrario de la guerra es la _____.

6. Un _____ es una persona que ha visto algo cuando ocurre.

7. Un _____ es lo mismo que un evento.

8. Una _____ es una persona que informa al público de un evento o noticia.

B. Las noticias. Complete las oraciones con la frase o palabra apropiada.

1. Saber las últimas noticias significa _____.
   a. comunicarse   **b.** luchar   **c.** estar al día

2. Una lucha entre dos o más grupos armados es _____.
   a. mantener la paz   **b.** una huelga   **c.** una guerra

3. La erupción de un volcán es _____.
   a. un medio de comunicación   **b.** un desastre natural   **c.** un asesinato

4. El acto de chocar dos coches es _____.
   a. un choque   **b.** una manifestación   **c.** una lucha

5. Los periódicos, las revistas, la televisión y la radio son _____.
   a. medios de comunicación   **b.** reporteros   **c.** testigos

6. Un programa de televisión o radio en el que (*which*) se transmiten las noticias es _____.
   a. una manifestación   **b.** un noticiero   **c.** una estación de radio

C. ¿Cómo se enteran de los acontecimientos? Ud. va a oír descripciones sobre cómo varias personas se enteran de los acontecimientos. Primero, lea las siguientes oraciones. Después empareje la letra de la descripción con el medio de comunicación que lógicamente utilizaría (*would use*) cada persona para estar al día.

1. _____ Escucha las noticias por radio mientras conduce.

2. _____ Mira el noticiero local en la televisión.

3. _____ Lee la sección de deportes del periódico.

4. _____ Lee *El Blog de Miguel Ángel.*

5. _____ Lee un periódico publicado en otro país.

D. El noticiero del Canal 10. Ud. va a oír un breve noticiero de un canal de televisión. Primero, escuche el **Vocabulario útil** y el noticiero. Después va a oír algunas oraciones sobre el noticiero. Luego indique **C, F** o **ND** (No lo dice).

Vocabulario útil

el Oriente Medio   the Middle East

1. C   F   ND   4. C   F   ND
2. C   F   ND   5. C   F   ND
3. C   F   ND

E. Mantenerse informados. En esta entrevista, Rubén, Karina, Tané y Miguel René hablan de los periódicos que leen y de los problemas actuales (*current*) de sus países respectivos. Primero, escuche el **Vocabulario útil** y la entrevista. Luego complete la tabla con información de la entrevista.

Vocabulario útil

la primera plana	front page
de espectáculos	entertainment
el paro	unemployment
la polémica	debate
que se le oponga	that can stand up to it

	Rubén	Karina	Tané	Miguel René
1. Parte del periódico que lee primero				
2. Problemas actuales de su país				

El gobierno y la responsabilidad cívica

A. Más definiciones. Complete las definiciones con la forma apropiada de las palabras de la lista.

| ciudadano | derecho | discriminación | ejército | reina | rey |

1. Un _____ es algo que la Constitución y las leyes garantizan a todos los

   _____.

2. El _____ / La _____ es el jefe / la jefa de una monarquía.

3. El _____ es una organización militar que defiende el país.

4. La _____ es el trato (*treatment*) desigual que se le da a una persona o a un grupo.

B. Las últimas noticias. Complete con las palabras apropiadas del vocabulario. Hay palabras que se repiten.

Buenas noches. El Canal 25 les ofrece el _____[1] (*news broadcast*) de las ocho, con

nuestros _____[2] (*reporters*) Teresa Frías y Jaime Cienfuegos.

TERESA: París. El _____[3] (*event*) más notable del día es la _____[4]

(*strike*) iniciada por los _____[5] (*workers*) de los transportes públicos, que ha paralizado

casi por completo la vida en la capital francesa. La huelga incluye a los trabajadores de los ferro-

carriles[a] y, por esta razón, los viajeros[b] a muchas ciudades francesas han perdido la

_____[6] (*hope*) de llegar hoy a su destino.[c] El Ministro del Interior ha declarado en

una rueda[d] de _____[7] (*press*) que la huelga significa un _____[8]

(*disaster*) económico de grandes proporciones; espera que no dure más de tres o cuatro días.

Cuando el jefe del Sindicato[e] de Trabajadores de Transporte _____[9] (*found out*) de

lo que había dicho el Ministro, comentó: —La huelga va a durar hasta que se resuelva la

_____[10] (*inequality*) de salarios ahora existente—. Como es de esperar[f] en estos

casos, ha habido[g] algunos incidentes de violencia, y Jaime Cienfuegos nos _____[11]

(*informs*) sobre lo que pasó esta mañana.

JAIME: Unos obreros en huelga atacaron esta mañana a tres camiones[h] de la Compañía Fran-

cesa de Petróleo cerca de la Estación de San Lázaro. Según varios _____[12] (*witnesses*),

los camiones fueron detenidos[i] cuando cruzaban las vías[j] del ferrocarril y fueron incendiados[k] por

tres obreros, mientras que los _____[13] (*rest*) aplaudían. El embotellamiento de tráfico[l]

que se produjo causó varios _____[14] (*collisions*) de automóviles. Felizmente no hubo

daños personales serios. El público espera que la _____[15] (*peace*) se restablezca

pronto entre los trabajadores y los dueños...

[a]*railroads* [b]*travelers* [c]*destination* [d]*conference* [e]*Union* [f]*Como... As might be expected* [g]*ha... there have been* [h]*trucks* [i]*stopped* [j]*tracks* [k]*set on fire* [l]*embotellamiento... traffic jam*

(Continúa.)

TERESA: ¡Últimas _____[16] (news)! Acabamos de enterarnos del

_____[17] (assassination) del _____[18] (dictator) de Maldivia.

No hay detalles todavía, pero se teme que este _____[19] (event) precipite una

_____[20] (war) civil entre los militares que apoyaban[m] al _____[21]

(dictator) y los izquierdistas radicales.

[m]supported

C. Opiniones

Paso 1. Ud. va a oír algunas oraciones sobre las noticias, el gobierno y la responsabilidad cívica. Primero, lea las siguientes frases. Después escuche las oraciones. Luego exprese su reacción a cada oración por escrito. Empiece cada reacción con una de las frases.

Dudo que...   Es cierto que...
Es verdad que...   No es cierto que...

1. _____

2. _____

3. _____

4. _____

5. _____

6. _____

Paso 2. Ahora Ud. va a oír las mismas oraciones del **Paso 1.** Después lea en voz alta las respuestas que escribió en el **Paso 1.** Luego escuche una respuesta posible y repítala.

MODELO: (Ud. oye) Uno. Todos los ciudadanos votan.
         (Ud. lee en voz alta) No es cierto que todos los ciudadanos voten.
         (Ud. oye y repite) No es cierto que todos los ciudadanos voten.

2. ...   3. ...   4. ...   5. ...   6. ...

PRONUNCIACIÓN Intonation and Review of Linking

Intonation

- Intonation is the rise or fall of one's voice in speech. As you have probably noticed throughout the audio program and from listening to your instructor in class, intonation plays an important role in Spanish. In the examples that follow, the arrows indicate a falling or rising intonation.

- Generally speaking, declarative statements in Spanish end in a falling intonation. Listen to the following declarative statements.

   Los reporteros están aquí.

   La periodista los entrevistó ayer.

   La señorita Garrido se postuló como candidata.

- In yes/no questions, the intonation rises at the end of the question. Yes/no questions can be formed in three ways in Spanish:

    1. You can invert the subject and the verb:

        ¿Es Ud. el candidato?

    2. You can keep the word order of a declarative statement and change your intonation when speaking:

        ¿Ud. es el candidato?

    3. You can add a "tag" question, such as ¿no? or ¿verdad? at the end of a declarative statement:

        Ud. es el candidato, ¿verdad? Ud. es el candidato, ¿no?

- Usually, information questions, i.e., questions with an interrogative word, end in a falling intonation. Listen to the following information questions.

    ¿Dónde están los reporteros?

    ¿Qué nos ofrecerán los candidatos?

    ¿Cuándo llegan los candidatos para el debate?

Linking

- Remember that in Spanish, words are linked together in native speech. Listen to the following sentences.

    El presidente ecuatoriano organizará el debate.

    ¿Con quién hablarán ustedes?

    ¿La unión de obreros está en huelga?

    El Internet es un medio importantísimo en nuestras elecciones, ¿verdad?

A. **Repeticiones.** Repita las siguientes oraciones, imitando lo que oye. Preste atención a la entonación y a los enlaces (*linking*).

    1. ¿Ya destruyeron el edificio?
    2. Es imposible que ofrezcan esos precios.
    3. ¿De dónde es el candidato Molina?
    4. Votaron por la mejor candidata, ¿verdad?
    5. Espero que nos ayuden con las elecciones.

B. **La entonación y los enlaces.** Cuando oiga el número correspondiente, lea las siguientes oraciones. Preste atención a la entonación y a los enlaces. Luego escuche la pronunciación correcta y repítala.

    1. La elección es el once de abril.
    2. No entiendo lo que me estás diciendo.
    3. ¿Trabajaron Uds. en esa campaña política?
    4. No olvides votar en las elecciones, ¿eh?
    5. ¿Dónde nació el señor Arango?
    6. La información que nos ofrecen no es imparcial.

C. **¿Pregunta o no?** Ud. va a oír las siguientes oraciones. Escriba signos interrogativos (*question marks and inverted question marks*) o puntos finales (*periods*) donde sean necesarios.

1. Cuál es tu profesión Te pagan bien
2. Tú no la conoces, verdad
3. Preferimos informarnos por medio del Internet
4. No sé dónde viven ahora
5. Quieren que les digamos los resultados ahora

GRAMÁTICA

¿Recuerda Ud.?

Repaso del presente de subjuntivo. Complete cada oración con la forma apropiada del verbo entre paréntesis: el infinitivo, el presente o pasado de indicativo o el presente de subjuntivo.

Verbs of Influence	1. Queremos que ellos nos _____. (llamar)
	2. Sugiere que _____ allí temprano. (*nosotros:* estar)
	3. Juan insiste en _____ allí. (estar)
Verbs of Emotion	4. Qué lástima que tú no _____. (ir)
	5. Siento que Uds. no _____. (ir)
	6. Me alegro de _____ contigo. (*yo:* ir)
Verbs of Doubt and Denial	7. Dudo que _____ ellos. (ser)
	8. María niega que Pepe _____ el dinero. (tener)
	9. No dudo que Pepe _____ el dinero. (tener)
Indefinite and Non-existent Antecedents	10. No hay nadie que _____ la verdad. (saber)
	11. ¿Conoces un restaurante que _____ paella? (servir)
	12. Conozco un restaurante que _____ paella. (servir)
Conjunctions of Purpose & Contingency	13. Llama a Eva en caso de que _____ en casa. (estar)
	14. No digas nada a menos que alguien te _____. (preguntar)
Conjunctions of Time	15. Llama a tu novia antes de que ella _____. (salir)
	16. Llama a tu novia antes de _____. (*tú:* salir)
	17. Debemos llamar cuando _____. (*nosotros:* volver)
	18. Firmaré (*I will sign*) el cheque después de que _____ al banco. (*yo:* llegar)
	19. Siempre firmo los cheques cuando _____ al banco. (*yo:* llegar, presente, habitual)
	20. Siempre firmaba los cheques cuando _____ al banco. (*yo:* llegar, pasado, habitual)

48. *Queríamos que todo el mundo votara* • The Subjunctive (Part 9): The Past Subjunctive

A. Formas verbales. Escriba la tercera persona plural (**ellos**) del pretérito y la forma indicada del imperfecto de subjuntivo.

		PRETÉRITO		IMPERFECTO DE SUBJUNTIVO
MODELO:	hablar →	hablaron	→ yo	hablara
1.	aprender	_____	yo	_____
2.	decidir	_____	yo	_____
3.	sentar	_____	tú	_____
4.	jugar	_____	tú	_____
5.	querer	_____	tú	_____
6.	hacer	_____	Ud.	_____
7.	tener	_____	Ud.	_____
8.	poner	_____	Ud.	_____
9.	traer	_____	nosotros	_____
10.	venir	_____	nosotros	_____
11.	seguir	_____	nosotros	_____
12.	dar	_____	Uds.	_____
13.	ser	_____	Uds.	_____
14.	ver	_____	Uds.	_____

B. ¿Qué querían todos? Complete las oraciones con la forma apropiada del imperfecto de subjuntivo de los verbos entre paréntesis.

1. Enrique quería que yo...
   a. _____ (ir) con él.
   b. _____ (almorzar) con él.
   c. _____ (empezar) la cena.
   d. _____ (hacer) el café.

2. Ellos esperaban que tú...
   a. _____ (poder) visitarlos.
   b. _____ (recordar) la fecha.
   c. _____ (estar) allí.
   d. _____ (venir) hoy.

3. Ellos nos pidieron que (*nosotros*)...
   a. _____ (despertarlos).
   b. _____ (poner) la mesa.
   c. _____ (sentarnos).
   d. _____ (llamarlos).

(Continúa.)

4. Pepe dijo que no iría (*wouldn't go*)
   a menos que ellos...

   a. le _____ (ofrecer) más dinero.

   b. le _____ (dar) otro empleo.

   c. le _____ (decir) la verdad.

   d. le _____ (conseguir) otro coche.

C. **Hablando de la escuela secundaria.** Ud. va a oír algunas oraciones generales sobre cómo era la escuela secundaria en este país hace veinte años. Indique si cada oración es cierta (**C**) o falsa (**F**).

   1. C F   5. C F
   2. C F   6. C F
   3. C F   7. C F
   4. C F   8. C F

D. **Antes de empezar la universidad.** ¿Qué consejos les dieron los padres a sus hijos antes de empezar su primer semestre/trimestre en la universidad?

   1. Los padres les pidieron que _____ (cuidarse) mucho.

   2. Insistían en que _____ (estudiar) mucho.

   3. (No) Querían que _____ (volver) a casa todos los fines de semana.

   4. Les recomendaron que _____ (asistir) a todas sus clases.

   5. Les dijeron que _____ (gastar) su dinero con cuidado.

E. **Más deseos.** Escriba lo que cada persona quería que la otra hiciera. Siga el modelo.

   MODELO: LUISA: Enrique, cómprame otra botella de vino. →

   Luisa quería que Enrique le comprara otra botella de vino.

   1. PEPE: Gloria, tráeme las llaves.

   _____

   2. ANA: Carla, dime la verdad.

   _____

   3. DAVID: Miguel, no hagas tanto ruido.

   _____

   4. RITA: Ernesto, no te enojes tanto y sé más paciente.

   _____

F. **Ojalá que no fuera así.** Exprese los siguientes deseos imposibles con **ojalá** y el imperfecto de subjuntivo.

   MODELO: Tengo que estudiar. → Ojalá (que) no tuviera que estudiar.

   1. Tengo que trabajar esta noche. _____

   2. Tenemos que gastar menos. _____

   3. Mis padres no pueden ir a España. _____

   4. Está lloviendo. _____

G. **Recuerdos de un viaje.** Imagine que Ud. acaba de regresar de un viaje a Madrid, y sus amigos quieren saber todos los detalles. Cuénteles, con las palabras que oye, algunas de las cosas que tuvo que hacer en Madrid. Empiece cada oración con **Fue necesario que... ¡OJO!** Use el imperfecto de subjuntivo en sus respuestas. Luego escuche la respuesta correcta y repítala.

> MODELO: (Ud. oye) ir a la agencia de viajes
>
> (Ud. dice) Fue necesario que fuera a la agencia de viajes.
>
> (Ud. oye y repite) Fue necesario que fuera a la agencia de viajes.

1. ... **2.** ... **3.** ... **4.** ... **5.** ... **6.** ...

H. **¿Qué quería Ud.?** Imagine que a Ud. nunca le gustan los planes que hace su familia. Diga lo que quería que Ud. y su familia hicieran. Empiece cada oración con **Yo quería que...** Luego escuche la respuesta correcta y repítala.

> MODELO: (Ud. ve y oye) Ayer cenamos en un restaurante.
>
> (Ud. oye) en casa
>
> (Ud. dice) Yo quería que cenáramos en casa.
>
> (Ud. oye y repite) Yo quería que cenáramos en casa.

1. Ayer vimos una obra de teatro.
2. El mes pasado fuimos a la playa.
3. Anoche miramos un noticiero.
4. Para mi cumpleaños, me regalaron un iPod.
5. Esta noche mi madre sirvió patatas en la cena.

I. **Tertulia** (*Gathering*) **política entre amigos**

Paso 1. En esta conversación, tres amigos —Maricarmen, Paco y Manolo— se encuentran en un bar para hablar de política. Paco y Maricarmen llegan al bar primero y hablan. Luego llega Manolo. Primero, escuche el **Vocabulario útil** y la conversación. Luego indique a quién se refieren las siguientes oraciones: **MC** (Maricarmen), **P** (Paco) o **M** (Manolo).

Vocabulario útil

el siglo	century
cuanto antes	as soon as possible
propuesto/a	proposed
anterior	former

Maricarmen, Paco y Manolo

(Continúa.)

1. _____ Su partido político acaba de ganar las elecciones.

2. _____ No le gusta la política del partido que está gobernando; esperaba que mejorara la situación del país más rápidamente.

3. _____ Vio las noticias anoche, y ahora piensa que el partido que está gobernando quería votar la nueva legislación cuanto antes.

4. _____ Está de acuerdo en que se necesitan nuevas leyes laborales, pero no las que (*those which*) propone el gobierno.

5. _____ Piensa que los problemas actuales de huelga y desempleo son problemas del gobierno anterior.

Paso 2. Escuche la conversación otra vez. Luego complete las siguientes oraciones.

1. Paco y Maricarmen empezaron a discutir la política antes de que Manolo _____ (llegar).

2. Maricarmen no creía que el partido de Paco _____ (estar) haciendo un buen trabajo en el gobierno.

3. Paco deseaba que las cosas _____ (ser) más sencillas (*simple*).

4. Está claro que estos amigos _____ (hablar) de política con frecuencia.

5. No es habitual que estos amigos _____ (estar) de acuerdo en política.

6. No hay un partido que _____ (ser) el favorito de los tres.

Nota: Verifique sus respuestas al **Paso 2** en el Apéndice antes de empezar el **Paso 3**.

Paso 3. Ahora Ud. va a oír algunas preguntas sobre la conversación. Contéstelas con las respuestas correctas al **Paso 2**. Luego escuche una respuesta posible y repítala.

1. …   2. …   3. …   4. …   5. …

¿Recuerda Ud.?

El futuro. Escriba la forma del futuro de los siguientes verbos.

1. (yo) votar _____

2. (ellos) ofrecer _____

3. (tú) vivir _____

4. (nosotros) poder _____

5. (Ud.) decir _____

6. (yo) querer _____

7. (Uds.) venir _____

8. (nosotros) saber _____

---

49. Expressing What You Would Do • Conditional Verb Forms

A. Situaciones. ¿Qué haría Ud. si estuviera en estas situaciones? Complete las oraciones con la forma apropiada del condicional del verbo entre paréntesis. Luego seleccione lo que *haría* Ud. en cada situación.

1. Si yo fuera testigo de un robo (*robbery*)…

   a. _____ (tratar) de parar al criminal.

   b. no _____ (decir) nada.

   c. _____ (llamar) a la policía.

2. Si hubiera un terremoto (*earthquake*)…

   a. _____ (meterme [*to get*]) debajo de la mesa del comedor.

   b. no _____ (saber) qué hacer.

   c. no _____ (moverme).

3. Si yo fuera presidente/a del país…

   a. _____ (cortar) las relaciones con todas las dictaduras del mundo.

   b. _____ (ofrecer) más ayuda a los pobres.

   c. _____ (eliminar) la desigualdad de salarios entre hombres y mujeres.

B. **¿Qué harían para mejorar las condiciones?** Diga, según las indicaciones, lo que harían las siguientes personas para mejorar el mundo. Luego escuche la respuesta correcta y repítala.

   MODELO: (Ud. oye) **1.** Gema
   (Ud. ve) eliminar las guerras
   (Ud. dice) Gema eliminaría las guerras.
   (Ud. oye y repite) Gema eliminaría las guerras.

   2. desarrollar otros tipos de energía
   3. construir viviendas para todos
   4. resolver los problemas domésticos
   5. eliminar el hambre
   6. protestar por el uso de las armas atómicas
   7. eliminar las desigualdades sociales

C. **¿Qué haría Ud. en Madrid?** Cuando oiga el número correspondiente, use las frases dadas para decir lo que haría Ud. en Madrid. Luego escuche la respuesta correcta y repítala.

   MODELO: (Ud. oye) Uno.
   (Ud. ve) **1.** quedarse en un buen hotel
   (Ud. dice) Me quedaría en un buen hotel.
   (Ud. oye y repite) Me quedaría en un buen hotel.

   2. comunicarse en español
   3. ir al Museo del Prado
   4. conocer la ciudad
   5. comer tapas y paella
   6. poder tomar el metro
   7. cenar muy tarde

D. **¿Qué dijo Rafael?** Dígale a Ana lo que Rafael acaba de decir, según el modelo. **¡OJO!** Tenga cuidado con los complementos pronominales.

   MODELO: RAFAEL: Los llevaré al cine mañana.
   ANA: ¿Qué dijo?
   UD.: Dijo que nos llevaría al cine mañana.

   1. RAFAEL: Saldré del trabajo a las siete.

   ANA: ¿Qué dijo?

   UD.: _____

   2. RAFAEL: Tendré que volver a casa antes de buscarlos (a Uds.).

   ANA: ¿Qué dijo?

   UD.: _____

   3. RAFAEL: Pasaré por Uds. a las ocho.

   ANA: ¿Qué dijo?

   UD.: _____

(Continúa.)

4. RAFAEL: Llegaremos al cine a las ocho y media.

    ANA: ¿Qué dijo?

    UD.: _____

5. RAFAEL: No habrá ningún problema en buscarlos (a Uds.).

    ANA: ¿Qué dijo?

    UD.: _____

E. Consejos apropiados. ¿Qué consejos les daría Ud. a estas personas famosas? Complete las oraciones con la forma apropiada del condicional del verbo indicado.

1. A Jodie Foster: Si yo fuera Ud., no _____ (aceptar) una invitación para cenar con Anthony Hopkins.

2. A Julio César: Si yo fuera Ud., no _____ (confiarse: *to trust*) de Bruto.

3. A Ana Bolena: Si yo fuera Ud., no _____ (casarse) con Enrique VIII.

4. A Abraham Lincoln: Si yo fuera Ud., no _____ (ir) al Teatro Ford.

5. A John Kennedy: Si yo fuera Ud., no _____ (hacer) ninguna visita a Dallas.

6. A Janet Leigh: Si yo fuera Ud., no _____ (ducharse) en el Motel Bates.

7. A John Lennon: Si yo fuera Ud., _____ (mudarse) lejos de Nueva York.

8. A George Armstrong Custer: Si yo fuera Ud., no _____ (luchar) contra los indios en la batalla de Little Bighorn.

 F. ¿Qué harían?

Paso 1. Ud. va a oír algunas oraciones. Escriba el número de cada oración al lado del dibujo descrito (*described*). Primero, mire los dibujos.

a. _____   **b.** _____

c. _____

d. _____

e. _____

Paso 2. Ahora Ud. va a oír algunas preguntas sobre los dibujos del **Paso 1.** Contéstelas y diga lo que harían las personas de cada dibujo. Luego escuche la respuesta correcta y repítala.

MODELO: (Ud. oye)   ¿Qué harían los amigos si estuvieran en el campo?

(Ud. ve)

(Ud. dice)   Si los amigos estuvieran en el campo, montarían a caballo.

(Ud. oye y repite)   Si los amigos estuvieran en el campo, montarían a caballo.

1. ...   2. ...   3. ...   4. ...   5. ...

G. **Consejos.** Imagine que su amigo Pablo tiene problemas con sus compañeros de cuarto. Diga lo que haría Ud. en su lugar, según las indicaciones. Empiece cada una de sus reacciones con **Si yo fuera Pablo...** Use la forma del condicional de los verbos que oye. Siga el modelo. Luego escuche la respuesta correcta y repítala.

MODELO: (Ud. oye)   llamar a mis padres

(Ud. dice)   Si yo fuera Pablo, llamaría a mis padres.

(Ud. oye y repite)   Si yo fuera Pablo, llamaría a mis padres.

1. ...   2. ...   3. ...   4. ...   5. ...

H. ¿Qué harían si... ?

Paso 1. En esta entrevista, Karina, Miguel René, Rubén y Tané hablan de lo que harían en ciertas circunstancias. Primero, escuche el **Vocabulario útil** y la entrevista. Luego indique con la primera letra del nombre de la persona —**K** (Karina), **MR** (Miguel René), **R** (Rubén) y **T** (Tané)— quién haría cada una de las siguientes cosas. **¡OJO!** En algunos casos hay más de una respuesta.

Vocabulario útil

una temporada	some time
cualquier	any
escoger (escojo)	to choose
la cuna	cradle
mismo/a	very
la raíz	root
poner	to establish
invertir (invierto) (i)	to invest
los bonos	bonds
la deuda	debt
la mitad	half

Karina   Miguel René   Rubén   Tané

1. _____ viviría en España.

2. _____ viviría en la India.

3. _____ viviría en la Argentina.

4. _____ no da ejemplos específicos de lo que haría con el dinero.

5. _____ viajaría mucho.

6. _____ invertiría dinero en bonos públicos.

7. _____ pondría su propia empresa.

8. _____ compraría una casa para su mamá.

❖ **Paso 2.** Ahora escriba cuatro preguntas, una para cada uno de los entrevistados, sobre la información que dieron en la entrevista. **¡OJO!** Las preguntas que Ud. escribe deben ser diferentes de las preguntas de la entrevista.

1. Para Karina: _____

2. Para Miguel René: _____

3. Para Rubén: _____

4. Para Tané: _____

Un poco de todo

A. Una manifestación. Complete la narración. Use la forma apropiada de los verbos indicados: el pasado de indicativo, el pasado de subjuntivo o el condicional. Cuando se dan dos posibilidades, escoja la correcta.

Ayer un amigo _____[1] (mi, mío), reportero de televisión, me llamó para ver si

_____[2] (yo: querer) ir con él y otros dos periodistas a la Plaza Mayor el próximo sábado

donde _____[3] (tener) lugar una manifestación. El propósito de la protesta era proteger el

medio ambiente y el interés público contra una compañía internacional. Esta compañía planeaba

destruir un bello parque y construir un centro comercial _____[4] (gran, grande) y

apartamentos de lujo.[a] Este plan solo _____[5] (beneficiar) a los dueños de la compañía.

Yo le _____[6] (decir) que me gustaría mucho acompañarlos, pero que primero

_____[7] (tener) que acabar un artículo _____[8] (para, por) ese mismo día.

Le prometí que _____[9] (hacer) todo lo posible para terminar antes de que

_____[10] (empezar) la protesta.

En caso de que no terminara el artículo a tiempo, yo le _____[11] (sugerir) que

_____[12] (ir) todos juntos a cenar en el restaurante El Atlántico a las diez de la noche y

allí ellos _____[13] (poder) informarme de todo lo que _____[14] (haber) pasado.

Le pedí que, de todas maneras,[b] me _____[15] (él: llamar) de su celular para que

_____[16] (enterarme) de lo que pasaba y en caso de que _____[17] (haber) algún

cambio de planes.

Desgraciadamente,[c] no recibí _____[18] (ningún, ninguna) llamada, y cuando yo

_____[19] (tratar) de llamarlo a él, no contestaba. Esta mañana, al abrir[d] el periódico, vi

su foto y su nombre en una lista de personas _____[20] (arrestados, arrestadas) por la

policía por protestar en la manifestación.

[a]de... *luxury* [b]de... *at any rate* [c]*Unfortunately* [d]al... *upon opening*

B. *Listening Passage:* **Resumen de las noticias**

Antes de escuchar. You will hear a news brief on the radio, just as it would be if you were listening to it in a Hispanic country. After you listen to the passage, you will be asked to complete the following statements about it. First listen to the **Vocabulario útil** and scan the statements to get a general idea of the information to listen for.

(Continúa.)

Vocabulario útil

la redacción	editorial desk
el maremoto	seaquake (an earthquakc below the sea)
asolar	to devastate
la decena	dozen
el herido	wounded
sin hogar	homeless
el desempleo	unemployment
el paro	**el desempleo**
la subida	increase
la propuesta	proposal
contar con	to count on
el apoyo	support
sintonizar	to tune in (to a broadcast)
amplio/a	comprehensive

Noticia 1: Fuerte maremoto en _____,[1] de más de _____[2] puntos en la escala Richter.

Noticia 2: Tema: _____[3]   Mes: _____[4]

Noticia 3: Visita de Juan Carlos I, _____[5] de _____.[6] Duración de la visita:

_____[7]

Noticia 4: Propuesta del partido de oposición para _____[8] el precio de la

_____,[9] el _____[10] y el _____,[11] el primero en un

_____[12] por ciento y los dos últimos en un _____[13] por ciento.

El próximo noticiero de amplio reportaje será a las _____.[14]

Listening Passage. Now listen to the passage.

Después de escuchar. Now complete the statements in **Antes de escuchar.**

C. Final feliz de un año en el extranjero

Paso 1. En esta conversación, Diego habla con Lupe de lo que a él le gustaría hacer ahora que las clases están a punto de (*about to*) terminar. Escuche la conversación. Luego complete las siguientes oraciones con información de la conversación.

1. Diego pensaba que era increíble que las clases _____ (estar) a punto de terminar.

2. A Diego le gustaría que Lupe lo _____ (acompañar) a la península de Yucatán para ver las ruinas de Chichen Itzá.

3. Después le dijo a Lupe que quería que ella _____ (ir) con él a California para que

ella _____ (conocer) a sus padres.

Paso 2. Ahora Ud. va a participar en una conversación con Lupe en la que hace el papel de **Ud.** Lupe va a invitarlo o invitarla a hacer algunas cosas. Primero, complete la conversación con las siguientes frases. Segundo, verifique sus respuestas en el Apéndice. Después haga la conversación en voz alta: Lea las líneas de **Ud.** en el diálogo y luego escuche la pronunciación correcta y repítala.

Nos vemos a las ocho en el restaurante Tapa Tapa.
¿A qué hora nos reunimos?
¡Me encantaría!
¡Y hay tantos restaurantes buenos!

LUPE: ¿Qué te parece Barcelona?

UD.: Es una ciudad magnífica. _____ 1

LUPE: Tienes razón. De hecho (*In fact*), ¿te gustaría ir de tapas esta noche?

UD.: _____ 2

LUPE: ¡Qué bien! Hay un lugar bueno para comer tapas cerca de tu hotel. Se llama Tapa Tapa.

UD.: ¡Perfecto! _____ 3

LUPE: A las ocho, más o menos... ¿Te parece bien?

UD.: Sí, ¡claro! _____ 4

CULTURA

España

A. Mapa. En el siguiente mapa identifique España y la capital de ese país.

B. **Comprensión.** Complete las siguientes oraciones con información de la **Lectura cultural: España** en la página 546 del libro de texto.

1. España es un país de mucha variedad geográfica y _____. Algunas regiones tienen su propia _____; por ejemplo, el gallego en _____, el vasco en el _____ y el catalán en _____.

2. La _____ de 1978 establece las diecisiete regiones como un Estado de Autonomías, similar al sistema federativo de los _____. Aunque este sistema es motivo de orgullo (*pride*), también produce _____ políticas y económicas.

3. La mayoría de las naciones latinoamericanas obtuvieron su _____ de España hace _____ años.

4. _____, _____, _____ y el Brasil formaron MERCOSUR, un acuerdo (*agreement*) con el propósito (*purpose*) de ofrecerse ayuda económica mutua.

5. En España, la Constitución de 1978 es un símbolo de la _____ española a pesar de (*in spite of*) la diversidad lingüística, política y económica.

6. Las tapas, pequeños _____ de comida, no solo son para comer sino (*but*) también son motivo para reunirse socialmente en los _____.

7. Aunque el _____ es la música propia del (*belonging to*) sur de España y de los gitanos, en el resto del mundo se identifica como símbolo de toda España.

PÓNGASE A PRUEBA

A. **Formas del imperfecto de subjuntivo.** Complete la siguiente tabla.

INFINITIVO	YO	TÚ	NOSOTROS	ELLOS
aprender	aprendiera			
decir		dijeras		
esperar			esperáramos	
poner				pusieran
seguir				

B. El condicional

1. Complete la siguiente tabla.

INFINITIVO	YO	UD.	NOSOTROS	ELLOS
comer		*comería*		
decir				
poder			*podríamos*	
salir				
ser				*serían*

2. Complete las oraciones con la forma apropiada del condicional.

a. Dije que _____ (*yo: ir*) con ellos el sábado.

b. Dije que _____ (*nosotros: hacerlo*) mañana.

c. Dije que _____ (*Uds: volver*) a las cuatro.

d. Dije que no _____ (*yo: tener*) tiempo.

C. Cláusulas con *si*. Complete las oraciones con el imperfecto de subjuntivo o el condicional, según las indicaciones.

1. Si yo _____ (ser) Ud., me mudaría.

2. Si yo _____ (tener) tiempo, iría.

3. Si (yo) supiera su número de teléfono, _____ (llamarlo).

4. Si no _____ (hacer) tanto frío, podríamos sentarnos afuera.

5. Si _____ (*yo: querer*) quedarme, me quedaría.

PRUEBA CORTA

A. El imperfecto de subjuntivo. Complete las oraciones con el imperfecto de subjuntivo.

1. El gobierno quería que todos _____ (obedecer) la ley.

2. Perdón, ¿_____ (poder) Ud. decirme a qué hora sale el autobús para Málaga?

3. Era necesario que los reporteros _____ (dar) más importancia a los problemas de los jóvenes.

4. Mis padres siempre insistían en que _____ (*yo: decir*) la verdad.

5. El rey Juan Carlos I prefería que la gente lo _____ (tratar) como a cualquier (*any*) otro ciudadano.

6. Pedro, ¿_____ (*tú: querer*) acompañarme a la estación de policía?

B. ¿El indicativo o el subjuntivo? Complete las oraciones con el indicativo (incluyendo el futuro y el condicional) o el subjuntivo.

1. Si él tenía tiempo, _____ (ir) al cine.

2. Si tengo dinero el verano próximo, _____ (viajar) a España.

3. Visitarían la Florida si allí no _____ (hacer) tanto calor.

4. Si viviera en San Diego, yo _____ (tener) un apartamento en la playa.

5. Si yo fuera ella, _____ (escribir) una novela sobre mi vida.

6. Si ellos tuvieran interés en trabajar, _____ (conseguir) cualquier tipo de trabajo.

7. Si estoy cansado/a, no _____ (hacer) ejercicio.

8. Si estudiaran más, _____ (salir) mejor en los exámenes.

C. Comentarios sobre la política y los acontecimientos. Haga oraciones sobre la política y los acontecimientos, según las indicaciones. **¡OJO!** Use los verbos en el pasado de subjuntivo. Haga todos los cambios necesarios. Luego escuche y repita la respuesta correcta. Siga el modelo.

MODELO: (Ud. oye) Uno. Insistíamos.

(Ud. ve) **1.** el gobierno / gobernar bien

(Ud. dice) Insistíamos en que el gobierno gobernara bien.

(Ud. oye y repite) Insistíamos en que el gobierno gobernara bien.

2. los reporteros / informarnos imparcialmente
3. el público / apoyarlos
4. el gobierno / castigar a los criminales
5. el gobierno / poder economizar
6. haber / una huelga
7. la huelga / durar tantos meses
8. los obreros / pedir un aumento tan grande

D. ¿Qué haría Ud. si... ? Ud. va a oír algunas preguntas. Para contestarlas, escoja la frase apropiada de la lista y use el verbo en el condicional . Luego escuche una respuesta posible y repítala.
votar por otro candidato (otra candidata) presidencial

acabar con (*to end*) la desigualdad
informar al público de los acontecimientos
postularse como candidato/a
hablar con la policía

MODELO: (Ud. oye) ¿Qué haría si fuera testigo de un accidente?

(Ud. dice) Hablaría con la policía.

(Ud. oye y repite) Hablaría con la policía.

1. ... **2.** ... **3.** ... **4.** ...

PUNTOS PERSONALES

A. Preguntas personales. Conteste con oraciones completas.

1. ¿Ve Ud. programas en la televisión pública? ¿Cuáles? _____

_____

2. ¿Cómo se informa Ud. de las noticias? ¿Lee Ud. un periódico local? _____

_____

3. ¿Cree Ud. que la libertad de prensa incluye también el derecho de distribuir material

pornográfico por el Internet? _____

_____

4. ¿Cree Ud. que votar debe ser obligatorio o voluntario? ¿Votó Ud. en las últimas

elecciones? _____

5. ¿Obedece Ud. la ley de manejar a un máximo de 70 millas por hora en las autopistas? _____

_____

6. ¿Ha sido Ud. alguna vez testigo o víctima de un crimen violento? ¿Qué pasó? _____

_____

7. ¿Cree Ud. que el servicio militar debe ser obligatorio o voluntario en este país? _____

_____

8. ¿Cree Ud. que el gobierno debe o no debe tener el poder para sacrificar nuestros derechos

civiles en la lucha contra el terrorismo? _____

_____

B. De niño/a. Ahora Ud. puede tomar sus propias decisiones, pero cuando era niño/a, casi todo lo que hacía dependía de la voluntad (*wishes*) de sus padres. Conteste las preguntas para indicar cómo era su niñez.

1. ¿Había algo en que sus padres insistían que Ud. hiciera antes de salir a jugar?

_____

2. ¿Su madre insistía en que Ud. recogiera su ropa antes de acostarse?

_____

3. ¿Qué quehaceres de la casa eran obligatorios que hiciera?

_____

4. ¿Le permitían que saliera de noche? _____

_____

5. ¿Qué restricciones había en su casa en cuanto al uso de la televisión?

_____

C. Cuando tenía 16 años...

Paso 1. Ud. va a oír algunas oraciones sobre su vida cuando Ud. tenía 16 años. Escoja la respuesta que corresponde a su propia experiencia.

1. ☐ Es cierto.   ☐ No es cierto.
2. ☐ Es cierto.   ☐ No es cierto.
3. ☐ Es cierto.   ☐ No es cierto.
4. ☐ Es cierto.   ☐ No es cierto.
5. ☐ Es cierto.   ☐ No es cierto.
6. ☐ Es cierto.   ☐ No es cierto.
7. ☐ Es cierto.   ☐ No es cierto.
8. ☐ Es cierto.   ☐ No es cierto.
9. ☐ Es cierto.   ☐ No es cierto.

Paso 2. Ahora Ud. va a oír algunas de las oraciones del **Paso 1** en forma de pregunta. Contéstelas por escrito.

1. _____
2. _____
3. _____
4. _____
5. _____

Paso 3. Ahora cuando oiga las preguntas del **Paso 2**, lea sus respuestas en voz alta.

1. ...   **2.** ...   **3.** ...   **4.** ...   **5.** ...

D. ¿Qué haría Ud.?

Paso 1. Complete las siguientes oraciones, según sus preferencias personales. Use verbos en el condicional y palabras adicionales.

1. Si tuviera más dinero, _____.

2. Si pudiera hablar español bien, _____.

3. Si me dieran un aumento de sueldo, _____.

4. Si viviera en Madrid, _____.

5. Si tuviera más tiempo, _____.

Paso 2. Ahora conteste en voz alta las preguntas que oye con la información del **Paso 1**.

1. ...   **2.** ...   **3.** ...   **4.** ...   **5.** ...

E. Guided Composition. En una hoja aparte, escriba una composición sobre algún acontecimiento que lo/la haya afectado profundamente. Describa ese acontecimiento y los efectos que tuvo en Ud. Mencione si este acontecimiento fue reportado en algún medio de comunicación. Puede empezar de la siguiente manera: Un acontecimiento que me ha afectado (afectó) profundamente ha sido (fue)...

Incluya la siguiente información:

- ¿Dónde ocurrió?
- ¿Cuándo ocurrió?
- ¿Hubo testigos de lo que ocurrió?
- ¿Hubo daños a la propiedad (*property*) o a las personas?
- ¿Intervino la policía o no?
- ¿Se reportó en la prensa?
- ¿Cómo terminó el incidente?

Puede usar las siguientes palabras, y otras, para conectar las ideas de su composición: **por eso, y, aunque** (*although*), **también, luego** y **porque.**

F. **Mi diario.** Imagine que Ud. es uno de «los ricos y famosos» y que le gustaría hacer un viaje espléndido. Planee su viaje, incluyendo los siguientes datos:

- adónde iría
- a quién invitaría
- cómo viajaría
- dónde se alojaría (*you would live*)
- qué ropa llevaría
- qué cosas haría en ese lugar

G. **Intercambios.** Escuche las siguientes preguntas y contéstelas por escrito.

1. _____

2. _____

3. _____

4. _____

5. _____

Capítulo 9 · Los días festivos

VOCABULARIO — Preparación

Appendix 1

Capítulo 9, which appears near the end of the first volume of the Workbook/ Lab Manual, *has been included here for instructors whose classes may not have completed this lesson in the first term.*

Una fiesta de cumpleaños para Javier

A. La quinceañera de Amanda. Lea el siguiente párrafo. Luego conteste las preguntas con oraciones completas. Use pronombres de complemento directo e indirecto si es posible.

El 14 de septiembre es el cumpleaños de Amanda. Va a cumplir 15 años. Para celebrarlo sus padres van a hacerle una quinceañera, la fiesta tradicional para las jóvenes que cumplen esa edad. Esta es una fiesta en la que[a] los padres a veces gastan mucho dinero. Para no gastar tanto, sus padres van a hacer la fiesta en casa, no en un hotel o restaurante. Los padres de Amanda ya le compraron un vestido elegante para la ocasión e invitaron a sus parientes y a los mejores amigos de su hija. Va a haber[b] cien invitados, y todos van a regalarle algo a Amanda. Todos los parientes van a ayudar a preparar botanas, como empanadas y croquetas[c] de jamón, y platos principales como arroz con pollo y chiles rellenos. De postre,[d] va a haber un magnífico pastel de cumpleaños y flan. Además,[e] tres amigos de ella van a tocar la guitarra y cantar en su honor. Amanda está muy emocionada.[f] Sin duda,[g] la quinceañera va a ser una fiesta muy divertida.[h]

[a]la... *which* [b]*to be* [c]*balls of meat or potato coated in breadcrumbs and deep-fried* [d]De... *For dessert* [e]*Moreover* [f]*excited* [g]Sin... *Without a doubt* [h]*fun*

1. ¿Por qué van a hacerle sus padres una fiesta a Amanda?
   _____

2. ¿Cómo se llama esa fiesta tradicional? _____

3. ¿Dónde va a ser la fiesta? _____

4. ¿Por qué decidieron los padres hacer la fiesta en ese lugar?
   _____

5. ¿Cuántos invitados van a ir a la fiesta?
   _____

6. ¿Qué van a hacer todos los invitados para Amanda?

_____

7. ¿Quiénes van a preparar la comida? _____

8. ¿Que tipo de botanas van a preparar?

_____

B. **¿Cuánto sabe Ud. de los días festivos?** Complete las oraciones con el día festivo apropiado.

el Día de la Raza (*Columbus Day / Hispanic Awareness Day*)
el Día de los Muertos (*Day of the Dead*)
la Navidad
la Nochebuena
la Nochevieja
la Pascua judía (*Passover*)

1. El día antes del primero de enero se llama _____.

2. El 25 de diciembre, los cristianos celebran _____.

3. _____ conmemora la huida (*escape*) de los judíos (*Jews*) de Egipto.

4. Muchos católicos asisten a la Misa del Gallo (*Midnight Mass*) el día antes de la Navidad, que

se conoce como _____.

5. _____ se celebra el 2 de noviembre.

6. _____ se celebra el 12 de octubre.

C. **Asociaciones.** Ud. va a oír algunas descripciones. Indique la fiesta o la celebración que se asocia con cada descripción. **¡OJO!** Hay más de una respuesta correcta en algunos casos.

1. _____ **a.** la Navidad   **b.** el Día de la Raza (*Columbus Day / Hispanic Awareness Day*)   **c.** el cumpleaños

2. _____ **a.** el Cinco de Mayo   **b.** la Pascua   **c.** el Día del Canadá

3. _____ **a.** el Día de los Reyes Magos (*Day of the Magi (Three Kings) / Epiphany* [Jan. 6])   **b.** el Día de Acción de Gracias (*Thanksgiving*)   **c.** el Día de los Muertos (*Day of the Dead*)

4. _____ **a.** el Día de San Patricio   **b.** el Día de los Reyes Magos   **c.** el día del santo (*saint's day* [*the saint for whom one is named*])

5. _____ **a.** el Cuatro de Julio   **b.** Janucá (*Hanukkah*)   **c.** la Semana Santa (*Holy Week*)

D. **¿Una fiesta típica?**

Paso 1. Ud. va a oír la descripción de una reunión (*gathering*) reciente (*recent*) de la familia de Sara. Primero, escuche el **Vocabulario útil** y la descripción. Luego escuche las siguientes oraciones e indique si son ciertas (**C**) o falsas (**F**), según lo que dice Sara. Si la información no se dio en la descripción, indique **ND** (No lo dice). **Nota:** Las palabras subrayadas (*underlined*) y las en cursiva (*italicized*) tienen que ver (*have to do*) con el **Paso 2.**

Vocabulario útil

portarse (mal)	to behave (badly)
el angelito	little angel
discutir	to argue
esta vez	this time
Dios	God
quejarse (de)	to complain (about)
fueran	would be, were

1. C   F   ND   Según lo que dice <u>Sara</u>, las fiestas de su familia normalmente son *muy divertidas.*

2. C   F   ND   A la tía Eustacia *le gusta discutir* con el padre de <u>Sara</u>.

3. C   F   ND   Normalmente, los primos de <u>Sara</u> *se portan mal* en las fiestas familiares.

4. C   F   ND   <u>Sara</u> nunca *lo pasa bien* en las fiestas familiares.

5. C   F   ND   Los hermanos de <u>Sara</u> *discuten mucho* con sus padres.

Paso 2. Ahora, cambie el nombre de **Sara** a **Antonio** para describir las fiestas familiares de Antonio. Sustituya (*Substitute*) las palabras en cursiva de las oraciones del **Paso 1** por la información que oye.

MODELO: (Ud. ve)   **1.** Según lo que dice <u>Sara</u>, las fiestas de su familia normalmente son *muy divertidas.*

         (Ud. oye)   Uno: en un hotel

         (Ud. dice)   Según lo que dice Antonio, las fiestas de su familia normalmente son en un hotel.

   (Ud. oye y repite)   Según lo que dice Antonio, las fiestas de su familia normalmente son en un hotel.

2. ...   **3.** ...   **4.** ...   **5.** ...

E. Entrevista cultural. Ud. va a oír una entrevista con Rocío en la que (*in which*) habla de su trabajo y de algunas celebraciones cubanas. Primero, escuche el **Vocabulario útil** y luego la entrevista. Después, complete el párrafo con información de la entrevista.

Vocabulario útil

el globo	balloon
la serpentina	paper streamer
el payaso	clown
disfrutar	to enjoy
el arroz con gris	rice cooked with black beans
la yuca con mojo	manioc (cassava) with citrus-garlic sauce
el buñuelo con almíbar	fried pastry covered in syrup

Rocío es de _____,[1] _____.[2] Pero ahora vive en

_____.[3] Trabaja en una _____[4] que vende

artículos _____[5] de _____.[6]

En su país, en las fiestas de _____[7] hay _____[8]

para beber y se come *cake*. Y para los niños hay payasos, globos y piñatas.

El día festivo favorito de Rocío es la _____[9] porque toda la familia

se reúne y se hace una gran _____[10] con _____[11]

típica cubana. Un plato típico es la carne de puerco _____.[12]

Las emociones y los estados afectivos

A. ¿Cómo reaccionan los profesores y los estudiantes? Escriba cómo reaccionan los profesores y los estudiantes con la forma apropiada de los verbos de la lista.

discutir   ponerse (avergonzado, irritado,   quejarse
enfermarse   nervioso, triste)   recordar
enojarse   portarse   reírse

1. Cuando Julián no contesta bien en clase, se ríe porque se pone nervioso. Cuando

   yo no _____ la respuesta correcta, yo _____.

2. Cuando nos olvidamos de entregar (*turn in*) la tarea a tiempo, los profesores

   _____.

3. Cuando llega la época de los exámenes, algunos estudiantes _____

   porque no duermen lo suficiente (*enough*). Y todos _____ porque

   dicen que tienen muchísimo trabajo.

4. Generalmente los estudiantes universitarios son responsables y _____

   bien en clase.

5. A los profesores no les gusta _____ con los estudiantes sobre las

   notas (*grades*) que les dan.

B. Enfáticamente. Complete las oraciones con la forma **–ísimo/a** del adjetivo apropiado.

cansado/a   difícil   rico
caro   largo

1. La novela *Guerra y paz* del autor ruso Tolstoi es _____.

2. Carlos Slim Helú, Bill Gates y Warren Buffett son _____.

3. Después de correr diez kilómetros me siento _____.

4. La vida en Tokio es _____.

5. Las preguntas del último examen fueron _____.

C. Reacciones. Describa cómo reaccionan estas personas en las siguientes situaciones, según las indicaciones. Use **cuando** en cada oración. Luego escuche la respuesta correcta y repítala.

       MODELO: (Ud. ve)   Mi novio olvida el cumpleaños de su madre.
                   (Ud. oye)   ponerse triste
                   (Ud. dice)   Mi novio se pone triste cuando olvida el cumpleaños de su madre.
                   (Ud. oye y repite)   Mi novio se pone triste cuando olvida el cumpleaños de su madre.

1. Los abuelos juegan con sus nietos.
2. Marta ve una película triste.
3. Nosotras sacamos buenas notas.
4. Tengo que hacer cola.
5. Los estudiantes tienen demasiada (*too much*) tarea.

PRONUNCIACIÓN *c* and *qu*

- The [k] sound in Spanish can be written two ways: before the vowels **a**, **o**, and **u** it is written as **c;** before **i** and **e**, it is written as **qu**. Note that the *kw* sound, spelled in English with *qu* (as in *quaint* and *quince*), is spelled in Spanish with **cu**, not **qu: cuando, cuento.** The letter **k** itself appears only in words that have come to Spanish from other languages.
- Unlike the English [k] sound, the Spanish sound is not aspirated; that is, no air is allowed to escape when it is pronounced. Compare the following pairs of English words in which the first [k] sound is aspirated and the second is not.

can / scan   cold / scold   kit / skit

A. Repeticiones

Paso 1. Repita las siguientes palabras, imitando lo que oye. No se olvide (*Don't forget*) de pronunciar el sonido [k] sin aspiración.

1. casa	cosa	rico	loca	roca
2. ¿quién?	Quito	aquí	¿qué?	pequeño
3. kilo	kilogramo	kerosén	kilómetro	karate

Paso 2. Cuando oiga el número correspondiente, lea las siguientes palabras y oraciones en voz alta. Luego escuche la pronunciación correcta y repítala.

1. paquete
2. quinceañera
3. química
4. ¿por qué?
5. cuaderno
6. comida
7. ¿Quién compró los camarones?
8. Carolina no come con Carlos.
9. Ricardo quiere ir a Querétaro.

B. El sonido [k]. Escriba las palabras que oye. **¡OJO!** Fíjese en los sonidos y no se distraiga (*don't get distracted*) por las palabras desconocidas (*unknown*) que oye.

1. _____
2. _____
3. _____
4. _____
5. _____
6. _____

GRAMÁTICA

¿Recuerda Ud.?

You have already learned the irregular preterite stem and endings for the verb **hacer.** All of the verbs presented in **Gramática 24** have irregular stems and use the same endings as **hacer.** Review the preterite endings for regular verbs and those for **hacer** by completing the following chart.

hablar:	yo habl _____	nosotros habl _____	Ud. habl _____	ellos habl _____
comer:	yo com _____	nosotros com _____	Ud. com _____	ellos com _____
vivir:	yo viv _____	nosotros viv _____	Ud. viv _____	ellos viv _____
hacer	yo **hic** _____	nosotros **hic** _____	Ud. **hiz** _____	ellos **hic** _____

24. Talking about the Past (Part 2) • Irregular Preterites

A. **Formas verbales.** Escriba la forma indicada de los verbos.

INFINITIVO	YO	UD.	NOSOTROS	UDS.
estar				
	tuve			
		pudo		
			pusimos	
				quisieron
saber				
	vine			
		dijo		
			trajimos	

B. **Situaciones.** Complete las oraciones con el pretérito de los verbos entre paréntesis.

Durante la Navidad: La familia Román _____¹ (tener) una reunión[a] familiar muy bonita para la Navidad. Todos sus hijos _____² (estar) presentes. _____³ (Venir) de Denver y Dallas, y_____⁴ (traer) regalos para todos. Su mamá pensaba[b] hacer una gran cena para la Nochebuena, pero todos le _____⁵ (decir) que no. Por la noche todos _____⁶ (ir) a un restaurante muy elegante donde _____⁷ (comer) bien, _____⁸ (poder) escuchar música y _____⁹ (pasarlo) bien.

[a]*gathering* [b]*was planning*

Otro terremoto[a] en California: Esta mañana _____¹ (*nosotros:* saber) que _____² (haber) un terremoto en California. Lo _____³ (*yo:* oír) primero en la radio y luego lo _____⁴ (*yo:* leer) en el periódico. Algunas casas _____⁵ (dañarse[b]), pero en general, este terremoto no _____⁶ (hacer) mucho daño.[c] Un experto _____⁷ (decir): «No _____⁸ (ser) el primero ni va a ser el último».

[a]*earthquake* [b]*to be damaged* [c]*damage*

C. **Después del examen.** Jorge y Manuel hablan en la cafetería. Complete las oraciones con la forma apropiada de los verbos entre paréntesis.

JORGE: ¿Cómo _____¹ (estar) el examen?

MANUEL: ¡Terrible! No _____² (poder) contestar las últimas tres preguntas porque no _____³ (tener) tiempo. ¿Por qué no _____⁴ (ir) tú?

JORGE: _____⁵ (Querer) ir, pero _____⁶ (estar) enfermo todo el día.

¿Qué preguntas _____⁷ (hacer) el profesor?

MANUEL: Muchas, pero ahora no recuerdo ninguna. ¿_____⁸ (*Tú:* Saber) que Claudia

_____⁹ (tener) un accidente y tampoco _____¹⁰ (ir) al examen?

JORGE: Sí, me lo _____¹¹ (decir) María Inés esta mañana... Bueno, tengo que irme...

¡Caramba! ¿Dónde _____¹² (poner) mi cartera?

MANUEL: ¿No la _____¹³ (traer) otra vez? Yo solo _____¹⁴ (traer) dos

dólares. Vamos a buscar a Ernesto. Él siempre tiene dinero.

D. ¿Qué pasó ayer?

Paso 1. Va a oír algunas oraciones sobre lo que pasó ayer. Primero, escuche el **Vocabulario útil,** luego escuche las oraciones. Escriba el número de la oración y el nombre de cada persona en el dibujo (*drawing*) debajo del dibujo correspondiente.

Vocabulario útil

jugar a videojuegos   to play videogames

a. _____

_____

b. _____

_____

c. _____

_____

d. _____

_____

e. _____

_____

Nota: Verifique (*Check*) sus respuestas al **Paso 1** en el Apéndice antes de empezar el **Paso 2.**

(Continúa.)

Paso 2. Ahora, va a oír algunas preguntas. Contéstelas, según los dibujos del **Paso 1.** Luego escuche la respuesta correcta y repítala.

MODELO: (Ud. oye) **1.** ¿Quién tuvo que hacer su maleta para un viaje?
                  (Ud. ve)

                  e. 1 - Ricardo
       (Ud. dice) Ricardo tuvo que hacer su maleta para un viaje.
  (Ud. oye y repite) Ricardo tuvo que hacer su maleta para un viaje.

2. … **3.** … **4.** … **5.** …

25. Talking About the Past (Part 3) • Preterite of Stem-Changing Verbs

A. Formas verbales. Escriba la forma indicada de los verbos.

INFINITIVO	YO	TÚ	UD.	NOSOTROS	UDS.
divertirse					
sentir					
dormir					
conseguir					
reírse					
vestir					

B. **Situaciones.** Complete las oraciones con la forma apropiada del pretérito de uno de los verbos de la lista, según el significado de la oración.

dormirse   **sentarse**

1. Yo _____ delante de la televisión y poco después _____ .

2. —¿A qué hora _____ Uds. a comer?

    —A las nueve y media. Y después de trabajar tanto, ¡nosotros casi _____ en la mesa!

3. Mi esposo se despertó a las dos y no _____ otra vez hasta las cinco de la mañana.

    reírse   **sentir** (*to regret*)   **sentirse**

4. Esa película fue tan divertida que (nosotros) _____ toda la noche. Solo Jorge no

    _____ mucho porque no la comprendió.

5. Rita y Marcial _____ mucho haber faltado (*having missed*) a tu fiesta, pero Rita se

    enfermó y _____ tan mal que se quedó en la cama todo el fin de semana.

C. Una mala noche

Paso 1. Cambie al pretérito los verbos indicados para describir la noche horrible de Juan.

Juan *entra*[1] en el restaurante y *se sienta*[2] a comer con unos amigos. *Pide*[3] una cerveza y el camarero le *sirve*[4] inmediatamente, pero después de tomar dos tragos[a] *se siente*[5] mal, *se levanta*[6] y *se despide*[7] de todos rápidamente. *Vuelve*[8] a casa y no *duerme*[9] en toda la noche.

[a]*sips*

1. _____   6. _____

2. _____   7. _____

3. _____   8. _____

4. _____   9. _____

5. _____

Paso 2. Esta vez la mala noche fue suya (*yours*). Complete el párrafo con la forma apropiada de los verbos en el pretérito. **¡OJO!** Tenga cuidado (*Be careful*) con los pronombres.

Yo _____[1] (entrar) en el restaurante y _____[2] (sentarse) a comer con unos

amigos. _____[3] (*yo:* Pedir) una cerveza y el camarero _____[4] (servirme)

inmediatamente, pero después de tomar dos tragos _____[5] (sentirse) mal,

_____[6] (levantarse[6]) y _____[7] (despedirse) de todos rápidamente.

_____[8] (Volver) a casa y no _____ (dormir) en toda la noche.

D. La fiesta de sorpresa (*surprise party*)

Paso 1. Ud. va a oír un breve párrafo narrado por Ernesto sobre una fiesta de sorpresa. Primero, mire la tabla, luego escuche el párrafo. Después, indique en la tabla las acciones de cada persona.

PERSONA	VESTIRSE ELEGANTEMENTE	SENTIRSE MAL	DORMIR TODA LA TARDE	PREFERIR QUEDARSE EN CASA
Julia				
Verónica				
Tomás				
Ernesto (el narrador)				

Paso 2. Ahora va a oír algunas oraciones sobre la narración del **Paso 1.** Indique si son ciertas (**C**) o falsas (**F**), según la narración. Si la información no se dio, indique **ND** (No lo dice).

1. C F ND   4. C F ND
2. C F ND   5. C F ND
3. C F ND

E. **¿Qué le pasó a Antonio?** Raquel invitó a Antonio a una fiesta en su casa. Antonio le dijo a Raquel que él asistiría (*would attend*), pero todo le salió mal. Cuando oiga el número y las indicaciones correspondientes, diga lo que le pasó a Antonio. Luego escuche la respuesta correcta y repítala.

> MODELO: (Ud. oye) Uno. no recordar
> (Ud. ve) llevar los refrescos
> (Ud. dice) No recordó llevar los refrescos.
> (Ud. oye y repite) No recordó llevar los refrescos.

2. la dirección de Raquel
3. muy tarde a la fiesta
4. en la fiesta
5. enfermo después de la fiesta
6. muy tarde
7. mal esa noche
8. a las cinco de la mañana
9. a clases de todos modos (*anyway*)

¿Recuerda Ud.?

Direct and Indirect Object Pronouns

Cambie las frases indicadas (*a Ud., a nosotros, a ellos, etcétera*) y los complementos directos indicados por complementos pronominales. Luego identifique la clase de pronombre (C.D. = complemento directo; C.I. = complemento indirecto). Siga los modelos.

> MODELOS: No dice la verdad. (*a Uds.*) → No les dice la verdad. (C.I.)
> No dice *la verdad*. → No la dice. (C.D.)

1. Yo traigo el café. (*a Ud.*) _____

2. Yo traigo *el café* ahora. _____

3. Ellos compran los boletos hoy. (*a nosotros*) _____

4. Ellos compran *los boletos* hoy. _____

5. No hablo mucho. (*a ellas*) _____

6. No conozco bien *a tus primas*. _____

7. Queremos dar una fiesta. (*a mis padres*) _____

8. Pensamos dar *la fiesta* en casa. _____

26. Avoiding Repetition • Expressing Direct and Indirect Object Pronouns Together

Recuerde:				
le **les**	lo la los las	→ **se**	lo la los las	

A. **¡Promesas, promesas!** (*Promises, promises!*) Estas personas prometen hacer las siguientes cosas. Vuelva a escribir lo que prometen, pero omita la repetición innecesaria del complemento directo.

MODELO: ¿Las flores? José nos trae *las flores* pronto. →
¿Las flores? José nos las trae pronto.

1. ¿El dinero? Te devuelvo (*I'll return*) *el dinero* mañana.

_____

2. ¿Las tapas? Te traigo *las tapas* esta noche.

_____

3. ¿El champán? Nos traen *el champán* esta tarde.

_____

4. ¿Los pasteles? Me prometieron *los pasteles* para esta tarde.

_____

5. ¿Las fotos? Les mando las fotos a Uds. con la carta.

_____

6. ¿La bicicleta? Le devuelvo la bicicleta a Pablo mañana.

_____

7. ¿El dinero? Le doy (a Ud.) el dinero el viernes.

_____

8. ¿Los regalos? Le muestro los regalos a Isabel esta noche.

_____

B. La herencia (*inheritance*). Imagine que un pariente rico murió y les dejó (*he left*) varias cosas a Ud. y a diferentes personas e instituciones. ¿Qué le dejó a quién?

Ana y Ernesto

Marta

Memo

la Cruz Roja

la biblioteca

yo

MODELO: ¿A quién le dejó su ropa? → Se la dejó a la Cruz Roja.

1. ¿A quién le dejó su coche? _____

2. ¿A quién le dejó su nueva cámara? _____

3. ¿A quién le dejó sus libros? _____

4. ¿A quién le dejó sus muebles? _____

5. ¿A quién le dejó su camioneta? _____

6. ¿A quién le dejó los $20.000 dólares? _____

C. Durante la cena

Paso 1. Durante la cena, su hermano le pregunta acerca de (*about*) la comida que sobra (*that is left*). Indique la comida a la que (*to which*) él se refiere en cada pregunta.

MODELO:　　　(Ud. oye)　¿Hay más? ¿Me la pasas, por favor?

　　　　　　　　(Ud. ve)　la sopa　el pan　el pescado

　　　　　　(Ud. indica)　(la sopa)

1. las galletas　　　la fruta　　　　el helado
2. la carne　　　　　el postre　　　　los camarones
3. la leche　　　　　el vino　　　　　las arvejas
4. las papas fritas　la cerveza　　　el pastel

Paso 2. Ahora va a oír las preguntas de su hermano otra vez. Contéstelas, según el modelo. Luego escuche la respuesta correcta y repítala.

MODELO:　　　　　(Ud. oye)　¿Hay más? ¿Me la pasas, por favor? →

　　　　　　　　　(Ud. ve)　(la sopa)

　　　　　　　(Ud. dice)　¿La sopa? Claro que (*Of course*) te la paso.

　　　(Ud. oye y repite)　¿La sopa? Claro que te la paso.

1. ...　2. ...　3. ...　4. ...

D. Una fiesta de sorpresa para Lupita

Paso 1. Ud. va a oír una descripción de la fiesta de sorpresa que Olivia hizo recientemente para su amiga Lupita. Mientras escucha, escriba las palabras que faltan (*are missing*).

El viernes pasado, mis amigos y yo dimos una fiesta de sorpresa para Lupita, una de nuestras

amigas. Yo escribí las invitaciones y _____ _____[1] mandé a todos. Carmen hizo un pastel

y _____ _____[2] dio antes de la fiesta. Anita preparó una comida elegante y _____

_____[3] sirvió en el comedor. Arturo y Patricio sacaron muchas fotos y _____ _____[4]

regalaron a Lupita. Todos llevamos regalos y _____ _____[5] presentamos a Lupita al final

de la fiesta. ¡Lupita nos dijo que fue una fiesta maravillosa!

Nota: Verifique sus respuestas al **Paso 1** en el Apéndice antes de empezar el **Paso 2.**

Paso 2. Ahora, va a oír algunas preguntas sobre la narración del **Paso 1.** Conteste cada pregunta, luego escuche la respuesta correcta y repítala.

1. ...　2. ...　3. ...　4. ...　5. ...　6. ...

E. ¿Dónde está?

¿Dónde está? Carolina quiere pedirle prestadas (*borrow*) algunas de las cosas que Ud. tiene. Dígale a quién ya le prestó Ud. las cosas que Carolina quiere.

MODELO:　　　　　(Ud. oye)　Oye, ¿dónde está tu diccionario?

　　　　　　　　　(Ud. ve)　Se (lo/la) presté a Nicolás. Él (lo/la) necesita para un examen.

　　　　　　　(Ud. dice)　Se lo presté a Nicolás. Él lo necesita para un examen.

　　　(Ud. oye y repite)　Se lo presté a Nicolás. Él lo necesita para un examen

1. Se (lo/la) presté a Nicolás. Él (lo/la) necesita para un viaje.
2. Se (los/las) presté a Teresa. Ella (los/las) necesita para llevar a una fiesta.
3. Se (la/las) presté a Juan. Él (la/las) necesita para escribir un trabajo.
4. Se (lo/la) presté a Nina. Ella (lo/la) necesita para ir al parque.

F. **En una tienda de música.** Ud. va a oír un diálogo en el que (*in which*) un empleado de una tienda de música atiende (*helps*) a una clienta y luego a un cliente. Primero, escuche el **Vocabulario útil,** luego escuche el diálogo. Después, indique si las siguientes oraciones se refieren al disco compacto, a los dos éxitos de un disco compacto o al recibo.

Vocabulario útil

el éxito	hit, success
el disco	album (*music*)
quisiera	I would like
devolver	to return (something)
el recibo	receipt
reembolsar	to refund
el reembolso	refund
Qué pena.	What a shame.
cambiar	to exchange

1. Puedes oírlos allá.   CD   éxitos   recibo
2. ¿Por qué quieres devolverlo?   CD   éxitos   recibo
3. No lo tengo.   CD   éxitos   recibo
4. Me lo regalaron para mi cumpleaños.   CD   éxitos   recibo
5. ¿Puedes cambiármelo?   CD   éxitos   recibo

G. **Preguntas y más preguntas.** Escriba una respuesta para cada pregunta. Use los pronombres de complemento directo y complemento indirecto juntos.

> MODELO: —¿Quién te regaló esta novela?
>
> —<u>Me la regaló</u> mi tía

1. —¿Quién te dio estas flores?

   — _____ mi amigo Samuel.

2. —¿A cuántas personas les mandaste las invitaciones de la fiesta?

   — _____ a treinta personas por lo menos.

3. —¿Puedo pedirte un favor?

   —¡Claro que puedes _____!

4. —Profesora, ¿le damos a Ud. la tarea ahora?

   —Sí, por favor, _____ ahora.

Un poco de todo

A. Un mensaje para un amigo

Paso 1. Complete el mensaje que Gerardo le escribe a un amigo que vive en La Habana. Use el pretérito de los verbos entre paréntesis. Cuando se presentan dos palabras entre paréntesis, escoja (*choose*) la más lógica.

Hola Pepe,

La semana pasada _____[1] (*yo:* hacer) un viaje corto a La Habana para reunirme con

Felipe Rubio, un director de _____[2] (nuestra / nuestro) compañía. _____[3]

(Ser) imposible verte ese día porque la reunión _____[4] (ser) muy _____[5]

(corta / larga) y luego él me _____[6] (invitar) a comer con otros miembros de la compañía. El día siguiente _____[7] (*yo: tener*) otras reuniones que _____[8]

(también / tampoco) _____[9] (acabar) muy tarde. Quería[a] visitarte, pero

_____[10] (saber) por Luis Dávila que estabas[b] de viaje. Cuando _____[11]

(*yo: encontrarse*) con Luis, le _____[12] (dar) unas fotos de la última vez que

_____[13] (*nosotros: estar*) juntos, y _____[14] (le / lo) _____[15]

(pedir) que te _____[16] (las / los) diera[c] a ti.

Espero verte durante mi próxima visita. Recibe un fuerte abrazo[d] de tu amigo,

Gerardo

[a]*I wanted* [b]*you were* [c]*he give* [d]*hug*

Paso 2. Conteste las preguntas con oraciones completas.

1. ¿Por qué fue Gerardo a La Habana?

2. ¿Por qué no pudo ver a Pepe el primer día?

3. ¿Cómo supo que Pepe estaba de viaje?

4. ¿A quién le dio las fotos?

B. *Listening Passage:* **El Carnaval**

Listening Passage. You will hear a passage about Carnival celebrations (**los Carnavales**). First, listen to the **Vocabulario útil.** Next, listen to the passage once to get a general idea of the content. Then listen again for details.

Vocabulario útil

la Cuaresma	Lent	**el disfraz**	costume
aun	even	**el monstruo**	monster
la gente	people	**caricaturesco/a**	cartoonish, satirical
la máscara	mask	**durar**	to last
pagano/a	pagan	**de maravilla**	great, wonderfully
se mezclan	are blended		

Después de escuchar. Indicate the statements that contain information that you *cannot* infer from the listening passage, then check your answers in the Appendix.

1. ☐ El Carnaval es una tradición exclusivamente europea.
2. ☐ A pesar de (*In spite of*) las diferencias, las celebraciones del Carnaval tienen muchas semejanzas (*similarities*).
3. ☐ El Carnaval celebra la llegada del buen tiempo.
4. ☐ Los mejores Carnavales se celebran en Europa.
5. ☐ La gran diferencia entre el Carnaval de Río y los otros Carnavales es que el de Río se celebra en un mes diferente.
6. ☐ La persona que habla tuvo gran dificultad con el idioma en Río de Janeiro.
7. ☐ La persona que habla quiere ir al *Mardi Gras* de Nueva Orleáns el próximo año.

C. **Charlando** (*Chatting*) **y preparando una fiesta**

Paso 1. Ud. va a oír una conversación entre Miguel René y Rubén, quienes charlan mientras preparan una fiesta. Primero, escuche el **Vocabulario útil.** Luego escuche la conversación e indique todos los temas que mencionan.

Rubén y Miguel René

Vocabulario útil

colgar (cuelgo) (gu)	to hang
el globo	balloon
para que la genta sepa	so that people know
juntarse	**reunirse (me reúno)**
las uvas de la suerte	the lucky grapes
nos agarramos de	we hold
el segundo	second

1. ☐ una fiesta para María
2. ☐ la celebración del Día de la Independencia
3. ☐ las tradiciones de la Nochevieja
4. ☐ la importancia de la familia

Paso 2. En el **Paso 3,** Ud. va a participar en una conversación similar a la del **Paso 1** en la que (*in which*) Ud. va a hacer el papel (*play the role*) de Enrique, quien habla con su amigo Juan sobre una fiesta que ellos están planeando para su amiga Ana. Primero, complete la conversación con las siguientes frases.

celebra tu familia la Navidad   gastamos mucho dinero
comemos las doce uvas de la suerte   le va a encantar

JUAN: Creo que los adornos para la fiesta están quedando muy bien.

ENRIQUE: ¡De acuerdo! Creo que a Ana _____,[1]

JUAN: Estos preparativos me recuerdan mucho a la Navidad.

ENRIQUE: ¿Cómo _____[2]?

JUAN: Pues nos juntamos toda la familia, hay mucho que comer, muchos regalos,... ¿Y tu familia?

ENRIQUE: Pues cosas similares, y siempre _____,[3]

JUAN: ¿Y hacen algo especial para la Nochevieja?

ENRIQUE: Sí. Tenemos una cena especial, y a la medianoche _____

_____.⁴

JUAN: ¡Ah! Esa es la costumbre española, ¿verdad?

Nota: Verifique sus respuestas al **Paso 2** en el Apéndice antes de empezar el **Paso 3.**

Paso 3. Ahora, haga el papel de Enrique en la conversación completa del **Paso 2.** Después de leer en voz alta cada línea del diálogo de Enrique, escúchela y repítala.

CULTURA

Cuba

A. Mapa. Identifique en el siguiente mapa Cuba y su capital.

B. Comprensión. Complete las siguientes oraciones con información de la **Lectura cultural: Cuba** de la página 286 del libro de texto.

1. En Cuba, el 10 de octubre se conoce como el Día de la _____ Nacional. En este

    día, Carlos Manuel de Céspedes declaró libres a todos los esclavos y también empezó la

    primera guerra por la independencia cubana de _____ (país).

2. Desde 1959 hasta 1998 el gobierno de Fidel Castro no permitió la celebración oficial de la

    _____.

(Continúa.)

3. Durante la _____, que termina el Domingo de Pascua, en casi todos los países hispanos se cierran los colegios y universidades porque muchas personas toman _____.

4. En muchos países como España, el Brasil, Colombia y Cuba se celebra el _____ con muchos bailes y música.

5. La _____, un tipo de árbol, es uno de los símbolos nacionales de Cuba y es parte de su escudo (*coat of arms*).

6. Cuba se conoce por producir el mejor _____ del mundo.

PÓNGASE A PRUEBA

A. **Irregular Preterites.** Escriba las formas apropiadas de los verbos en el pretérito.

1. **estar:** yo _____
2. **poder:** tú _____
3. **poner:** Ud. _____
4. **querer:** nosotros _____
5. **saber:** ellos _____
6. **tener:** yo _____
7. **venir:** tú _____
8. **traer:** Ud. _____
9. **decir:** ellos _____
10. **ir:** nosotros _____

B. **Preterite of Stem-Changing Verbs.** Complete la siguiente tabla.

	dormir	pedir	preferir	recordar	sentirse
él / ella / Ud.					
ellos / ellas / Uds.					

C. **Double Object Pronouns.** Sustituya (*Substitute*) los complementos directos e (*and*) indirectos por sus respectivos pronombres.

MODELO: Alberto le sirvió café a Jimena. → Alberto se lo sirvió.

1. Ricardo le pidió dinero a su padre.   Ricardo _____ _____ pidió.
2. Clara le sugirió la idea a Enrique.   Clara _____ _____ sugirió.
3. Carmen les puso los suéteres a sus hijos.   Carmen _____ _____ puso.

PRUEBA CORTA

A. ¿Qué pasó? Complete las oraciones con la forma correcta del pretérito de un verbo de la lista.

conseguir	dormir	reírse
despedirse	hacer	traer
divertirse	ponerse	vestirse

1. Cuando vimos esa película todos (nosotros) _____ mucho.

2. Después de comer ese pescado, Martín _____ enfermo y se acostó, pero no

   _____ en toda la noche.

3. Yo _____ un boleto extra para el concierto de mañana. ¿Quieres ir?

4. Marcos _____ de sus amigos y volvió a su casa.

5. Para celebrar el Año Nuevo, Mirasol _____ con ropa elegante: pantalones negros

   y una blusa de seda. Ella _____ muchísimo bailando con sus amigos.

6. Para celebrar el Año Nuevo, nosotros _____ una fiesta y unos amigos nos

   _____ champán.

B. Preguntas y respuestas. Conteste las preguntas con la respuesta más apropiada.

1. ¿Cuándo nos traes el café?

   a. Se lo traigo en seguida (*right away*).
   b. Te los traigo en seguida.
   c. Te lo traigo en seguida.

2. ¿Cuándo me van a lavar (*wash*) el coche?

   a. Se lo vamos a lavar esta tarde.
   b. Me lo voy a lavar esta tarde.
   c. Te lo voy a lavar esta tarde.

3. ¿Quién te sacó estas fotos?

   a. Julio me los sacó.
   b. Julio te las sacó.
   c. Julio me las sacó.

4. ¿Quién les mandó estas flores a Uds.?

   a. Ceci nos los mandó.
   b. Ceci nos las mandó.
   c. Ceci se las mandó.

5. ¿A quién le vas a regalar esa camisa?

   a. Te la voy a regalar a ti.
   b. Se lo voy a regalar a Uds.
   c. Me las vas a regalar a mí.

6. ¿A quién le sirves ese vino?

   a. Se los sirvo a Uds.
   b. Se lo sirvo a Uds.
   c. Mario nos lo sirve.

C. Preparativos para la fiesta de Gilberto. Va a oír algunas preguntas sobre el cumpleaños de Gilberto. Escoja la letra de la mejor respuesta para cada pregunta. Preste (*Pay*) atención a los pronombres y los complementos directos que oye en las preguntas.

1. **a.** Sí, voy a mandártela. **b.** Sí, voy a mandártelos.
2. **a.** Sí, se lo tengo que hacer. **b.** Sí, te lo tengo que hacer.
3. **a.** Sí, nos los van a traer. **b.** Sí, se los voy a traer.
4. **a.** No, no van a traértelas. **b.** No, no van a traérmelas.
5. **a.** Sí, te las sirvo. **b.** Sí, se las sirvo.

D. El cumpleaños de Gilberto. Imagine que Ud. le hizo una fiesta de sorpresa para su cumpleaños a su amigo Gilberto. Cuando oiga el sujeto, forme oraciones con las palabras que se dan. Use el pretérito de los verbos. Luego escuche la respuesta correcta y repítala. ¡OJO! Si el sujeto es un pronombre de sujeto, no lo use.

MODELO:	(Ud. ve)	**1.** hacerle una fiesta de sorpresa a Gilberto
	(Ud. oye)	Uno: yo
	(Ud. dice)	Le hice una fiesta de sorpresa a Gilberto.
	(Ud. oye y repite)	Le hice una fiesta de sorpresa a Gilberto.

2. venir
3. querer venir, pero no poder
4. traer o mandar regalos
5. tener que preparar todo
6. servir los refrescos
7. contar chistes como siempre
8. divertirse y reírse
9. quejarse
10. tener que bailar con todas las muchachas
11. ¡ponerse muy nervioso!

PUNTOS PERSONALES

❖ **A. Ud. y las fiestas.** Conteste las preguntas con oraciones completas.

1. ¿Cómo celebra Ud. el Día de Acción de Gracias?

_____

2. ¿Qué hace Ud. para celebrar la Nochevieja? ¿Se queda en casa o va a algún lugar?

_____

3. ¿Hace algo para celebrar el Día de San Patricio?

_____

4. ¿Celebra Ud. la Pascua?

_____

5. En su familia, ¿se gasta mucho dinero para los regalos de Navidad o Janucá (*Hanukkah*)?

_____

Nombre _____ Fecha _____ Clase _____

❖ **B. Reacciones.** ¿Cómo reacciona o cómo se pone Ud. en estas circunstancias? Use por lo menos uno de los verbos útiles en cada respuesta. Puede usar la forma enfática (**-ísimo/a**) de los adjetivos.

Verbos útiles

enojarse   quejarse
llorar   reírse
ponerse contento/a (avergonzado/a, enojado/a, feliz, triste)   sonreír

1. Alguien le hace una broma un poco pesada (*in bad taste*).

   _____

2. Alguien le cuenta un chiste gracioso (*funny*).

   _____

3. En un restaurante le traen a Ud. la cuenta y ve que no tiene su cartera (*wallet*).

   _____

4. Ud. acaba de oír que su perro (gato) murió (*died*) en un accidente.

   _____

5. Le sirven una comida malísima en un restaurante muy caro.

   _____

6. Ud. acaba de saber que recibió la nota (*grade*) más alta de la clase en el examen de historia.

   _____

❖ **C. ¿Qué pasó la última vez que... ?** Conteste estas preguntas con oraciones completas.

1. La última vez que Ud. se enfermó, ¿tuvo que guardar cama (*stay in bed*)? ¿Cuánto tiempo?

   _____

2. La última vez que Ud. y su familia celebraron algo especial, ¿vinieron de lejos (*from far away*) algunos parientes (tíos, abuelos, hermanos)? ¿Quién vino y de dónde vino? ¿O no vino de lejos ningún pariente?

   Para celebrar _____ , _____

3. ¿Pudo Ud. contestar todas las preguntas del último examen de español? ¿Fue fácil o difícil el examen?

   _____

4. ¿Conoció Ud. a alguien durante sus últimas vacaciones? ¿A quién conoció?

   _____

D. Días de fiesta

Paso 1. Ud. va a escuchar una entrevista en la que (*in which*) Karina (de Venezuela), Rubén (de España) y Miguel René (de México) hablan de las fiestas que celebran. Primero, escuche el **Vocabulario útil,** luego escuche la entrevista una vez para tener una idea general de su contenido (*content*). Después, escuche la entrevista otra vez (*again*). Mientras la escucha, empareje (*match*) la letra del nombre de cada persona (**K** = Karina, **R** = Rubén, **MR** = Miguel René) con la oración apropiada.

Karina

Rubén

Miguel René

Vocabulario útil

la boda	wedding
el bautizo	baptism
el Día de Muertos	Day of the Dead (Nov. 2)
festejar	celebrar
entregar	dar
la bendición	blessing

1. _____ Su familia celebra los Carnavales.

2. _____ Su familia celebra el Día de Muertos.

3. _____ En su país el Niño Jesús trae regalos.

4. _____ En su país, hay diferencias entre las tradiciones navideñas del norte y las del sur.

5. _____ En su país, en Nochebuena viene Papá Noel

6. _____ y _____ (¡OJO! dos personas) En sus países los Reyes Magos (*Magi*) vienen con regalos el 6 de enero.

❖ **Paso 2.** Ahora, escuche la primera pregunta que se hace, y contéstela por escrito.

❖ **E. Guided Composition.** En hoja aparte (*On a separate sheet of paper*), conteste las siguientes preguntas sobre su último cumpleaños. Luego organice y combine sus respuestas en una composición. Recuerde usar palabras conectivas como, por ejemplo, **por eso, como...** , (*since . . .*), **porque, aunque** (*although*) y **luego.**

1. ¿Cuántos años cumplió en su último (*last*) cumpleaños?
2. ¿Qué hizo para celebrarlo?
3. ¿Dio una fiesta? ¿Salió con su pareja (*partner*), amigos y/o con su familia?
4. ¿Qué comidas y bebidas se sirvieron?
5. ¿Se sirvió un pastel de cumpleaños?
6. ¿Qué le regalaron sus amigos y su familia?
7. ¿Se divirtió en el día de su cumpleaños?

❖ F. **Mi diario.** En su diario, escriba sobre el día festivo más importante para su familia o sus amigos. ¿Cuándo se celebra? ¿Se celebra con una cena especial o con una fiesta? ¿Dónde se celebra? ¿Quiénes asisten? ¿Qué comidas y bebidas se sirven? ¿Es una actividad cooperativa la preparación de la comida? ¿O lo prepara todo una sola persona? ¿Cuáles son las costumbres (*customs*) y tradiciones más importantes relacionadas con este día festivo?

Vocabulario útil

dar las doce	to strike twelve	**el globo**	balloon
decorar el árbol		**normalmente**	normally
los fuegos artificiales	fireworks		

G. **Intercambios.** Escuche las siguientes preguntas y contéstelas por escrito (*in writing*).

1. _____

   _____

2. _____

   _____

3. _____

   _____

4. _____

   _____

5. _____

   _____

APPENDIX 2: ANSWER KEY

CAPÍTULO 10: EL TIEMPO LIBRE

VOCABULARIO: Preparación

Los pasatiempos, diversiones y aficiones

A. **1.** el golf **2.** el basquetbol **3.** el fútbol **4.** el ciclismo **5.** el tenis **6.** el béisbol

B. **1.** Está paseando en bicicleta. **2.** Está patinando en línea. **3.** Está nadando (en la piscina). (Está haciendo natación.) **4.** Está jugando al fútbol. **5.** Están haciendo un picnic. **6.** Está dando un paseo (con su perro). **7.** Están corriendo.

E. **Paso 2.** **1.** Bogotá **2.** Colombia **3.** juega **4.** liga **5.** fines **6.** equipo **7.** fueron **8.** natación **9.** selección **10.** mundial **11.** maestro

Los quehaceres domésticos

A. **1.** Está lavando los platos. **2.** Está barriendo el piso. **3.** Está haciendo la cama **4.** Está pasando la aspiradora.

B. **1.** La estufa se usa para cocinar. **2.** El café se prepara en la cafetera. **3.** Lavamos la ropa. **4.** Para lavar los platos usamos el lavaplatos. **5.** No, usamos la aspiradora. **6.** Tostamos el pan en la tostadora. **7.** Usamos el horno de microondas.

PRONUNCIACIÓN: *p* and *t*

C. **Paso 1.** **1.** Paco toca el piano para sus parientes. **2.** Los tíos de Tito son de Puerto Rico. **3.** ¿Por qué pagas tanto por la ropa? **4.** Tito trabaja para el padre de Pepe.

GRAMÁTICA

¿Recuerda Ud.? Paso 1. **1.** me desperté **2.** me duché **3.** me vestí **4.** salí **5.** tuve **6.** pude **7.** dejé
Paso 2. 1. se despertó **2.** se duchó **3.** se vistió **4.** salió **5.** tuvo **6.** pudo **7.** dejó

27. Talking About the Past (Part 4) • Descriptions and Habitual Actions in the Past: Imperfect of Regular and Irregular Verbs

A. *cantar:* cantabas / cantábamos / cantaban *tener:* tenía / tenía / tenían *salir:* salía / salías / salíamos *ser:* eras / era / eran *ir:* iba / iba / íbamos *ver:* veía / veías / veíamos / veían

B. **1.** tenía **2.** vivíamos **3.** Iba **4.** volvía **5.** prefería **6.** venían **7.** era **8.** celebrábamos **9.** hacía **10.** cocinaba **11.** visitaban **12.** se quedaban **13.** dormíamos **14.** nos acostábamos **15.** había **16.** pasábamos **17.** eran

C. **1.** Antes tenía menos independencia. Ahora se siente más libre. **2.** Antes dependía de su esposo. Ahora tiene más independencia económica. **3.** Antes se quedaba en casa. Ahora prefiere salir a trabajar. **4.** Antes solo pensaba en casarse. Ahora piensa en seguir su propia carrera. **5.** Antes pasaba horas cocinando. Ahora sirve comidas más fáciles de preparar. **6.** Antes su esposo se sentaba a leer el periódico. Ahora (su esposo) la ayuda con los quehaceres domésticos.

D. **1.** éramos / veíamos / venían / íbamos **2.** estábamos / daban / saludaban / despedían **3.** almorzaba / Servían / veían / llevaban / traían / comía

E. Paso 1. *Gustavo:* estar en el aeropuerto, ir a San Juan, sentirse triste. *La madre de Gustavo:* estar en el aeropuerto, estar nerviosísima. *El padre de Gustavo:* estar en el aeropuerto, estar preocupado

¿Recuerda Ud.? **1.** d **2.** e **3.** a **4.** b **5.** f **6.** c **7.** g

28. Getting Information (Part 2) • Summary of Interrogative Words

A. **1.** ¿Cómo se llama Ud.? **2.** ¿De dónde es Ud.? **3.** ¿Dónde vive Ud.? **4.** ¿Adónde va Ud. ahora? **5.** ¿Qué va a hacer? **6.** ¿Cuáles son sus pasatiempos favoritos? **7.** ¿Cuándo empezó a jugar? **8.** ¿Quiénes son sus jugadores preferidos? **9.** ¿Por qué (son sus preferidos)?

B. **1.** Cómo **2.** Qué **3.** Quién **4.** De dónde **5.** cuántos **6.** Cómo **7.** Cuándo **8.** Por qué **9.** cómo **10.** Qué

C. (*Possible answers*) **1.** ¿Por qué hace frío en la Argentina en agosto? **2.** ¿Qué ropa llevan las chicas? **3.** ¿Sabían ellas que era invierno en la Argentina? **4.** ¿Cuáles son los meses de invierno? **5.** ¿Qué piensan comprar el próximo día?

¿Recuerda Ud.? **1.** ...tanto dinero como... **2.** ...tantas clases como... **3.** ...tanto como... **4.** ...más dinero que... **5.** ...menos clases que... / ...más clases que... **6.** ...mayor que.../ ...menores que...

29. Expressing Extremes • Superlatives

A. (*Opinions will vary.*) **1.** El béisbol es el más emocionante de todos. **2.** Kobe Bryant es el mejor jugador del mundo. **3.** El equipo de los Dallas Cowboys es el peor equipo de todos. **4.** El estadio de Río de Janeiro es el más grande del mundo.

B. **1.** el Carnaval **2.** mayo **3.** patinar en línea **4.** *Diarios de motocicleta* **5.** pasar la aspiradora

UN POCO DE TODO

A. **1.** pasaba **2.** esquiando **3.** conoció **4.** visitaba **5.** vivían **6.** esquiaba **7.** estaba **8.** vio **9.** Dobló **10.** perdió **11.** se puso **12.** Te hiciste **13.** esperando **14.** sacudiéndose **15.** sonriendo **16.** se hicieron

B. Después de escuchar. **1.** F (*Possible correction*) No todos los hispanos tienen otra casa fuera de la ciudad. **2.** F (*Possible correction*) Normalmente los abuelos de una familia hispana (sí) pasan tiempo con sus hijos y nietos. **3.** F (*Possible correction*) La comida dura dos o tres horas porque mientras comen, los miembros de la familia charlan. **4.** C

CULTURA

A. **1.** Puerto Rico **2.** San Juan

B. **1.** libre / playa **2.** acuáticos **3.** dominó **4.** sobremesa **5.** polo **6.** taínos / españoles **7.** española / colonial **8.** boricua **9.** coquí

PÓNGASE A PRUEBA

A. **1.** *cantar:* cantábamos *ir:* iba / íbamos *leer:* leía / leíamos *ser:* era / éramos *ver:* veía / veíamos **2.** **1.** d **2.** e **3.** c **4.** b **5.** f **6.** a

B. **1.** Qué **2.** Cuál **3.** Cuáles **4.** Qué **5.** Cuál

C. **1.** Soy la persona más feliz del mundo. **2.** Son los mejores jugadores del equipo. **3.** Es el peor estudiante de la clase.

PRUEBA CORTA

A. **1.** era **2.** asistía **3.** estaba **4.** ayudaba **5.** vivían **6.** iban **7.** jugaban **8.** servía **9.** se cansaban **10.** volvían

B. **1.** Adónde **2.** Quién **3.** Cómo **4.** Dónde **5.** Cuál **6.** Cuánto

C. **1.** ...el mejor jugador del... **2.** ...los (las) mejores estudiantes de la... **3.** ...el peor día de... **4.** ...la mejor película del... **5.** ...el deporte más emocionante de...

PUNTOS PERSONALES

D. Paso 1. *Rubén:* dormir, ir al cine, leer; *Karina:* bailar, ir de compras, leer; *Tané:* descansar, dormir, ver sus fotos; *Miguel René:* hablar con sus amigos, ir a tomar un café, ir a un bar, ir al cine, leer, salir con sus amigos

CAPÍTULO 11: LA SALUD

VOCABULARIO: Preparación

La salud y el bienestar

A. **1.** la boca / el cerebro **2.** los ojos / los oídos **3.** los pulmones / la nariz (la boca) **4.** el corazón **5.** la garganta **6.** el estómago **7.** los dientes

D. *Answers will vary. Some possibilities:* **1.** **a.** Hace ejercicio. **b.** Lleva una vida sana. **c.** Sí, (No, no) hago tanto ejercicio como ella. **2.** **a.** No, no se cuida mucho. **b.** Debe dejar de fumar. **c.** Sí, debe hacer más ejercicio.

E. Paso 1.

PERSONA	DEPORTE(S)	RAZÓN POR LA CUAL SE PRACTICA
Clara	correr	puedes hacerlo con amigos; a veces es emocionante
Antonio	todo tipo de deporte, especialmente el tenis	es entretenido y tiene mucha acción
Gabriela	yoga	es buenísimo para todo el cuerpo
Patricia	el tenis	es bueno para la salud
Teresa	caminar, nadar	son excelentes para todo el cuerpo; no permiten que uno se engorde
José	el fútbol	es saludable, divertido y muy emocionante
Xiomara	levantar pesas, nadar	son importantes para mantenerse en forma
Erick	nadar, hacer ejercicios aeróbicos	sirven de ejercicio físico y mental

Paso 2. **1.** nadar (la natación) **2.** seis (6)

F. ¿Una vida sana? **1.** T, MR **2.** T, K **3.** T, K, MR **4.** R, K **5.** MR **6.** K, R, T, MR

En el consultorio del médico

A. **1.** **a.** Está en el consultorio del médico. **b.** Le toma la temperatura. **c.** Le va a poner una inyección. **2.** **a.** Tiene dolor de cabeza y dolor de estómago. **b.** Le hace preguntas sobre su salud. **c.** Se lava las manos.

B. **1.** abrir la boca / sacar la lengua **2.** comer comidas sanas / cuidarnos / dormir lo suficiente / hacer ejercicio **3.** respirar / fiebre (tos) / tos (fiebre) **4.** jarabe **5.** llevar lentes **6.** antibióticos

D. Paso 1. *(Possible answers)* **1.** Darío tiene dolor de estómago. (A Darío le duele el estómago) **2.** Rebeca tiene fiebre. **3.** Toño tiene dolor de muela. (A Toño le duele la (una) muela (el/un diente.) (A Toño le duelen los dientes.) **4.** Gabi está mareada.

E. (*Possible answers*) **1.** Los síntomas de Juan Carlos son dolor de garganta y está resfriado. **2.** Fue al médico esta mañana. **3.** (El médico) Le recetó un antibiótico. **4.** (Si toma el jarabe) Juan Carlos (Él) no puede manejar. **5.** (Al llegar a casa) Juan Carlos (Él) va a acostarse y dormir.

GRAMÁTICA

¿Recuerda Ud.?

A. 1. nos cuidábamos / nos cuidamos **2.** comíamos / comimos **3.** hacía / hice **4.** eras / fuiste **5.** decían / dijeron **6.** sabía / supe **7.** jugaba / jugué **8.** iba / fue **9.** ponía / puso **10.** venías / viniste

B. 1. I **2.** I **3.** I **4.** P

30. Narrating in the Past (Part 5) • Using the Preterite and the Imperfect

A. 1. Eran **2.** llegué **3.** entró **4.** tenía **5.** dije **6.** dolían **7.** examinó **8.** dijo **9.** era **10.** dio **11.** sentía

B. 1. compré **2.** quería **3.** quería **4.** me desperté **5.** facturé **6.** estaba

C. 1. T **2.** MR **3.** R **4.** K **5.** T **6.** R **7.** K **8.** MR **9.** R **10.** MR **11.** T **12.** K

D. 1. a / b **2.** b /a **3.** b / a **4.** b/ a **5.** a / b **6.** b / a **7.** a / b

E. Paso 1. 1. imperfect **2.** preterite **3.** imperfect **4.** preterite **5.** imperfect **6.** preterite **7.** imperfect

Paso 2. 1. tenía **2.** vivía **3.** asistía **4.** trabajaba **5.** se quedaba **6.** viajaron **7.** nos quedamos **8.** iba **9.** se rompió **10.** supieron **11.** querían **12.** aseguró **13.** estaba

F. 1. supimos / tuvo **2.** se sentía / iba **3.** pudo / fue **4.** pude / tenía **5.** estuve / estaba **6.** iba

H. 1. Los niños se estaban pegando (estaban pegándose) cuando su madre los vio. **2.** Graciela estaba durmiendo cuando sonó el teléfono. **3.** Yo me estaba despidiendo (estaba despidiéndome) de Raúl cuando entraste. (Raúl se estaba despidiendo [estaba despidiéndose] de mí cuando entraste.)

I. 1. se despertó **2.** dijo **3.** se sentía **4.** pudo **5.** dolía **6.** hizo **7.** Estaba **8.** temía **9.** examinó **10.** dijo **11.** era **12.** estaba **13.** debía **14.** dio **15.** llegó **16.** se sentía

¿Recuerda Ud.? 1. Qué / que **2.** quién / que **3.** lo que **4.** Lo que

31. Recognizing *que, quien(es), lo que* • Relative Pronouns

A. 1. lo que **2.** que **3.** lo que **4.** quien **5.** quienes **6.** que

B. 1. que **2.** que / que **3.** quien **4.** quienes **5.** quienes **6.** que / quien **7.** lo que

C. 1. Esa es la doctora que me cuidó cuando me resfrié gravemente. **2.** Aquella es la paciente de quien te hablaba ayer. **3.** Esa es Susana Preciado, con quien compartí mi cuarto. **4.** Estas son las flores que me mandaron al hospital. **5.** ¡Esta es la cuenta que recibí hoy!

¿Recuerda Ud.? 1. me **2.** te **3.** se **4.** nos **5.** se

32. Expressing *each other* • Reciprocal Actions with Reflexive Pronouns

A. (*Possible answers*) **1.** Entre el profesor y los estudiantes **2.** Entre el profesor y los estudiantes **3.** Entre los estudiantes **4.** Entre los estudiantes **5.** Entre los estudiantes **6.** Entre los estudiantes **7.** Entre el profesor y los estudiantes

B. Paso 2. 2. Francisco y Raúl (Ellos) también se mandan mensajes. **3.** El Sr. Barrios y la Srta. Castán (Ellos) se saludan. **4.** Isabel y Paco (Ellos) se miran.

UN POCO DE TODO

A. **1.** fue **2.** tuve **3.** estuve **4.** me levanté **5.** sentía **6.** quería (quise) **7.** se puso (se ponía) **8.** dolía **9.** dormí **10.** empecé **11.** llamaste **12.** los **13.** conocía **14.** llamé **15.** a **16.** llamó **17.** llevaron **18.** lo **19.** despertaba (despertaron) **20.** lo **21.** el **22.** hablaba **23.** el

B. **Después de escuchar.** **1.** F: (*Possible answer*) El sistema médico más común en los países hispanos no es el sistema privado. (El sistema médico más común en los países hispanos es el sistema público o el sistema de medicina socializada.) **2.** F: (*Possible answer*) El gobierno controla el sistema médico en muchos países hispanos. **3.** C **4.** C

C. **Paso 2.** **1.** dolor de cabeza **2.** estoy muy cansado/a **3.** el lunes pasado **4.** no tengo fiebre

CULTURA

A. **1.** Venezuela **2.** Caracas

B. **1.** público **2.** social **3.** pagar **4.** privada **5.** barato **6.** (la) Argentina / Cuba / Costa Rica **7.** largas **8.** Miss Universo / Miss Mundo **9.** tortilla

PÓNGASE A PRUEBA

A. **1.** I **2.** P **3.** I **4.** I **5.** I

B. **1. a.** quien(es) **b.** que **c.** lo que **2.** **1.** c **2.** b **3.** a **4.** a **5.** b

C. **1.** Mi novio/a y yo nos queremos. **2.** Mi mejor amigo y yo nos conocemos bien. **3.** Marta y sus padres se llaman todos los domingos.

PRUEBA CORTA

A. **1.** era **2.** tenía **3.** pagaban **4.** preguntó **5.** quería **6.** pude **7.** me dieron **8.** creían **9.** era **10.** tenía **11.** conseguí **12.** empecé

B. **1.** que **2.** quien **3.** lo que **4.** quien **5.** que

C. **1.** se despiden / se dan **2.** se hablan **3.** se respetan **4.** se ven **5.** se ayudan

CAPÍTULO 12: CONECTAD@S

VOCABULARIO: Preparación

La ciudad y el barrio

A. **1.** alquilar **2.** dirección **3.** barrio **4.** alquiler **5.** piso **6.** ascensor **7.** vista **8.** centro **9.** afueras **10.** ancianos **11.** inquilinos **12.** electricidad (calefacción) **13.** calefacción (electricidad) **14.** dueños **15.** portero **16.** planta baja **17.** vecinos

D. **Paso 1.** **1.** b **2.** d **3.** g **4.** e **5.** a **6.** c **7.** f **8.** h

Paso 2. **1.** bienes raíces **2.** San José **3.** mostrar **4.** trámites **5.** vivienda **6.** centro **7.** apartamentos **8.** amueblados **9.** patio **10.** aves

Tengo... Necesito... Quiero... (Part 3)

A. **1.** correo electrónico **2.** pantalla / remoto **3.** guardar **4.** fotocopia **5.** grabar **6.** bajar / imprimir

B. **1.** falló / almacenar **2.** DVD **3.** cámara / impresora **4.** entrar en Facebook / contraseña **5.** teléfono fijo / buzón de voz **6.** descargué / app **7.** GPS / paradas

C. **1.** jefa / aumento / cambiar de trabajo / conseguir **2.** sueldo **3.** falló **4.** manejar / funcionaba

GRAMÁTICA

¿Recuerda Ud.?

A. **2.** Escríbanlo / lo escriban   **3.** Juéguelo / lo juegue   **4.** Dígamelo / me lo diga   **5.** Dénselo / se lo den

B. **1.** No se vayan todavía.   **2.** Consiga otro trabajo.   **3.** No se cansen.   **4.** No se olvide.

33. Influencing Others (Part 2) • *Tú* (Informal) Commands

A. **1.** Sube   **2.** cambies   **3.** uses / usa   **4.** Apaga   **5.** te quejes   **6.** le mandes / mándale   **7.** Préstame   **8.** Dime / me digas

B. (*Possible answers*)   **1.** juegues en la sala   **2.** deja de mandar mensajes   **3.** llegues tarde   **4.** vístete bien (mejor)   **5.** lávate las manos antes de comer   **6.** seas pesado   **7.** pongas los pies en el sofá   **8.** toques la pantalla   **9.** ten cuidado al cruzar la calle

C. **1.** ponla / no la pongas   **2.** sírvesela / no se la sirvas   **3.** tráemela / no me la traigas   **4.** lávamelos / no me los laves

34. Expressing Subjective Actions or States • Present Subjunctive (Part 1): An Introduction

A. lleguemos / empiece / conozcamos / juegue / consigamos / divirtamos / duerma

B. **1.** a, c   **2.** b, c   **3.** a, b   **4.** a, b   **5.** a, c   **6.** b, c

C. **1.** pueda / olvide / sepa   **2.** empiecen / manden / digan   **3.** llegues / seas / busques   **4.** vayamos / alquilemos / perdamos

D. **Paso 1.** *su hermana:* no usar su coche, prestarle su iPad; *su hermano menor:* bajarle el volumen a su música; *sus hermanitos:* no jugar con su Wii hasta las doce de la noche

35. Expressing Desires and Requests • Use of the Subjunctive (Part 2): Influence

A. **Paso 1.** **1.** digan la verdad / lleguen a tiempo / acepten responsabilidad / sepan usar la computadora / no entren en Facebook en el trabajo   **2.** resulte interesante / me guste / no esté lejos de casa / me dé oportunidades para avanzar

Paso 2. **1.** trabajemos / trabajar   **2.** almorcemos / almorzar   **3.** traer / traigamos   **4.** pidamos / pedir   **5.** obtengo / obtenga

B. **1.** se lo mandes   **2.** pedírselo   **3.** buscarlo   **4.** lo empiece   **5.** me lo traiga

C. **1.** ¿Qué quieres que traiga?   **2.** ¿Qué quieres que prepare?   **3.** ¿Qué quieres que busque?   **4.** ¿Qué quieres que cocine?

F. **Paso 1.** **1.** puedas   **2.** sea

Paso 2. **1.** venga   **2.** escriba   **3.** cuidar   **4.** sea

UN POCO DE TODO

A. **1.** mudarse   **2.** les   **3.** está   **4.** usar   **5.** que   **6.** sus   **7.** ayuden   **8.** les   **9.** vengan   **10.** enseñarles   **11.** funciona   **12.** vayas   **13.** ve   **14.** ponte   **15.** te olvides   **16.** te quedes

B. **Después de escuchar.** *You should have checked the numbers 2 and 5.*

C. **Paso 1.** **1.** quieran   **2.** estés   **3.** (te) alejes   **4.** pueda

Paso 2. **1.** Busco un apartamento amueblado con dos cuartos.   **2.** Pues, no tengo coche. Por eso es necesario que yo encuentre un apartamento en el centro.   **3.** Necesito que el apartamento esté cerca de la universidad.   **4.** Sí, claro. Cuanto antes, mejor.   **5.** A mi celular, por favor.   **6.** Sí, muy bien. Gracias. Hasta luego.

CULTURA

A. **1.** Colombia **2.** Bogotá **3.** Cartagena **4.** Medellín

B. **1.** conocen **2.** fiestas **3.** nombres **4.** social **5.** trabajan **6.** mayores (ancianas) **7.** plaza **8.** metro **9.** sur **10.** la Ciudad de México (México, D.F.) **11.** estaciones (paradas) **12.** cumbia **13.** orquídea **14.** Juan Valdez

PÓNGASE A PRUEBA

A. *decir:* di; *escribir:* no escribas; *hacer:* haz / no hagas; *ir:* ve / no vayas; *salir:* sal / no salgas; *ser:* sé / no seas; *tener:* no tengas; *trabajar:* trabaja

B. **1. a.** busque **b.** dé **c.** escriba **d.** esté **e.** estudie **f.** vaya **g.** oiga **h.** pueda **i.** sepa **j.** sea **k.** traiga **l.** viva **2.** *comenzar:* comience / comencemos; *dormir:* durmamos; *perder:* pierda; *sentirse:* sienta / sintamos

C. **1.** prefiere / vengan **2.** Es / comience **3.** prohíbe / entremos **4.** insisten / se queden **5.** Es / traigas

PRUEBA CORTA

A. **1.** Ven **2.** apagues **3.** Llama / dile **4.** pongas / ponla **5.** te preocupes / descansa

B. **1.** busques **2.** comprar **3.** vayamos **4.** hablar / hablemos **5.** compres / pierdas

CAPÍTULO 13: EL ARTE Y LA CULTURA

VOCABULARIO: Preparación

Las artes

A. Paso 1. **2.** directora **3.** arquitecta **4.** cantante **5.** pintor (artista) **6.** escultora (artista) **7.** director (de orquesta) **8.** músico

B. Paso 1. **1.** escritora / novelista **2.** fotógrafo **3.** dramaturga **4.** el guion **5.** compositor **6.** poeta **7.** música **8.** la obra maestra

C. **1.** Gabriel García Márquez escribió *Cien años de soledad.* **2.** Diego Rivera pintó murales. **3.** Plácido Domingo cantó óperas italianas. **4.** Guillermo del Toro dirigió *El laberinto del fauno.* **5.** Frank Gehry diseñó casas y museos muy modernos.

D. Paso 1. **1.** K **2.** T **3.** MR **4.** K **5.** T

Paso 2. **1.** escritor **2.** pintor (moderno) **3.** escritor poeta **4.** compositor **5.** poeta, ensayista, dramaturgo

Ranking Things: Ordinals

A. **1.** primera **2.** cuarto **3.** segundo **4.** Primero / Quinto **5.** Tercero / Cuarto **6.** Octavo / segunda / quinta **7.** Décimo **8.** primer **9.** noveno

C. Paso 2. (*Possible answers*) **1.** Junio es el sexto mes del año. (El sexto mes del año es junio.) **2.** Agosto es el octavo mes del año. (El octavo mes del año es agosto.) **3.** El primer día de la semana en el calendario hispánico es (el) lunes. (El lunes es el primer día de la semana en el calendario hispánico.)

PRONUNCIACIÓN: *y* and *ll*

C. **1.** Aquella mujer se llama Yolanda. **2.** La señorita Camillo es de Castilla. **3.** ¿Llueve o no llueve allá en Yucatán? **4.** El señor Muñoz es de España y habla español.

GRAMÁTICA

¿Recuerda Ud.?

1. a. sentarme **b.** que / se sienten   **2. a.** estar **b.** que / estés   **3. a.** venir **b.** que / venga

36. Expressing Feelings • Use of the Subjunctive (Part 3): Emotion

A. 1. Me alegro de que (nosotros) vayamos al museo esta tarde.   **2.** Espero que (ellos) vendan entradas con precios rebajados para estudiantes.   **3.** Siento que tus amigos no puedan venir.   **4.** Es una lástima que el museo no muestre más obras de Frida Kahlo.   **5.** Es extraño que no exhiban más esculturas indígenas.

B. 1. Es una lástima que mis amigos no puedan salir con nosotros.   **2.** Me sorprende que ellos no vayan nunca al teatro.   **3.** Espero que sepas dónde está el teatro.   **4.** Temo que haya mucho tráfico a estas horas.   **5.** Me molesta que estas entradas sean tan caras.

E. 1. Es una lástima que Juanes no cante esta noche.   **2.** Es terrible pagar tanto por las entradas al espectáculo.   **3.** Me sorprende que tú no conozcas las novelas de García Márquez.   **4.** Sentimos no poder ayudarlos a Uds.   **5.** Me molesta que haya tanta gente que habla durante una película.   **6.** Es absurdo que algunos actores y atletas ganen tanto dinero.

37. Expressing Uncertainty • Use of the Subjunctive (Part 4): Doubt and Denial

A. 1. I **2.** S **3.** S **4.** I **5.** S **6.** I **7.** S **8.** S

B. 1. Dudo que a mis amigos les encante el *jazz*.   **2.** Creo que el museo está abierto los domingos.   **3.** No estoy seguro/a de que todos los niños tengan talento artístico.   **4.** No es cierto que mi profesor vaya al teatro todas las semanas.   **5.** No creo que mi profesor siempre exprese su opinión personal.

C. 1. Creo que hoy vamos a visitar el Museo del Prado.   **2.** Es probable que lleguemos temprano.   **3.** Estoy seguro/a de que hay precios especiales para estudiantes.   **4.** Es probable que tengamos que dejar nuestras mochilas en la entrada del museo.   **5.** Dudo que podamos ver todas las obras de Velázquez.   **6.** Creo que los guardias van a prohibir que saquemos fotos.   **7.** ¿Es posible que volvamos a visitar el museo mañana?

F. Paso 1. 1. pintor **2.** Bolivia **3.** abstractos / emociones **4.** padres **5.** hermanos

38. Expressing Influence, Emotion, Doubt, and Denial • The Subjunctive (Part 5): A Summary

A. 1. ofrezca (Negación) **2.** sean (Emoción) **3.** sepas (Emoción) **4.** haya (Duda) **5.** permitan / paguemos (Emoción / Influencia) **6.** empaqueten (Influencia)

B. 1. apagues / pagar **2.** es / sepa / es **3.** estés / te sientas **4.** hablemos / tratemos / hacerlo **5.** estudies / guste / hagas **6.** estaciones / caminar **7.** empieza / recuerde

C. 1. Les sorprende que desee estudiar para ser bailarina.   **2.** Les molesta que vuelvan tarde de las fiestas.   **3.** Le prohíben a Carlitos que juegue en la calle con sus amigos.   **4.** No les gusta que vaya de viaje con su novia y otros amigos.   **5.** Se oponen a que busque un apartamento para vivir con otra amiga.   **6.** Temen que quiera ser músico.   **7.** Dudan que sean una influencia positiva.

F. 1. interesa **2.** ir **3.** pueda **4.** sea **5.** salga

UN POCO DE TODO

A. Paso 1. 1. antropología física / lingüística / arqueología **2.** investiga **3.** capacidad **4.** iguales **5.** culturas **6.** vivir

B. Después de escuchar. 1. C **2.** F: (*Possible answer*) Las cooperativas artesanas ayudan a las tejedoras a conseguir precios buenos.   **3.** ND **4.** F: (*Possible answer*) Chaska y las otras tejedoras usan lana para hacer bufandas, bolsos y cinturones.   **5.** F: (*Possible answer*) El tejer es un oficio principalmente de las mujeres.   **6.** C

C. Paso 1. (*Possible answers*) **1.** Ellos van a ir al Museo de Arte Moderno el (próximo) sábado. **2.** Varios artistas mexicanos del siglo XX (veinte) están representados en el museo. **3.** Hay una colección de esculturas en el jardín. **4.** Hay un mural (de Orozco). **5.** Ella está segura de que va a haber mucha gente porque las familias van los sábados al Bosque de Chapultepec. **6.** Lupe desea que no llueva el sábado.

Paso 2. **1.** vayamos a un concierto de música clásica. **2.** es más emocionante **3.** haya entradas

CULTURA

A. **1.** (el) Ecuador **2.** Quito **3.** Bolivia **4.** La Paz **5.** Sucre

B. **1.** cultura / Quito / museo / pintor (artista) **2.** publica / escritores **3.** Prado / pintores (artistas) / Antropología / artesanía **4.** indígena / variedad / Bolivia / Islas / Ecuador

PÓNGASE A PRUEBA

A. **1.** llegues **2.** estén **3.** veamos **4.** puedan **5.** se aburran

B. **1.** sea **2.** es **3.** sepas **4.** guste **5.** dicen

C. **1.** atrae (Es cierto que) **2.** haya (Me alegro de que) **3.** vayan (Dudamos que) **4.** estudien (Los padres quieren que) **5.** consigamos (Es una lástima que) **6.** lleguen (Les recomiendo que) **7.** cocine (Mi padre no cree que)

PRUEBA CORTA

A. **1.** Espero que Uds. puedan acompañarnos al mercado esta tarde. **2.** Quiero comprar algunos recuerdos de nuestro viaje. **3.** Es probable que Julia no vaya con nosotros. **4.** Es una lástima que pierda esta oportunidad de visitar este mercado. **5.** No creo que el mercado esté abierto los domingos. **6.** Me sorprende que Marcos no esté aquí. **7.** Es posible que encontremos a Marcos luego. **8.** Es obvio que este mercado tiene los mejores precios para comprar tejidos indígenas.

B. **1.** tercer **2.** primera **3.** segunda **4.** séptimo **5.** quinto

PUNTOS PERSONALES

D. **1.** el Museo del Pueblo **2.** tejidos y objetos de cerámica (auténticos) **3.** el lunes, 31 (treinta y uno) de julio **4.** Arturo Rosa **5.** a las 6 (seis) de la tarde **6.** no **7.** sí

CAPÍTULO 14: LAS PRESIONES DE LA VIDA MODERNA

VOCABULARIO: Preparación

Las presiones de la vida académica

A. **1.** d **2.** f **3.** h (c, e) **4.** g **5.** c (e) **6.** a **7.** e (c, a) **8.** b

B. **1.** d **2.** e **3.** c **4.** f **5.** b **6.** a

C. **1.** e **2.** d **3.** b **4.** c **5.** a

D. CAUSAS DE ESTRÉS: *los exámenes:* K, MR, T; *los trabajos de clase:* MR; *el tráfico en la ciudad:* MR; LAS PERSONAS QUE AYUDAN: *los amigos:* MR, T; *los padres:* K

¡Qué mala suerte!

A. **1.** d **2.** e **3.** a **4.** b **5.** c

B. **1.** torpe **2.** me caí **3.** me hice daño **4.** duele **5.** no se equivoca **6.** me rompí **7.** se siente **8.** ¡Qué mala suerte! **9.** me acuerdo de (recuerdo)

C. Paso 2. **1.** chocó con **2.** se hizo daño **3.** se equivocó **4.** se cayó, se rompió **5.** se pegó la cabeza

Nota comunicativa: Más sobre los adverbios: *adjetivo* + *-mente*

A. **1.** fácilmente **2.** inmediatamente **3.** impacientemente **4.** lógicamente **5.** totalmente **6.** rápidamente **7.** directamente

B. **1.** tranquilamente **2.** finalmente **3.** Posiblemente **4.** aproximadamente (solamente) **5.** sinceramente **6.** solamente (aproximadamente)

GRAMÁTICA

¿Recuerda Ud.? **1.** hace / Hace **2.** haga **3.** hiciste **4.** hace **5.** Haz **6.** hiciste

39. Telling How Long Something Has Been Happening or How Long Ago Something Happened • *Hace… que:* Another Use of *hacer*

A. *Presente:* **1.** Hace / vivo; Vivo / hace **2.** Hace / estudio; Estudio / hace *Pretérito:* **3.** Hace / conocí; Conocí / hace

B. **1.** Pizarro fundó la ciudad de Lima hace más de 450 años. (Hace más de 450 años que Pizarro fundó la ciudad de Lima.) **2.** Los Estados Unidos declaró su independencia de Inglaterra hace más de 230 años. (Hace más de 230 años que los Estados Unidos declaró su independencia de Inglaterra.) **3.** El primer hombre pisó la luna hace más de cuarenta años. (Hace más de cuarenta años que el primer hombre pisó la luna.) **4.** Los terroristas atacaron a los Estados Unidos hace más de diez años. (Hace más de diez años que los terroristas atacaron a los Estados Unidos.) **5.** El Canal de Panamá se abrió hace casi cien años. (Hace casi cien años que el Canal de Panamá se abrió.)

C. **1.** ¿Cuánto tiempo hace que estudias español? **2.** ¿Cuánto tiempo hace que asistes a esta universidad? **3.** ¿Cuánto tiempo hace que vives en el mismo lugar? **4.** ¿Cuánto tiempo hace que no vas al cine? **5.** ¿Cuánto tiempo hace que no recibes dinero de tu familia?

E. Paso 1. (*Answers may vary slightly.*) **1.** Hace un semestre que estudio español. (Estudio español desde hace un semestre). **2.** Hace dos semanas que estoy en el Perú. (Estoy en el Perú desde hace dos semanas. **3.** Hace una semana que estoy en Lima. (Estoy en Lima desde hace una semana.) **4.** Hace cinco días que empecé el curso intensivo de español. (Empecé el curso intensivo de español hace cinco días.) **5.** Hace una semana que recibí noticias de mis padres. (Recibí noticias de mis padres hace una semana.)

¿Recuerda Ud.?

A. **1.** duelen **2.** gusta **3.** gustan **4.** moleste

B. **1.** c **2.** d **3.** a **4.** b

40. Expressing Unplanned or Unexpected Events • Another Use of *se*

A. **1.** b **2.** d **3.** a **4.** c **5.** e

B. **1.** olvidaron **2.** cayeron **3.** acabó **4.** rompió

C. **1. a.** Se le quedó en casa. **b.** No, se le quedó el libro en casa. **c.** No, se le quedó a Pablo. **2. a.** Se me olvidaron los papeles. **b.** Se me olvidaron en la biblioteca. **c.** No, se me olvidaron los papeles. **3. a.** Se le perdió el paraguas. **b.** Se le perdió ayer. **c.** Se le perdió en el cine. **d.** Se le perdió a Carla.

D. **1.** se les olvidó **2.** se le perdieron **3.** se nos quedó **4.** se les rompieron

E. **a.** 1 **b.** 4 **c.** 5 **d.** 3 **e.** 2

41. ¿Por o para? • **A Summary of Their Uses**

A. 1. para / d 2. por / e 3. para / g 4. por / b 5. para / f 6. para / a 7. por / c

B. 1. Por Dios / por 2. por primera 3. por eso / por ejemplo 4. por si acaso 5. Por lo general 6. por 7. por lo menos 8. por / Por fin

C. 1. Mi hermano y yo fuimos al Perú por primera vez en el verano de 2009. 2. Fuimos al Perú por la celebración del Inti Raymi en Cusco. 3. Viajamos desde (de) San Francisco hasta (a) Lima por avión. 4. Fuimos por Miami. 5. Pasamos por lo menos doce horas en el avión.

D. 1. (Lo necesita) Para ir a recoger a María Rosa. 2. Viene para esquiar. 3. No, son para ella. 4. Sí, es muy lista para (una chica de) su edad. 5. Estudia para (ser) sicóloga. 6. Sí, trabaja para la compañía de teléfonos.

E. 1. por 2. por 3. por 4. para 5. para 6. por 7. para 8. para 9. por 10. para 11. para 12. para 13. por

UN POCO DE TODO

A. 1. a 2. está 3. le 4. Se (le) perdió 5. dimos 6. su (el) 7. supo 8. se escapó 9. se despertó 10. se vistió 11. salió 12. encontró 13. hizo 14. pudo 15. se olvidó 16. por 17. se sintió 18. durmió 19. para

B. Después de escuchar. (*Answers may vary.*) 1. Liliana es de Colombia (es colombiana). 2. Estudia antropología y arqueología. 3. Llegó al Perú hace cuatro meses. (Hace cuatro meses que llegó al Perú.) 4. Viajó por tren y autobús. 5. Viajó por más de cinco horas. 6. La comida peruana es una mezcla de la comida española y amerindia y hasta tiene influencias chinas, japonesas y africanas.

C. Paso 1. 1. a 2. d 3. c 4. b 5. d 6. a

Paso 2. 1. ¡Lo siento! Fue sin querer. 2. No se preocupe. 3. Discúlpeme.

CULTURA

A. 1. (el) Perú 2. Lima

B. 1. educación / dinero / salario / gastos (cotidianos) 2. estrés (ansiedad) / tráfico / transporte 3. supersticiones / romper / mala / suerte / viernes 4. cajón / africanos / uva / hace / años / marinera

PÓNGASE A PRUEBA

A. 1. a. Hace diez años que vivimos en esta casa. b. ¿Cuánto tiempo hace que estudias español? 2. a. Hace dos días que entregué mi trabajo. b. Haca una hora que recogieron los documentos.

B. 1. Se me perdió la cartera. 2. Se nos perdió la llave. 3. Se le rompieron los lentes. 4. Se les olvidó poner el despertador.

C. 1. a. 3 b. 4 c. 1 d. 2 2. a. 3 b. 1 c. 2 d. 4

PRUEBA CORTA

A. 1. Fui a ver al doctor (médico) hace una semana. (Hace una semana que fui a ver al doctor [médico].) 2. Tomé mis pastillas hace una hora. (Hace una hora que tomé mis pastillas.) 3. Estoy enfermo/a desde hace tres semanas. (Hace tres semanas que estoy enfermo/a.) 4. Me siento mejor desde hace dos días. (Hace dos días que me siento mejor.)

B. 1. b 2. b 3. a 4. a 5. a

C. 1. por 2. para 3. para 4. por 5. para 6. para

PUNTOS PERSONALES

D. Paso 1. **1.** antropología **2.** universidad (UP, Universidad de Puerto Rico) **3.** San Juan
4. Puerto Rico **5.** se despierta **6.** va **7.** trabaja **8.** hace **9.** estrés **10.** estudiantes **11.** exámenes
12. obligaciones **13.** hace **14.** ejercicio **15.** va (sale)

CAPÍTULO 15: LA NATURALEZA Y EL MEDIO AMBIENTE

VOCABULARIO: Preparación

La ciudad y el campo

A. **1.** reciclar **2.** bello **3.** conservar **4.** salvaje **5.** contaminar **6.** el rascacielos **7.** desarrollar
8. destruir **9.** la finca **10.** proteger **11.** el medio ambiente **12.** la naturaleza **13.** el delito

B. **1.** puro / bella **2.** fábricas / medio ambiente **3.** ritmo de la vida **4.** falta / población
5. transportes **6.** destruyen **7.** proteja / desarrollar

D. Paso 1. **1.** las ciudades estadounidenses **2.** las ciudades hispanas **3.** las ciudades estadounidenses
4. las ciudades hispanas **5.** las ciudades hispanas **6.** las ciudades hispanas

Los autos

B. **1.** manejar (conducir) / funcionan / parar **2.** doblar / seguir **3.** gasta **4.** estacionar **5.** licencia
6. arrancar **7.** manejas (conduces) / carretera / chocar **8.** circulación / semáforos **9.** autopistas

C. (*Possible answers*) **1.** Lave el auto, por favor. **2.** Revise (Cambie) el aceite, por favor. **3.** Cambie
(Revise) la llanta, por favor. **4.** Limpie el parabrisas, por favor. **5.** Llene el tanque, por favor.

E. Paso 2. (*Possible answers*) **1.** arrancar **2.** arregle su carro **3.** funcione (arranque) **4.** se calme
5. tiene que tomar la vida con más calma

Nota comunicativa: Frases para indicar cómo llegar a un lugar

A. (*Possible answers*) **1.** Siga todo derecho (recto) en la Avenida Prado hasta llegar a la esquina de la
Calle Ocho. **2.** Doble a la derecha en la Calle Ocho y siga todo derecho (recto) hasta llegar al
segundo semáforo. **3.** Luego doble a la izquierda en la Avenida Miranda y siga todo recto (derecho)
hasta llegar a la Plaza Mayor. **4.** Mire a la izquierda. El museo está al lado de la Plaza Mayor.

PRONUNCIACIÓN: More Cognate Practice

B. **1.** *fos*fato **2.** a*t*ención **3.** cantida*d* **4.** *t*eología **5.** *op*osición **6.** *f*otogra*f*ía **7.** colec*c*ión
8. ar*qu*itecta

GRAMÁTICA

¿Recuerda Ud.? **1.** a **2.** b **3.** b **4.** b **5.** a **6.** b **7.** a **8.** a

42. *Más descripciones* • Past Participle Used as an Adjective

A. **1.** preparado **2.** salido **3.** corrido **4.** roto **5.** vuelto **6.** dicho **7.** puesto **8.** muerto
9. visto **10.** hecho

D. **1.** Las invitaciones están escritas. **2.** La comida está preparada. **3.** La mesa está puesta.
4. La limpieza está hecha. **5.** La puerta está abierta. **6.** ¡Yo estoy muerto/a de cansancio!

F. Paso 1. **1.** C **2.** C **3.** F: (*Possible answer*) La Patagonia es un territorio muy extenso, que es todo
el sur de Argentina. **4.** C **5.** F: (*Possible answer*) Muchos turistas visitan la Patagonia.

Paso 2. **1.** preocupados **2.** reflejado **3.** poblada **4.** centradas

43. ¿Qué has hecho? • Perfect Forms: Present Perfect Indicative and Present Perfect Subjunctive

A. *beber:* han bebido; *vivir:* has vivido / hayas vivido; *romper:* ha roto; *ver:* hemos visto / hayamos visto

B. **1.** ha escrito **2.** ha dado **3.** ha jugado **4.** ha dirigido **5.** ha construido **6.** se ha hecho

D. **1.** TINA: Raúl quiere que vayas al centro. UD.: Ya he ido. **2.** TINA: Raúl quiere que hagas las compras. UD.: Ya las he hecho. **3.** TINA: Raúl quiere que prepares la comida. UD.: Ya la he preparado. **4.** TINA: Raúl quiere que le des nuestra dirección a Bernardo. UD.: Ya se la he dado. **5.** TINA: Raúl quiere que le devuelvas el libro a Marta. UD.: Ya se lo he devuelto.

F. **1.** Es increíble que lo hayan construido. **2.** Es bueno que los hayan plantado. **3.** Es terrible que lo hayan cerrado. **4.** Es una lástima que se hayan mudado. **5.** Siento que la haya perdido. **6.** Me alegro de que lo haya conseguido.

G. **1. a.** Han vuelto al coche. **b.** (Ella) Piensa que ha perdido su (la) llave (del carro). **2. a.** Se le ha caído el café. **b.** Es una lástima que haya malgastado su dinero. **3. a.** Han comido en un restaurante elegante. **b.** Es posible que no hayan traído suficiente dinero. **4.** El policía ha visto el accidente. **b.** No hay duda de que el conductor ha conducido demasiado rápido.

I. **1.** Antes (del año pasado), (nunca) se habían construido tantos rascacielos. **2.** Antes (del año pasado), (nunca) nos habíamos preocupado por el medio ambiente. **3.** Antes (del año pasado), mi madre (nunca) había cambiado una llanta. **4.** Antes (del año pasado), mi hermana (nunca) había visto una ballena.

UN POCO DE TODO

A. **1.** preocupados **2.** diversos **3.** puertorriqueña **4.** esta **5.** hecha **6.** dicho **7.** pintado **8.** incluido **9.** construidos **10.** inspirado **11.** tratado **12.** preservar **13.** verdes **14.** cubiertas

B. **Después de escuchar.** **1.** F: (*Possible answer*) En general, los autos son más pequeños en los países hispanos. **2.** F: (*Possible answer*) No hay muchos autos japoneses en España. **3.** F: (*Possible answer*) Sí, se venden marcas europeas en Latinoamérica. **4.** C **5.** C

C. Paso 1. *You should have checked:* 2, 3, 5, and 6.

Paso 2. **1.** tenga algo serio **2.** Ha comenzado **3.** sea el motor **4.** Es un auto nuevo **5.** les revise las llantas y los frenos **6.** muchísimas gracias

CULTURA

A. **1.** (la) Argentina **2.** Buenos Aires **3.** (el) Uruguay **4.** Montevideo

B. **1.** de la belleza y la diversidad de su naturaleza **2.** la Argentina, el Brasil, el Paraguay **3.** el río Uruguay **4.** la Pampa **5.** (Son) tierras cubiertas de agua **6.** las energías eólica y solar **7.** el mate **8.** el tango **9.** el gaucho

PÓNGASE A PRUEBA

A. **1. a.** dicho **b.** ido **c.** leído **d.** puesto **e.** roto **f.** visto **2. a.** cerradas **b.** abierto **c.** investigados **d.** resueltos

B. *cantar:* que haya cantado; *conducir:* has conducido / habías conducido; *decir:* hemos dicho / que hayamos dicho / habíamos dicho; *tener:* han tenido / que hayan tenido / habían tenido

C. **1.** Había descubierto la causa. **2.** Habían contaminado el agua. **3.** Luis había hecho investigaciones. **4.** Habíamos parado en la esquina.

PRUEBA CORTA

A. 1. las fábricas destruidas **2.** las luces rotas **3.** la energía conservada **4.** las montañas cubiertas de nieve **5.** las flores muertas

B. 1. b **2.** b **3.** a **4.** c **5.** c

CAPÍTULO 16: LA VIDA SOCIAL Y AFECTIVA

VOCABULARIO: Preparación

Las relaciones sentimentales

A. 1. boda **2.** novia **3.** noviazgos / matrimonio / esposos **4.** cariñosa **5.** soltera **6.** lleva / divorciarse **7.** amistad **8.** luna de miel **9.** viudo

C. 1. Rompió con ella hace poco. **2.** La novia y sus padres habían invitado a muchas personas, y los padres habían perdido mucho dinero en contratos con el Country Club y la florista. **3.** (Le) Pide que le devuelva el anillo de compromiso. **4.** Según ella, «Indignada» debe guardar el anillo. **5. a.** «Indignada» **b.** los padres / gastos

D. Paso 1. 1. *Miguel René:* no; *Karina:* sí; *Tané:* sí; *Rubén:* sí **2.** *Miguel René:* bonita, chaparrita, morenita, ojos grandotes, muy inteligente; *Karina:* superatractivo, supernoble; *Tané:* fuerte de espíritu, grande, niño, necesario, bello; *Rubén:* muy inteligente, muy simpática, guapa **3.** *Miguel René:* sí; *Karina:* sí; *Tané:* sí; *Rubén:* sí **4.** *Miguel René:* sí; *Karina:* sí; *Tané:* sí; *Rubén:* sí

Paso 2. 1. K **2.** K **3.** MR **4.** R **5.** T **6.** MR

Las etapas de la vida

A. 1. juventud **2.** adolescencia **3.** nacimiento / muerte **4.** infancia **5.** madurez **6.** vejez **7.** niñez

PRONUNCIACIÓN: More Cognate Practice

B. Paso 1. (*Answers may vary*) El <u>ministro</u> de <u>Transportes</u> y <u>Comunicaciones</u>, Abel Caballero, ha <u>declarado</u> que el gobierno está dando los primeros pasos para la <u>construcción</u> de un <u>satélite</u> español de <u>telecomunicaciones</u> que, de tomarse la <u>decisión final, comenzará</u> a ser <u>operativo</u> el año que viene. Muchos de los <u>componentes</u> del <u>satélite</u> tendrían que ser <u>importados,</u> pero al menos el 36 <u>por ciento</u> los podría construir la <u>industria</u> española.

GRAMÁTICA

¿Recuerda Ud.? 1. vayan **2.** volvamos **3.** llames **4.** sepa **5.** estén **6.** puedas **7.** tenga **8.** se case **9.** sean

44. *¿Hay alguien que... ? ¿Hay un lugar donde... ?* • The Subjunctive (Part 6): The Subjunctive After Nonexistent and Indefinite Antecedents

A. 1. a **2.** e **3.** f **4.** c **5.** b **6.** d

B. a. 1. sea **2.** esté **3.** tenga **4.** cueste **5.** encuentren **b. 1.** sepa **2.** se lleve **3.** fume **4.** pase **5.** llegue **6.** se ponga **7.** se enferme **c. 1.** practiquen **2.** jueguen **3.** escuchen **4.** hagan **5.** guste

C. 1. viven en la playa / viva en las montañas **2.** le enseñe a hablar / viene a visitar **3.** son bonitos / le hacen / sean cómodos / estén de moda / vayan bien con su falda rosada / le guste **4.** acaban de divorciarse / quiere / sea soltero / busque

45. *Lo hago para que tú...* • **The Subjunctive (Part 7): The Subjunctive After Conjunctions of Purpose and Contingency**

A. 1. salgamos   2. no malgastemos   3. lo recuerdes   4. se lo digas

B. 1. tengas un buen trabajo   2. te enfermes o haya una emergencia   3. se conozcan   4. se amen y se lleven bien   5. antes de casarte (antes de que se casen)

E. Paso 1. 1. funcione / haya   2. existan   3. comparta   4. tengan   5. sientan   6. duren / planee

UN POCO DE TODO

A. 1. se llevan bien   2. se odian   3. por   4. sepa   5. ha   6. por   7. hecho   8. se conozcan   9. se encuentran   10. se enamoran   11. los vean   12. se encuentran   13. Por   14. descubren   15. rompan   16. lo obedezca   17. va   18. se termine   19. se escapan   20. lejos   21. han   22. vuelvan   23. acaben

B. Después de escuchar. 1. España   2. los Estados Unidos   3. España   4. los Estados Unidos   5. España   6. España y los Estados Unidos

C. Paso 1. 1. Lola   2. Eva   3. Eva   4. Lola   5. Lola   6. Eva

Paso 2. 1. Estás libre esta tarde   2. venir conmigo a tomar un café

CULTURA

A. 1. (el) Paraguay   2. Asunción

B. 1. formal y seria   2. se casa / está casada (acaba de casarse)   3. andan (salen)   4. pareja / casarse   5. parques   6. grupos   7. Paraguay   8. guaraní

PÓNGASE A PRUEBA

A. 1. es   2. sepa   3. conoce   4. haga   5. piense

B. 1. **a.** a menos que   **b.** para que   **c.** con tal (de) que   **d.** antes (de) que   **e.** sin que
2. **a.** poder   **b.** salga   **c.** tengas   **d.** llamarme   **e.** sea

PRUEBA CORTA

A. 1. quiera   2. vaya / viajan   3. nacen   4. acaba   5. sea

B. 1. casarse   2. poder   3. necesites   4. hayas   5. consigas   6. se vayan

CAPÍTULO 17: ¿TRABAJAR PARA VIVIR O VIVIR PARA TRABAJAR?

VOCABULARIO: Preparación

Las profesiones y los oficios

A. 1. hombre/mujer de negocios   2. obrero/a   3. plomero/a   4. enfermero/a   5. abogado/a   6. siquiatra   7. maestro/a   8. ingeniero/a   9. médico/a   10. periodista   11. bibliotecario/a

D. 1. (del) Uruguay   2. consejera (en la universidad)   3. recibirse (graduarse)   4. buscar trabajo   5. solicitudes (una solicitud)   6. actuar   7. entrevistas   8. negociaciones   9. encanta

El mundo laboral

A. 1. currículum   2. empleos   3. entrevista   4. empresa   5. mujer de negocios   6. Llena / solicitud   7. renunciar / dejes

B. Paso 1. 3 –llenar la solicitud;   4 –ir a la entrevista;   5 –contestar preguntas sobre mi experiencia;   6 –aceptar el nuevo puesto;   7 renunciar a mi puesto actual

C. Paso 2. (*Answers will vary slightly.*) **1.** (Ella) Se encarga de recibir las solicitudes de empleo para su empresa. **2.** El hecho de que no todas las solicitudes ni todas las personas son seleccionadas. **3.** (Ella piensa que) Mentir y cometer errores tipográficos en una solicitud de empleo son dos de los errores más graves.

Una cuestión de dinero

A. 1. gastado **2.** ahorrar **3.** presupuesto **4.** alquiler **5.** corriente **6.** facturas **7.** devolver **8.** te quejas

B. 1. en efectivo **2.** a plazos **3.** préstamo **4.** cobran **5.** tarjeta de crédito **6.** cajera

C. Paso 1. 1. Es posible que estén en una librería. **2.** Ha pagado en efectivo. **3.** Nina va a pagar con su tarjeta de crédito. **4.** Nina va a comprar muchos libros.

Nota comunicativa: Más pronombres posesivos

A. 1. las mías **2.** el nuestro (los nuestros) **3.** El mío **4.** Los míos

PRONUNCIACIÓN: More on Stress and the Written Accent

C. 1. cobró **2.** cobro **3.** toque **4.** toqué **5.** describe **6.** descríbemela **7.** levántate **8.** levanta **9.** franceses **10.** francés

D. 1. Creo que ese regalo es para mí. **2.** Aquí está tu té. ¿Qué más quieres? **3.** Él dijo que te iba a llamar a las ocho. **4.** Sí, mi amigo compró un auto alemán.

GRAMÁTICA

¿Recuerda Ud.? 1. b, c **2.** a, b **3.** c **4.** a, c

46. Talking About the Future • Future Verb Forms

A. *estar:* estarás / estará / estaremos / estarán; *comer:* comeré / comerá / comeremos / comerán; *seguir:* seguiré / seguirás / seguiremos / seguirán; *decir:* diré / dirás / dirá / dirán; *hacer:* haré / harás / hará / haremos; *poder:* podrás / podrá / podremos / podrán; *poner:* pondré / pondrá / pondremos / pondrán; *querer:* querré / querrás / querremos / querrán; *saber:* sabré / sabrás / sabrá / sabrán; *salir:* saldré / saldrás / saldrá / saldremos; *venir:* vendrás / vendrá / vendremos / vendrán

B. 1. buscaré / compraré **2.** Harás / vivirás **3.** vendrá / estará **4.** Iremos / nos divertiremos **5.** tendrán / podrán **6.** Saldremos / volveremos

C. 1. cobrará / lo pondrá **2.** querrán / se sentarán **3.** sabrá / se quedará **4.** les dirá **5.** tendremos / iremos / bailaremos

D. 1. Ahora será ingeniero. **2.** Ahora será programadora. **3.** Ahora estará casado. **4.** Ahora jugará con (para) un equipo profesional.

E. Paso 2. 1. (*Possible answer*) empezará a entrevistarse con varias compañías químicas **2.** Vivirá **3.** grande y elegante **4.** un jardín fabuloso **5.** será / gastará **6.** Pasará **7.** será

¿Recuerda Ud.? 1. después de **2.** hasta **3.** antes de **4.** para

47. Expressing Future or Pending Actions • The Subjunctive (Part 8): The Subjunctive and Indicative After Conjunctions of Time

A. 1. Habitual: a **2.** Futuro: b **3.** Futuro: b **4.** Habitual: a **5.** Futuro: b

B. 1. a. Cuando me casé **b.** Cuando me case **2. a.** Tan pronto como vuelvo **b.** Tan pronto como volví **c.** Tan pronto como vuelva **3. a.** hasta que nos llaman **b.** hasta que nos llamaban **c.** hasta que nos llamen **4. a.** Después (de) que nos vamos **b.** Después (de) que nos fuimos **c.** Después (de) que nos vayamos

C. 1. Elena hará su viaje en cuanto reciba su pasaporte. **2.** Ellos no se casarán hasta que encuentren casa. **3.** Roberto nos llamará tan pronto como sepa los resultados. **4.** Mario vendrá a buscarnos después de que vuelva su hermano. **5.** Mí hermana y yo iremos a México cuando salgamos de clases.

D. 1. Cuando viaje a México, tendré que cambiar los dólares a pesos. **2.** Iré a la Casa de Cambio Génova, en el Paseo de la Reforma. **3.** Firmaré los cheques de viajero en cuanto entre en el banco. **4.** Haré cola hasta que sea mi turno. **5.** Le daré mi pasaporte al cajero tan pronto como me lo pida. **6.** Después de que le dé 200 dólares, él me dará un recibo. **7.** Me devolverán el pasaporte cuando me den el dinero. **8.** Iré al restaurante La Tecla en cuanto salga de la Casa de Cambio.

UN POCO DE TODO

A. 1. preocuparse **2.** manejar **3.** propias **4.** abrir **5.** propia **6.** ahorre **7.** tenga **8.** abrirá **9.** pedir **10.** empezará (empezar) **11.** propias **12.** gaste **13.** tendrá (tiene) **14.** necesitará **15.** segunda **16.** será (es) **17.** cobrará **18.** suyo **19.** considerar

B. Después de escuchar. 1. los Estados Unidos **2.** el mundo hispano **3.** el mundo hispano **4.** los Estados Unidos **5.** el mundo hispano **6.** el mundo hispano **7.** los Estados Unidos

C. Paso 2. 1. Fantástico. **2.** un puesto estupendo **3.** Es muy amable **4.** tres semanas **5.** ya encontraste trabajo

CULTURA

A. 1. Chile **2.** Santiago

B. 1. trabajo (empleo, puesto) **2.** salario, sueldo **3.** (*Answers will vary. Must include three of the following.*) abogados, médicos, ingenieros, ejecutivos de bancos, congresistas **4.** (*Order of answers will vary.*) obreros / profesores / empleados públicos **5.** trabaja / buena / vivir **6.** beneficios / mes / maternidad / salud **7.** mapuches **8.** (la) Argentina **9.** Gracias a la vida

PÓNGASE A PRUEBA

A. 1. se jubilará **2.** Trabajaré **3.** Vendrán **4.** Podrás **5.** darás **6.** saldremos

B. 1. a **2.** c **3.** a **4.** b **5.** c **6.** b

PRUEBA CORTA

A. 1. iré **2.** hará **3.** habrá **4.** pondré **5.** devolverá

B. 1. manden **2.** deposite **3.** podamos **4.** fui **5.** terminen **6.** tenía **7.** pase

PUNTOS PERSONALES

C. Paso 1. (*Possible answers*) *Miguel René:* **1.** Le fue muy bien. **2.** Ve su futuro muy bien: casado con una mujer linda, dos hijos maravillosos y una empresa propia. **3.** Es bastante bueno con sus finanzas. Sí, es bueno para ahorrar.; *Tané:* **1.** Le fue satisfactoria. **2.** Ve su futuro hogareño y profesional. **3.** Nació con un instinto para las finanzas (que le asombra). Sí, es muy ahorrativa.; *Rubén:* **1.** Le fue muy bien. **2.** Ve su futuro de color de rosa: con una hermosa mujer, unos lindos niños y mejor posicionado en su trabajo. **3.** Las lleva bastante mal. No es nada bueno para ahorrar.

CAPÍTULO 18: LA ACTUALIDAD

VOCABULARIO: Preparación

Las noticias

A. 1. enterarse **2.** prensa **3.** huelga **4.** asesinato **5.** paz **6.** testigo **7.** acontecimiento **8.** reportera

B. 1. c **2.** c **3.** b **4.** a **5.** a **6.** b

E. *Rubén:* **1.** la primera página **2.** la política, el paro y la intolerancia hacia el inmigrante; *Karina:* **1.** la primera plana **2.** Venezuela tiene diversas opiniones y acciones y esto causa una crisis económica, política y social.; *Tané:* **1.** la sección de espectáculos **2.** la poca democracia que hay: los medios de comunicación y la libertad de prensa es todo con un solo partido—es como una manipulación de la información; *Miguel René:* **1.** la primera plana **2.** la pobreza, el poco acceso a la educación, la delincuencia, la inseguridad, pero sobre todo, la corrupción

El gobierno y la responsabilidad cívica

A. **1.** derecho / ciudadanos **2.** rey / reina **3.** ejército **4.** discriminación

B. **1.** noticiero **2.** reporteros **3.** acontecimiento (evento) **4.** huelga **5.** trabajadores **6.** esperanza **7.** prensa **8.** desastre **9.** se enteró **10.** desigualdad **11.** informa **12.** testigos **13.** demás **14.** choques **15.** paz **16.** noticias **17.** asesinato **18.** dictador **19.** acontecimiento (evento) **20.** guerra **21.** dictador

C. Paso 1. (*Possible answers*) **1.** No es cierto que todos los ciudadanos voten. **2.** Es cierto que los políticos usan el Internet durante las elecciones. **3.** Es cierto que hay guerras en el mundo. **4.** Dudo que todos los reporteros sean imparciales. **5.** Es verdad que las huelgas pueden durar mucho tiempo. **6.** Dudo que las dictaduras respeten los derechos individuales.

PRONUNCIACIÓN: Intonation and Review of Linking

C. **1.** ¿Cuál es tu profesión? ¿Te pagan bien? **2.** Tú no la conoces, ¿verdad? **3.** Preferimos informarnos por medio del Internet. **4.** No sé dónde viven ahora. **5.** Quieren que les digamos los resultados ahora.

GRAMÁTICA

¿Recuerda Ud.? **1.** llamen **2.** estemos **3.** estar **4.** vayas **5.** vayan **6.** ir **7.** sean **8.** tenga **9.** tiene **10.** sepa **11.** sirva **12.** sirve **13.** esté **14.** pregunte **15.** salga **16.** salir **17.** volvamos **18.** llegue **19.** llego **20.** llegaba

48. *Queríamos que todo el mundo votara* • The Subjunctive (Part 9): The Past Subjunctive

A. **1.** aprendieron / aprendiera **2.** decidieron / decidiera **3.** sentaron / sentaras **4.** jugaron / jugaras **5.** quisieron / quisieras **6.** hicieron / hiciera **7.** tuvieron / tuviera **8.** pusieron / pusiera **9.** trajeron / trajéramos **10.** vinieron / viniéramos **11.** siguieron / siguiéramos **12.** dieron / dieran **13.** fueron / fueran **14.** vieron / vieran

B. **1. a.** fuera **b.** almorzara **c.** empezara **d.** hiciera **2. a.** pudieras **b.** recordaras **c.** estuvieras **d.** vinieras **3. a.** los despertáramos **b.** pusiéramos **c.** nos sentáramos **d.** los llamáramos **4. a.** ofrecieran **b.** dieran **c.** dijeran **d.** consiguieran

D. **1.** se cuidaran **2.** estudiaran **3.** volvieran **4.** asistieran **5.** gastaran

E. **1.** Pepe quería que Gloria le trajera las llaves. **2.** Ana quería que Carla le dijera la verdad. **3.** David quería que Miguel no hiciera tanto ruido. **4.** Rita quería que Ernesto no se enojara tanto y (que) fuera más paciente.

F. **1.** Ojalá (que) no tuviera que trabajar esta noche. **2.** Ojalá (que) no tuviéramos que gastar menos. **3.** Ojalá (que) mis padres pudieran ir a España. **4.** Ojalá (que) no estuviera lloviendo.

I. Paso 1. **1.** P **2.** MC **3.** M **4.** MC **5.** P

Paso 2. **1.** llegara **2.** estuviera **3.** fueran **4.** hablan **5.** estén **6.** sea

¿Recuerda Ud.? **1.** votaré **2.** ofrecerán **3.** vivirás **4.** podremos **5.** dirá **6.** querré **7.** vendrán **8.** sabremos

49. Expressing What You Would Do • Conditional Verb Forms

A. (*Answers to what students would do will vary.*) **1. a.** trataría **b.** diría **c.** llamaría **2. a.** me metería **b.** sabría **c.** me movería **3. a.** cortaría **b.** ofrecería **c.** eliminaría

D. **1.** Dijo que saldría del trabajo a las siete. **2.** Dijo que tendría que volver a casa antes de buscarnos. **3.** Dijo que pasaría por nosotros a las ocho. **4.** Dijo que llegaríamos al cine a las ocho y media. **5.** Dijo que no habría ningún problema en buscarnos.

E. **Consejos apropiados.** **1.** aceptaría **2.** me confiaría **3.** me casaría **4.** iría **5.** haría **6.** me ducharía **7.** me mudaría **8.** lucharía

H. **Paso 1.** **1.** MR, T **2.** K **3.** R **4.** R **5.** MR **6.** K **7.** MR **8.** T

UN POCO DE TODO

A. **1.** mío **2.** quería (quisiera) **3.** tendría **4.** grande **5.** beneficiaría **6.** dije **7.** tenía (tendría) **8.** para **9.** haría **10.** empezara **11.** sugerí **12.** fuéramos **13.** podrían **14.** había **15.** llamara **16.** me enterara **17.** hubiera **18.** ninguna **19.** traté **20.** arrestadas

B. **Después de escuchar.** **1.** Nicaragua **2.** siete (7) **3.** el desempleo **4.** agosto **5.** rey **6.** España **7.** tres (3) días **8.** subir **9.** gasolina **10.** tabaco **11.** alcohol **12.** cinco (5) **13.** diez (10) **14.** dos (2) de la tarde

C. **Paso 1.** **1.** estuvieran **2.** acompañara **3.** fuera / conociera

Paso 2. **1.** ¡Y hay tantos restaurantes buenos! **2.** ¡Me encantaría! **3.** ¿A qué hora nos reunimos? **4.** Nos vemos a las ocho en el restaurante Tapa Tapa.

CULTURA

A. **1.** España **2.** Madrid

B. **1.** cultural / lengua / Galicia / País Vasco / Cataluña **2.** Constitución / Estados Unidos / tensiones **3.** independencia / 200 (doscientos) **4.** la Argentina / el Paraguay / el Uruguay **5.** cohesión (unidad) **6.** platos / bares **7.** flamenco

PÓNGASE A PRUEBA

A. *aprender:* aprendieras / aprendiéramos / aprendieran; *decir:* dijera / dijéramos / dijeran; *esperar:* esperara / esperaras / esperaran; *poner:* pusiera / pusieras / pusiéramos; *seguir:* siguiera / siguieras / siguiéramos / siguieran

B. **1.** *comer:* comería / comeríamos / comerían; *decir:* diría / diría / diríamos / dirían; *poder:* podría / podría / podrían; *salir:* saldría / saldría / saldríamos / saldrían; *ser:* sería / sería / seríamos **2. a.** iría **b.** lo haríamos **c.** volverían **d.** tendría

C. **1.** fuera **2.** tuviera **3.** lo llamaría **4.** hiciera **5.** quisiera

PRUEBA CORTA

A. **1.** obedecieran (obedeciéramos) **2.** pudiera **3.** dieran **4.** dijera **5.** tratara **6.** quisieras

B. **1.** iba **2.** viajaré **3.** hiciera **4.** tendría **5.** escribiría **6.** conseguirían **7.** hago (haré) **8.** saldrían

APPENDIX 1: CAPÍTULO 9: LOS DÍAS FESTIVOS

VOCABULARIO: Preparación

Una fiesta de cumpleaños para Javier

A. (*Possible answers*) **1.** Van a hacerle una fiesta porque es su cumpleaños. **2.** Se llama la quinceañera. **3.** Va a ser en la casa de Amanda. **4.** Decidieron hacerla en casa para no gastar tanto dinero. **5.** Van a ir cien invitados. **6.** Todos van a regarle a Amanda algo. **7.** Todos los parientes van a prepararla. **8.** Los botanas que van a preparar son empanadas y croquetas de jamón.

B. **1.** la Nochevieja **2.** la Navidad **3.** La Pascua judía **4.** la Nochebuena **5.** El Día de los Muertos **6.** El Día de la Raza

E. Paso 2. **1.** La Habana **2.** Cuba **3.** México **4.** tienda **6.** típicos **6.** fiesta **7.** cumpleaños **8.** refrescos **9.** Navidad **10.** fiesta **11.** comida **12.** asada

Las emociones y los estados afectivos

A. (*Possible answers*) **1.** recuerdo / me pongo avergonzado/a **2.** se enojan (se ponen irritados) **3.** se enferman / se quejan **4.** se portan **5.** discutir

B. **1.** larguísima **2.** riquísimos **3.** cansadísimo/a **4.** carísima **5.** dificilísimas

PRONUNCIACIÓN: *c* and *qu*

B. **1.** quemar **2.** quince **3.** campaña **4.** compras **5.** coqueta **6.** comedor

GRAMÁTICA

¿Recuerda Ud.? *hablar:* hablé / hablamos / habló / hablaron; *comer:* comí / comimos / comió / comieron; *vivir:* viví / vivimos / vivió / vivieron; *hacer:* hice / hicimos / hizo / hicieron

24. Talking about the Past (Part 2) • Irregular Preterites

A. *estar:* estuve / estuvo / estuvimos / estuvieron; *tener:* tuvo / tuvimos / tuvieron; *poder:* pude / pudimos / pudieron; *poner:* puse / puso / pusieron; *querer:* quise / quiso / quisimos; *saber:* supe / supo / supimos / supieron; *venir:* vino / vinimos / vinieron; *decir:* dije / dijimos / dijeron; *traer:* traje / trajo / trajeron

B. *Durante la Navidad:* **1.** tuvo **2.** estuvieron **3.** Vinieron **4.** trajeron **5.** dijeron **6.** fueron **7.** comieron **8.** pudieron **9.** lo pasaron *Otro terremoto en California:* **1.** supimos **2.** hubo **3.** oí **4.** leí **5.** se dañaron **6.** hizo **7.** dijo **8.** fue

C. **1.** estuvo **2.** pude **3.** tuve **4.** fuiste **5.** Quise **6.** estuve **7.** hizo **8.** Supiste **9.** tuvo **10.** fue **11.** dijo **12.** puse **13.** trajiste **14.** traje

D. **a.** 4 (Antonio y Mario) **b.** 2 (Laura y Marcos) **c.** 5 (Norma) **d.** 3 (María) **e.** 1 (Ricardo)

25. Talking About the Past (Part 3) • Preterite of Stem-Changing Verbs

A. *divertirse:* me divertí / te divertiste / se divirtió / nos divertimos / se divirtieron; *sentir:* sentí / sentiste / sintió / sentimos / sintieron; *dormir:* dormí / dormiste / durmió / dormimos / durmieron; *conseguir:* conseguí / conseguiste / consiguió / conseguimos / consiguieron; *reír:* me reí / te reíste / se rio / nos reímos / se rieron; *vestir:* vestí / vestiste / vistió / vestimos / vistieron

B. **1.** me senté / me dormí **2.** se sentaron / nos dormimos **3.** se durmió **4.** nos reímos / se rio **5.** sintieron / se sintió

C. Paso 1. 1. entró **2.** se sentó **3.** Pidió **4.** sirvió **5.** se sintió **6.** se levantó **7.** se despidió **8.** Volvió **9.** durmió

Paso 2. 1. entré **2.** me senté **3.** Pedí **4.** me sirvió **5.** me sentí **6.** me levanté **7.** me despedí **8.** Volví **9.** dormí

D. Paso 1. *Vestirse elegantemente:* Julia, Verónica, Ernesto; *sentirse mal:* Tomás; *dormir toda la tarde:* Tomás; *preferir quedarse en casa:* Tomás

¿Recuerda Ud.?

1. Yo le traigo el café. (C.I.) **2.** Yo lo traigo ahora. (C.D.) **3.** Ellos nos compran los boletos hoy. (C.I.) **4.** Ellos los compran hoy. (C.D.) **5.** No les hablo mucho. (C.I.) **6.** No las conozco bien. (C.D.) **7.** Queremos darles una fiesta. (Les queremos dar una fiesta.) (C.I.) **8.** Pensamos darla en casa. (C.D.)

26. Avoiding Repetition • Expressing Direct and Indirect Object Pronouns Together

A. 1. ¿El dinero? Te lo devuelvo mañana. **2.** ¿Las tapas? Te las traigo esta noche. **3.** ¿El champán? Nos lo traen esta tarde. **4.** ¿Los pasteles? Me los prometieron para esta tarde. **5.** ¿Las fotos? Se las mando a Uds. con la carta. **6.** ¿La bicicleta? Se la devuelvo a Pablo mañana. **7.** ¿El dinero? Se lo doy (a Ud.) el viernes. **8.** ¿Los regalos? Se los muestro a Isabel esta noche.

B. (*Possible answers*) **1.** Se lo dejó a Memo. **2.** Se la dejó a Marta. **3.** Se los dejó a la biblioteca. **4.** Se los dejó a la Cruz Roja. **5.** ¡Me la dejó a mí! **6.** Se los dejó a Ana y Ernesto

D. Paso 1. 1. se las **2.** me lo **3.** nos la **4.** se las **5.** se los

G. 1. Me las dio **2.** Se las mandé **3.** pedírmelo **4.** dénmela

UN POCO DE TODO

A. Paso 1. 1. hice **2.** nuestra **3.** Fue **4.** fue **5.** larga **6.** invitó **7.** tuve **8.** también **9.** acabaron **10.** supe **11.** me encontré **12.** di **13.** estuvimos **14.** le **15.** pedí **16.** las

Paso 2. (*Possible answers*) **1.** Fue para reunirse con un director de su compañía. **2.** No pudo verlo porque la reunión fue muy larga. **3.** Lo supo porque se lo dijo su amigo Luis Dávila. **4.** Se las dio a Luis.

B. Después de escuchar. *You should have checked* 1, 3, 4, 5, 6, *and* 7.

C. Paso 2. 1. le va a encantar **2.** celebra tu familia la Navidad **3.** gastamos mucho dinero **4.** comemos las doce uvas de la suerte

CULTURA

A. 1. Cuba **2.** La Habana

B. 1. Independencia / España **2.** Navidad **3.** Semana Santa / vacaciones **4.** Carnaval **5.** palmera **6.** tabaco

PÓNGASE A PRUEBA

A. 1. estuve **2.** pudiste **3.** puso **4.** quisimos **5.** supieron **6.** tuve **7.** viniste **8.** trajo **9.** dijeron **10.** fuimos

B. *él/ella/Ud.:* durmió / pidió / prefirió / recordó / se sintió; *ellos/ellas/Uds.:* durmieron / pidieron / prefirieron / recordaron / se sintieron

C. 1. se lo **2.** se la **3.** se los

PRUEBA CORTA

A. **1.** nos reímos (nos divertimos)   **2.** se puso / durmió   **3.** conseguí (traje)   **4.** se despidió
5. se vistió / se divirtió   **6.** hicimos / trajeron (consiguieron)

B. **1.** a   **2.** a   **3.** c   **4.** b   **5.** a   **6.** b

PUNTOS PERSONALES

D. Paso 1. **1.** K   **2.** MR   **3.** K   **4.** MR   **5.** R   **6.** MR y R